Next Level Leadership Training

—— Volume Two ——

RICK JOHNSTON

Copyright © 2015 Rick Johnston.

*All rights reserved. No part of this book may be reproduced, stored, or transmitted by any means—
whether auditory, graphic, mechanical, or electronic—without written permission of both
publisher and author, except in the case of brief excerpts used in critical articles and reviews.
Unauthorized reproduction of any part of this work is illegal and is punishable by law.*

*Scripture taken from the Holy Bible, NEW INTERNATIONAL VERSION®. Copyright ©
1973, 1978, 1984, 2011 by Biblica, Inc. All rights reserved worldwide. Used by permission. NEW
INTERNATIONAL VERSION® and NIV® are registered trademarks of Biblica, Inc. Use of either
trademark for the offering of goods or services requires the prior written consent of Biblica US, Inc.*

Scripture taken from the King James Version of the Bible.

*Scripture taken from the New Century Version. Copyright © 2005 by Thomas
Nelson, Inc. Used by permission. All rights reserved.*

*Scripture quotations are from The Holy Bible, English Standard Version® (ESV®), copyright © 2001 by
Crossway, a publishing ministry of Good News Publishers. Used by permission. All rights reserved.*

*Scripture taken from The Living Bible copyright © 1971 by Tyndale House Foundation. Used by permission
of Tyndale House Publishers Inc., Carol Stream, Illinois 60188. All rights reserved. The Living Bible,
TLB, and the The Living Bible logo are registered trademarks of Tyndale House Publishers.*

*Scripture taken from the Amplified Bible, copyright © 1954, 1958, 1962, 1964,
1965, 1987 by The Lockman Foundation. Used by permission.*

*Scripture quotations taken from the Holy Bible, New Living Translation, Copyright © 1996, 2004. Used
by permission of Tyndale House Publishers, Inc., Wheaton, Illinois 60189. All rights reserved.*

*Scripture quotations taken from the New American Standard Bible®, Copyright © 1960, 1962, 1963, 1968,
1971, 1972, 1973, 1975, 1977, 1995 by The Lockman Foundation. Used by permission. (www.Lockman.org)*

*Scripture taken from the New King James Version. Copyright © 1979, 1980, 1982
by Thomas Nelson, Inc. Used by permission. All rights reserved.*

*All Scripture quotations in this publications are from The Message. Copyright © by Eugene H. Peterson
1993, 1994, 1995, 1996, 2000, 2001, 2002. Used by permission of NavPress Publishing Group.*

*All Scripture text in **bold** throughout the book is the author's emphasis and is not used in the particular Bible version
quoted. The **bold** text used in Scripture references at the end of each chapter (also not found in the published versions
of the particular Scripture version) is used to show the thread of truth being referred to in the body of the text.*

*ISBN: 978-1-4834-3017-1 (sc)
ISBN: 978-1-4834-3016-4 (e)*

*Because of the dynamic nature of the Internet, any web addresses or links contained in this book may have changed
since publication and may no longer be valid. The views expressed in this work are solely those of the author and do
not necessarily reflect the views of the publisher, and the publisher hereby disclaims any responsibility for them.*

*Any people depicted in stock imagery provided by Thinkstock are models,
and such images are being used for illustrative purposes only.
Certain stock imagery © Thinkstock.*

Lulu Publishing Services rev. date: 04/27/2015

This book is dedicated to my dear wife, Merilee, who has supported me, walked with me and added to me, through all the years of learning and teaching. It is dedicated to my children who have contributed an immeasurable source of wisdom and encouragement and joy to me as a father. It is also dedicated to my spiritual fathers, Dick Iverson, Kevin Conner, and Bob Stricker who taught me and helped shape who I am today. Their legacy lives on, not only through me but through the contributions they have made to the development of leaders around the world. It is also dedicated to many sons and daughters in the gospel that God has privileged me with, that have taught me so much beyond their knowing. Special thanks to Michael Praverman for his tireless efforts in reading and editing the manuscript. Finally, it is a recognition that all that is good and eternal is as the Scripture says, "from Him, through Him, and to Him…" -- to Him be the glory. May any insight received from this text lead the leader into more of the Word and more of Him, for the Scripture says, "…in the volume of the book it is written of **Me**." (KJV emphasis mine)

To The Teacher

Leadership is meant to be developed in the same way as children are to be matured through the training of their parents. These lessons are meant to be used as a basis for instruction and discussion and can be taken in any order that the teacher believes is best. Scripture references for all Bible passages, not quoted in full, in the lesson, are all given at the end of each lesson, for reference in teaching. The teacher, in preparation for teaching, would be well advised to look at all the Scriptures so as to capture the full message of the lesson.

Turning to the Scriptures and referring to them in the teaching process is vital, as it is the Word of God that the Holy Spirit places into the hearts of leaders in training. All Scripture references used are the New International Version (2011 Anglicised version) except where specifically stated otherwise.

There are some project or implementation tips given at the end of some of the lessons. These tips can help would-be leaders to more fully integrate, what they have come to understand, into their lives. As the teacher will be training leaders for the rest of his life, there is no hurry to get through the material. Plants that grow the fastest are often weak and unstable. Any lessons that include concepts that are unsuitable to a particular context can simply be accommodated by saying, "in our context, we would do the following rather than what the text states."

The lessons endeavour to focus on five primary areas of leadership development: character issues, practical issues, relational issues, theological foundations and principles of supernatural ministry. The goal of this course is two-fold: 1) to develop total life maturity in the men and women being trained and 2) to develop a culture of love, unity and power among the "team" of those being trained. As a leader, you will only have the team that is powerful, loving and unified, if you train them to be so. Go for it! The wisdom and enablement that was His, in making a team of leaders that turned "the world upside down," is on you!

Contents

Leadership is xi

1. The Leader and Responding to Authority 1
2. The Leader and Wisdom 7
3. The Leader and Testing 12
4. The Leader and Lifelong Friendships 40
5. The Leader and Work..51
6. The Leader and Health 57
7. The Leader and Lust 74
8. The Leader and Identity 88
9. The Leader and Exercising Your Spiritual Authority in Ministry 112
10. The Leader and Self-Discipline 125
11. The Leader and Money 132
12. The Leader and Attitude..141
13. The Leader and Destiny...147
14. The Leader and Team Dynamics 160
15. The Leader and The Supernatural..172
16. The Leader and Criticism 180
17. The Leader and Judgment...190
18. The Leader and Legalism 218
19. The Leader and The Fear of The Lord 231
20. The Leader and Favour and Grace 246
21. The Leader and Fathers..257
22. The Leader and The Authority You Possess and Use...270

Summary 281

Leadership is...

Many people think of leadership as simply a role one is asked to fill in the context of the local church. Such a concept is fraught with unforeseen dangers. Leadership is fundamentally, spiritual maturity. As we grow up into Christ in all things, we model character, lifestyle and functions that are consistent with that increasing maturity or spiritual development. I can inspire others to stretch out after God but their spiritual development (which includes taking up certain biblical tasks), is limited by my own spiritual development. Parents cannot reasonably expect their children to act more wisely or more maturely than they do. Many do not discover that leadership is more than a man with a message. The man becomes the message even as Christ, who **is** the Word, spoke the Word. Leaders are meant to be and to become, the message they trumpet.

This course is designed to focus on the nature of this spiritual development as it is defined in our personal, family, and corporate life. No matter your age or experience, you will always be a "learner" and growing into greater spiritual maturity like Paul, who near the end of his amazing life, aspired to "know Him" in even greater ways. Next level leadership is "on the table" for the rest of your life. To develop a role or function without the corresponding character and Spirit-development is a road to ruin. Many leaders have had awe-inspiring talents but didn't last the course in integrity and honour. Let us set our hearts to follow Him, pursue Him, find Him, love Him and obey Him. Learning from the greatest leader and teacher of all time, we will lean into the One who draws us on and draws others on, through us. Paul said, "… that you may stand firm in all the will of God, mature and fully assured." Col. 4:12.

Some leaders will, like the first disciples, leave their careers and take up leadership responsibility and receive financial compensation for it. Jesus **called** His disciples. It is reasonable to believe that He still does so. Gal. 1:1. Whether the time and circumstances are such that a leader is to leave his or her career and take up leadership, in such a quantity of time, that it necessitates getting paid for it, is not the fundamental issue. Every genuine leader is one who has heard or sensed the call to "become" a fisher of men by responding to the discipline of training. Becoming what He said He would make them, is a process that is more than instruction, although it includes instruction. Whether you came into leadership responsibility because you came forward and asked for something to do or you were asked to do a certain task, you will inevitably have to recognise that it is God that has called you to serve Him. When and if you do, you will also see that it is His calling that must be supreme in your life. Using

His wisdom, you can integrate everything else He requires, to fulfil His mission for your life.

Saying "Yes!" to the call of God on your life is far more consequential than you realise. It is an adventure of faith, full of exciting challenges, and glorious privilege. Once you have said, "Yes" to the Master, He takes you forward in relationship, training and service fruitfulness beyond what you could ever dream. Leaders get tired, frustrated, upset, de-motivated and feel uninspired at times. If they submit to those feelings and make decisions on the basis of them, they will drift away from what they have acquired. Sometimes they even drift away from God entirely. God is always leading His people to take up a mandate outside of themselves that is impossible. Only He can sustain and enable what He has designed for each leader. Your leadership will find the greatest level of your endurance and motivation and then call you beyond it. Only then, do you "stretch" to become a greater expression of the capacity that He in His wisdom has placed within you.

There are two great entities that God is passionate about: His Church and His Kingdom. These lessons are designed to help the leader grow in his partnership with Christ in building His Church and in demonstrating His Kingdom.

John 15:16 NLT says, "You didn't choose me. I chose you. **I appointed you to go and produce lasting fruit**, so that the Father will give you whatever you ask for, using my name."

"Love the Lord your God with all your heart, all your soul, and all your mind." This is the first and most important command." Matt. 22:37-38 NCV.

"Do your best in the job you received from the Master. Do your very best." Col. 4:17 TMV

"See to it that you complete the ministry you have received in the Lord." Col. 4:17 NIV

The Leader and.....

Responding to Authority

Introduction
In this age of grace, sometimes, people wrongfully assume that there are no rules, boundaries, or authorities that are clear, inviolable, and right. All absolutes are questioned and cast away or redefined so as to make them more palatable. Any authority figure, who acts in their authority, to adjust or attempt to get them to do something, is viewed as harsh, controlling and unreasonable. Sometimes leaders are even negatively described as "legalistic" simply because they insist on what they require. Legalism is not, however, the existence of laws that must be obeyed, but more to do with *how* laws or requirements are to be obeyed.

Christian leaders, however, model their complete submission to all authorities, not justifying any behaviour that is illegal or not submissive. Rom. 13:1-8. Any leader who walks in rebellion will sow that rebellion into others and without repentance, eventually self-destruct. In John 15:14 Jesus says, "You are my friends if you do what I **command**." The leader also cannot resist the Devil if he fails to submit to God. James 4:7. Inherent in every command that we receive from the Lord is the power to fulfill or comply with that command. That inherent power is the power of grace.

Submission and Agreement
Sometimes leaders who disagree with their leader, refuse to comply. They justify their lack of obedience and submission as acceptable because they hold the "correct view" of the matter and their leader does not. They can fail to see that even if they are right in their judgment of a matter, that they are wrong in their attitude and approach to authority. Being right in one matter does not justify being wrong in another. If a leader is asking another to **violate Scripture**, the one asked, can justifiably decline obeying **but** with a submissive attitude as the disciples did when they were commanded not to preach. Their submissive attitude was revealed when they were arrested. They did not resist the authorities but believed that even their arrest would serve God's purpose. Acts 4:17-19; 5:17-20. It is the rare exception, however, that a leader is asked to violate a specific Bible principle or command.

Submission and Compliance
There are two words contrasted with each other that help to define the internal and external nature of response to authority: submission and compliance. Submission, is first an **internal** response to authority and then an **external** response to authority. Compliance (in one definition), is appearing to obey outwardly, while opposing the command or instruction in inward thoughts and plans. This hidden rebellious attitude

Leaders live under all authorities that they might exercise authority.

serves to achieve one's own goals or desires, or exercise one's own judgment. Eph. 6:5-6; Col. 3:22-25 NASU. True submission takes place when you choose to obey with a right attitude towards authority, even though you may intellectually disagree. Every person should consider that they themselves could be wrong—strange as it may seem to us—and God's will, either way, is worked out for you when you obey. Two wrongs never make a right.

1 Peter 3:1 says, "Wives, in the same way submit yourselves to your own husbands, so that if any of them do not believe the word, they may be won over, without words, by the behaviour of their wives…." In this passage, a godly wife submits to her husband even if he fails to obey God's Word. Submission, then, becomes a matter of trust—trusting in the Lord that as you submit to authorities in your life, His will is worked out in you and for you and for others. Her submission to her erring husband does not include violating the Word of God, however.

The Struggle to Obey
It is the old nature, the nature of sin and rebellion that hates to obey. Only one thing you do not have to teach children: how to disobey. Rom. 8:7-8. They know how to do this instinctively and how to avoid punishment for disobeying by lying. The leader understands that all disobedience comes from the person that he used to be, his old nature. He knows that he is to obey all authorities even as he would obey Christ. Rom. 13:1-7. Yet he may find at times a struggle to obey. It is most often because he unwittingly places his own logic and reasoning above the command to obey. Submission is not to be done because we agree with the authority figure's reasoning but because they are the authority over us. You may disagree with the government's right and calculation of your taxes but you are not allowed to disobey them simply because you believe they are wrong. The following are some of the reasonings that undermine submission to authority.

- I disagree with the authority figure's decision and thus their command

- I don't like to feel that someone else is controlling my life

- I don't like someone else telling me what to do

- No one is getting hurt by my disobeying or not complying with this command

- I think the instruction I have received should be an option and not a command because it is totally unreasonable and may have negative consequences if I do obey it

- Who would ever know if I did disobey in this instance? If no one would ever know that I disobeyed and thus there was no negative consequence for others or me, then I should be free to do as I desire

Leaders live under all authorities that they might exercise authority.

- I am not given the place of authority I should be given so I will resist some of the exercise of authority of the one over me

Leaders in Submission and Obedience

Leaders are commanded to submit and obey:

- Those over them in the Lord

- The laws of the land

- All established authorities

- Wives to husbands

- Husbands to Christ

- Children to parents

- Children to teachers

Succeeding in Submission

Christ was submissive and has placed that nature in us to submit and obey. Heb. 5:7. Leaders are to model a yieldedness to all authority and meekly respect and obey them. They do not react in anger and defensiveness, resisting authority, for that is connecting to the spirit of the first rebellious one, the Devil. Walking in the Spirit, they yield to all authorities as they would yield to Christ and obey Him.

Living in self-consciousness and self-dependence, a leader will rationalise or attempt to legitimise disobedience. Only as the leader chooses to live in vital relationship with Christ by the Spirit can he operate in the death of the old person (the person I used to be) and live the life of the person Christ has made him to be.

Correction, Adjustment, and Change

God uses circumstances, pressures, failures, His Word, the voice of the Holy Spirit, loving confrontation of peers, and the authority figures in our lives, to help us make course corrections in attitude, behaviour, and practice. If we respond positively to the authority figures in our lives when they correct us, we are truly sons. Heb. 12:5-11 NASU. If we fail to respond correctly to adjustments and find grace to make changes, we halt our progress in God and simply "go around in circles" like Israel did, until we get to that same point again and "get it right." Sometimes behind what seems a small area of correction, is a great well or reservoir of resistance and/or resentment. This is a sign of an unyielded spirit and a basic problem with authority. This kind of behaviour does not exhibit the person God has made the leader to be and it must be recognised and forsaken. The yielding, submissive, authority-embracing person is the new self He has made the leader to be.

Leaders live under all authorities that they might exercise authority.

Application

- Examine your whole life and reflect on situations you have been tempted to disobey or disregard some authorities' instruction or mandate. What does this tell you about your relationship to authority?

- Read the lesson on Authority in the book "Church Life Course," by Rick Johnston.

- Ask God to forgive you of any sins of rebellion and set a plan in motion to obey in all of the areas where you have failed.

Leaders live under all authorities that they might exercise authority.

Responding To Authority Scriptures

Rom. 13:1-8
"Let everyone be subject to the governing authorities, for **there is no authority except that which God has established**. The authorities that exist have been established by God. Consequently, whoever rebels against the authority is rebelling against what God has instituted, and those who do so will bring judgment on themselves. For rulers hold no terror for those who do right, but for those who do wrong. Do you want to be free from fear of the one in authority? Then do what is right and you will be commended. For the one in authority is God's servant for your good. But if you do wrong, be afraid, for rulers do not bear the sword for no reason. They are God's servants, agents of wrath to bring punishment on the wrongdoer. Therefore, it is necessary to submit to the authorities, not only because of possible punishment but also as a matter of conscience. This is also why you pay taxes, **for the authorities are God's servants**, who give their full time to governing. Give to everyone what you owe them: if you owe taxes, pay taxes; if revenue, then revenue; if respect, then respect; if honour, then honour. Let no debt remain outstanding, except the continuing debt to love one another, for whoever loves others has fulfilled the law."

James 4:7
"**Submit** yourselves, then, **to God**. Resist the devil, and he will flee from you."

Acts 4:17-20
"But so that it will not spread any further among the people, let us warn them to speak no longer to any man in this name." And when they had summoned them, **they commanded them not to speak or teach at all in the name of Jesus**. But Peter and John answered and said to them, "Whether it is right in the sight of God to give heed to you rather than to God, you be the judge; for we cannot stop speaking about what we have seen and heard."

Acts 5:17-20
"Then the high priest and all his associates, who were members of the party of the Sadducees, were filled with jealousy. They **arrested the apostles** and put them in the public jail. But during the night an angel of **the Lord opened the doors of the jail** and brought them out. '**Go**, stand in the temple courts,' he said, 'and **tell the people all about** this new life.'

Eph. 6:5-6
"Slaves, obey your earthly masters with respect and fear, and with sincerity of heart, just as you would obey Christ. Obey them not only to win their favour **when their eye is on you,** but as slaves of Christ, doing the will of God from your heart."

Col. 3:22-25 NASU
"Slaves, in all things obey those who are your masters on earth, not with external service, as those who *merely* please men, but with sincerity of heart, fearing the

Leaders live under all authorities that they might exercise authority.

Lord. Whatever you do, **do your work heartily, as for the Lord rather than for men**, knowing that from the Lord you will receive the reward of the inheritance. **It is the Lord Christ whom you serve.** For he who does wrong will receive the consequences of the wrong which he has done, and that without partiality."

Acts 5:29 NASU
"But Peter and the apostles answered: "We must obey God rather than men….""

Rom. 8:7-8
"For the sinful nature is always hostile to God. It never did obey God's laws, and it never will. That's why those who are still under the control of their sinful nature can never please God."

Rom. 13:1-7
"Let everyone be **subject to the governing authorities, for there is no authority except that which God has established. The authorities that exist have been established by God. Consequently, whoever rebels against the authority is rebelling against what God has instituted, and those who do so will bring judgment on themselves.** For rulers hold no terror for those who do right, but for those who do wrong. Do you want to be free from fear of the one in authority? Then do what is right and you will be commended. For the one in authority is God's servant for your good. But if you do wrong, be afraid, for rulers do not bear the sword for no reason. They are God's servants, agents of wrath to bring punishment on the wrongdoer. Therefore, it is necessary to submit to the authorities, not only because of possible punishment but also as a matter of conscience. This is also why you pay taxes, for the authorities are God's servants, who give their full time to governing. Give to everyone what you owe them: if you owe taxes, pay taxes; if revenue, then revenue; if respect, then respect; if honour, then honour….""

Heb. 5:7
"During the days of Jesus' life on earth, he offered up prayers and petitions with fervent cries and tears to the one who could save him from death, and he was heard because of his **reverent submission**."

Heb. 12:5-11 NASU
"…and you have forgotten the exhortation which is addressed to you as sons, "my son, do not regard lightly the discipline of the lord, nor faint when you are reproved by him; for those whom the lord loves he disciplines, and he scourges every son whom he receives." It is for discipline that you endure; God deals with you as with sons; for what son is there whom *his* father does not discipline? But if you are without discipline, of which all have become partakers, then you are illegitimate children and not sons. Furthermore, we had earthly fathers to discipline us, and we respected them; shall we not much rather be subject to the Father of spirits, and live? For they disciplined us for a short time as seemed best to them, but He *disciplines us* for *our* good, so that we may share His holiness. All discipline for the moment seems not to be joyful, but sorrowful; yet to those who have been trained by it, afterwards it yields the peaceful fruit of righteousness."

Leaders live under all authorities that they might exercise authority.

The Leader and...

Wisdom

Leaders and Wisdom
Every leader is involved in personal decisions and decisions that involve others. The impact of those decisions, whether minor or major decisions, impacts his or her life and the lives of others. Life quality, is in many ways, determined by our decisions. If we make poor decisions, we have disappointments and sometimes, major unnecessary consequences. Everyone uses wisdom. We use wisdom from one or two sources, Heaven or earth. One is sensual and devilish and the other is spiritual and godly. James 3:15-17.

As leaders, we pursue God, healing, provision, growth, deliverance, change and so many other dimensions of grace in order to secure the abundant life we have been given. Yet, in all of our pursuits, we must pursue the wisdom of God, so that our blessings and benefits are not overshadowed by poor decisions. Solomon, the wisest man who ever lived, made *some* poor decisions that affected his life in radical ways. Solomon's wisdom was not sourced in himself, but in the One who is Wisdom. Isa. 11:3-4.

Wisdom is: God's intelligence, God's solutions, and God's plan of procedure for every circumstance, condition, and problem. It is spoken of as, a "wisdom from Heaven" as contrasted with a wisdom from earth. (James 3:15-17). There is no earthly challenge or problem outside of the provision of God's wisdom. The instinct to rely on our own wisdom or ignorantly depend on the wisdom of this world, denies our dependence upon Him and sets us up for loss and disappointment. Matthew 12:42 tells us that our world will ultimately be judged by the wisdom that the Queen of Sheba sought and the world has forsaken. 1 Cor. 1:20-21; 3:19-20. A wise person receives Christ as Saviour, the foolish person does not. 2 Tim. 3:15. Our modern world glorifies its own research-based wisdom and scoffs at the timeless, senseless-appearing wisdom of God.

Realms in which Wisdom is Vital
Decision-making in all the seasons of life and in relation to the ministry demands the wisdom of God. Gen 41:38-39 says, "Can we find anyone like this man, one in whom is the spirit of God?" Then Pharaoh said to Joseph, "Since God has made all this known to you, there is no-one so discerning and wise as you." Wisdom in all the seasons of life and in all circumstances is found in the **Spirit** of wisdom. Prov. 24:3-5 says, "**By wisdom a house is built**, and through understanding it is established; through knowledge its rooms are filled with rare and beautiful treasures. **A wise man has great power**, and a man of knowledge increases strength." As a leader, you are

Leaders have wisdom to discern what to do.

always "building with Him, your own personal 'house'," and the collective House of the Lord. Leaning on Him in prayer, conversing with other wise people, studying the Word of God, and maintaining an enquiring heart, are vital to having success in the following areas:

- Handling success in ministry
- Financial accountability
- Handling financial blessing and giving to others
- Financial trial
- Mediation of relational problems
- Relating to the opposite sex
- Raising a family
- Making a marriage last a lifetime
- Selection of leaders
- Correcting and adjusting others
- Responding to insult, rejection, and being judged falsely or being misunderstood
- Enduring delay
- Conflicts that you are not directly responsible for solving – Prov. 26:17 ESV
- Parenting teenagers through the course of testing and trial
- Counselling

The Provision of Wisdom
There are sources of God's wisdom available to every leader. A leader has a lifestyle that seeks the wisdom of God for his entire life, embracing the One who is all wisdom. The wisdom of God comes to us from the following sources:

- Our own devotional relationship with The Wise One. Isa. 11:2. The same Spirit that rests on Him, rests on us, giving us wisdom in all the dimensions of life, as we look to Him.

- Wise men and women who have lived and received from God what we have not yet received…parents, older people, spiritual fathers and mothers, and other believers. Prov. 13:20; Eccl. 9:17; Prov. 10:13.

Leaders have wisdom to discern what to do.

- Observation of cause and effect in the course of our lives. Prov. 1:20.

- Experience, both positive and negative can provide for us wisdom for living. Gen. 30:27 NKJV; Prov. 15:31 NKJV says, "The ear that hears the rebukes of life will abide among the wise." Someone has said, "Experience is expensive; wisdom is far, far cheaper."

- The Book of Proverbs is a source of wisdom for many, many things. Prov. 1:1-7.

- Instruction is also a source of wisdom. Ps. 105:22. Wisdom can come from the mouths of the most unlikely. God has ways of imparting to us His thoughts and strategies in unique and effective ways. We must always be open to them.

Application

Discuss with two other members of the team **the places** you have found wisdom and how it has changed your life. Reveal in specific terms what that wisdom has taught you. It may be how to stay out of debt, budget your finances, teach your children to obey, become a punctual person, structure your life to enable a devotional life, solve family and marriage problems, succeed in your work relationships, demonstrate the Gospel, juggle all of your responsibilities successfully, organize your life, clean your home, relate to difficult or interfering relatives, etc.

Spend an hour with a wise person. Ask them five questions that you would like the answers for, from their life experience.

Leaders have wisdom to discern what to do.

Wisdom Scriptures

James 3:15-17
"Such "wisdom" does not come down **from heaven but is earthly, unspiritual, of the devil**. For where you have envy and selfish ambition, there you find disorder and every evil practice. But the **wisdom that comes from heaven** is first of all pure; then peace-loving, considerate, submissive, full of mercy and good fruit, impartial and sincere."

Isa 11:3-4
"…and he will delight in the fear of the Lord. He will **not judge by what he sees with his eyes, or decide by what he hears with his ears**; but with righteousness he will judge…."

James 3:15-17
"Such **"wisdom"** does not come down from heaven but is earthly, unspiritual, **of the devil**. For where you have envy and selfish ambition, there you find disorder and every evil practice. But the **wisdom that comes from heaven** is first of all pure; then peace-loving, considerate, submissive, full of mercy and good fruit, impartial and sincere."

Matt 12:42
"The Queen of the South will rise at the judgment with this generation and condemn it; for she came from the ends of the earth to listen to Solomon's **wisdom**, and now one greater than Solomon is here."

1 Cor. 1:20-21
"Where is the wise man? Where is the scholar? Where is the philosopher of this age? Has not God made foolish the **wisdom of the world**? For since in the **wisdom of God** the world through its wisdom did not know him, God was pleased through the foolishness of what was preached to save those who believe."

1 Cor. 3:19-20
"For the **wisdom of this world is foolishness** in God's sight. As it is written: "He catches the wise in their craftiness"; and again, "The Lord knows that the thoughts of the wise are futile.""

2 Tim. 3:15
"…and how from infancy you have known the holy Scriptures, which are able to make you **wise for salvation** through faith in Christ Jesus."

Prov. 26:17 ESV
"**Whoever meddles in a quarrel not his own** is like one who takes a passing dog by the ears."

Leaders have wisdom to discern what to do.

Isa 11:2
"The Spirit of the Lord **will rest on him** — the **Spirit of wisdom** and of understanding, the Spirit of counsel and of power, the Spirit of knowledge and of the fear of the Lord...."

Prov. 13:20
"He who **walks with the wise grows wise**, but a companion of fools suffers harm."

Eccl. 9:17
"The **quiet words of the wise are more to be heeded** than the shouts of a ruler of fools."

Prov. 10:13
"**Wisdom is found on the lips of the discerning**, but a rod is for the back of him who lacks judgment."

Prov. 1:20
"**Wisdom calls aloud in the street**, she raises her voice in the public squares...."

Gen. 30:27 NKJV
"...and Laban said to him, "Please *stay*, if I have found favor in your eyes, *for* I have **learned by experience** that the Lord has blessed me for your sake."

Prov. 1:1-7
"The **proverbs** of Solomon son of David, king of Israel: **for understanding words of insight attaining wisdom** and **discipline; for acquiring a disciplined and prudent life**, **doing what is right and just and fair; for giving prudence to the simple, knowledge and discretion to the young** — let the wise listen and add to their learning, and let the discerning get guidance — for understanding proverbs and parables, the sayings and riddles of the wise. The fear of the Lord is the beginning of knowledge, but fools despise wisdom and discipline."

Ps 105:22
"...to **instruct** his princes as he pleased and **teach** his elders **wisdom**."

Leaders have wisdom to discern what to do.

The Leader and.....

Testing

Introduction -- 1 Cor. 1:8-9.
Every leader is tested. Tests reveal:

- What we have learned…
- What we haven't learned…
- What we believe…
- Our character under pressure…
- What value we place on our relationship to the Lord.

Matt. 7:25. 1 Thes. 3:3 says, "…so that no one would be unsettled by these trials. You know quite well that **we were destined for them.**"

Job 23:10-12 says, "But he knows the way that I take; **when he has tested me**, I shall come forth as gold. My feet have closely followed his steps; I have kept to his way without turning aside. I have not departed from the commands of his lips; I have treasured the words of his mouth more than my daily bread."

Rev 3:10-11 says, "Because you have obeyed **my command to persevere**, I will protect you from the great **time of testing** that will come upon the whole world to test those who belong to this world."

We make spiritual progression through passing tests…we enter spiritual stagnation by *not* passing tests. Life is a continual series of tests…whether they are tests of blessing or tests of difficulty and opposition. It was, in one sense, Goliath, that brought David to the throne. If we face our opposition with the kind of approach that David did, we will move to the next level in God and in our destiny.

The Fact of Testing
The Bible clearly states that God tests believers. How does He test them? He allows the attacks of Satan, He allows the unfolding of difficult or impossible circumstances, and He allows the presentation of options for our careful selection (e.g. Solomon).

- God tested Abraham – Gen. 22:1; Heb. 11:17

- God tested Israel – Ex. 15:23-25; Ex. 16:4; Ex. 20:20; Jer. 6:27

- God tested David – Ps. 17:3; Ps. 66:10-14

Leaders are regularly "tested and approved."

- God tested Christ – Isa. 28:16; Luke 22:28

- God tested Jeremiah – Jer. 12:3

- God tests us – Luke 8:13; 1 Thes. 2:4; 1 Pet. 4:12

- God tests the whole world – Rev. 3:10-11 NASU

The Nature of Testing
Tests are comprised of the following:

1. Opposing, contradictory, threatening or humanly impossible circumstances.

2. Pressure on the spirit, mind, and emotions to bow to the "message" of the test – what you hear in your mind during the time of testing is the *essence of the test*. It is this "message" that you must manage in wisdom in order to pass. While Abraham waited for Isaac to be born, he, no doubt, had to deal with introducing himself with his new name that meant "father of many nations" for a number of years.

3. The apparent necessity of making a decision about what is occurring based on current or available input. We lean on ourselves and our experience, or we hear from Heaven how to live this portion of the journey.

The Reasons For The Testing of Leaders
Leaders are to live in advance of those they are meant to lead. They must have more maturity, more sanctification in evidence, more wisdom and more faith in operation. The challenge to respond to difficult circumstances, causes a leader to pursue God at a greater level and discover His faithfulness, His power, His enablement, His mercy and His wisdom. The general testing of all believers **applies to leaders. However, even greater tests are given to leaders to pass.** Luke 12:48 says, "From everyone who has been given much, much will be demanded; and from the one who has been entrusted with much, much more will be asked."

Testing is part of the maturing process. Infants have no significant tests. All the challenges they face are dealt with by the parents. Spiritual parents have a successful experience of life and maturity that enables them to guide their spiritual children through the challenges they, too, will face as they mature. Where there is no testing, there is no application of resources and subsequent development of maturity. Parents who are "over-protective" of their children in raising them, deprive them of the maturity that facing and responding to some challenges and hardships provides.

Deut. 8:2-5
Deut. 13:3
Judg. 2:22
Judg. 3:1-4

Leaders are regularly "tested and approved."

1 Chron. 29:17
2 Chron. 32:31
James 1:3, 12

Rom 16:10 says, "Greet Apelles, **tested and approved** in Christ." Apelles was, according to some historians, to later have been a bishop of Smyrna. It is our goal as leaders, that having been tested in the furnace of testing, that we, too, are labelled by God as "approved." We are "approved" by God as to who we are in Christ. We also desire to be "approved" as having passed the tests that make us more like Him and reveal Him in greater ways.

The Tests Leaders Face
During the course of a leader's life, he or she will face the following tests or connect with other leaders who are facing these tests. How we respond to the tests that we face will determine our ongoing and ultimate success. If we quit our leadership when the tests come, we fail to finish our mission and we reveal our lack of depth in God. Prov. 17:3. 1 Peter 1:6-7 says, "In this you greatly rejoice, though now for a little while you may have had to suffer grief in all kinds of trials. **These have come so that your faith** — of greater worth than gold, which perishes even though refined by fire — may be proved genuine and may result in praise, glory and honour when Jesus Christ is revealed." You gain *refined faith* only as your faith is tested.

Prov. 24:10
"If **you falter in times of trouble**, how small is your strength!"

Prov. 24:10 NLT
"If **you fail under pressure**, your strength is too small."

Prov. 24:10 TMV
"If **you fall to pieces in a crisis**, there wasn't much to you in the first place."

Prov. 24:10 NCV
"**If you give up** when trouble comes, it shows that you are weak."

Prov. 24:10 NASB
"**If you are slack** in the day of distress, your strength is limited."

Prov. 24:10 TLB
"You are **a poor specimen** if you can't stand the pressure of adversity."

When tests come, the leader is tempted to become soul-led or let his emotions rule his thought life and decision-making. Whenever emotions turn downward, it is a signal to examine one's thoughts and get into the Word and prayer. In so doing the leader discovers his perspective and wisdom are renewed and equilibrium and strength are restored. Sometimes a test seems like a major "spiritual surgery without anaesthetic."

Leaders are regularly "tested and approved."

The following are some of the tests that leaders face:

- The test of impossible circumstances – Ex. 14:15 God told Moses to tell the people to "move on" or "go forward." Moses then had to wait, to hear, and then to act in co-operation with the supernatural display.

- The test of health -- Philippians 2:25-27. Satan attacks our bodies so we will lose our health and our leadership effectiveness. Often leaders die prematurely or leave aside their leadership due to ill health. This is not God's plan. Every leader must know now to secure and maintain Divine health as well as bring healing to others. 2 Kings 5:1 says,"…He (Naaman) was a valiant soldier, but he had leprosy." Many leaders are great leaders but disease threatens their longevity and success. How will you approach any attack of sickness upon your continued service for the Lord?

- The test of opportunity – Esther 4:8-14. God calls men and women from their current status in life to serve Him. Like the disciples, who were fishermen, who left their nets and followed Him, leaders are those who say "Yes!" to the Master when He calls them from their natural careers to serve Him in full-time employment. The natural fears concerning job security, alleged inadequacy and financial compensation level, are all swept aside to pass this test of faith. When a local church leadership calls a "David" from the "stuff," he or she hears the Master's voice and receives the Master's anointing to "step up" into this new phase of obedience and faith.

- The test of finances…poverty and wealth -- 2 Cor. 8:2; John 6:5-6. Jesus tested His disciples regarding supernatural provision for the ministry and showed them how they were to provide. Matt. 10:9-10. When ministries become large and prosperous they face the test of depending on their own financial strength and the test of maintaining expansion beyond their 'income borders.' They become God's resource to enable a wider global expansion or a self-serving empire. Knowing how to secure the blessing of God and knowing how to use that blessing to further His Kingdom, are vital foundations of leadership life at a personal and family level.

- The test of public acclaim – Prov. 27:21 NCV. 3 John 9. To do a job well means you will not only have more work but you will also have more acclaim, commendation and glory that goes with it. The glory of success is a gift of influence to be used for His glory. It is also an opportunity to praise Him for the privilege of partnership, not the occasion of self-deification or pride. No one thinks he or she would ever be guilty of pride, but the truth is, that everyone is capable of it. An angel, who lived in the Presence of God Almighty, *became* the Devil through self-exaltation or pride.

Leaders are regularly "tested and approved."

- The test of criticism – 1 Pet. 4:14; Acts 6:1; 11:2. Everyone who lives and breathes receives criticism. Leaders receive even more criticism as their position and their decisions invite more scrutiny from people and more attacks from Satan. Without a clear and confident sense of personal identity, the insecure leader falls into the trap of mishandling the test of criticism. His lack of discernment in what is really taking place when he is criticised, is often because the "filter" of his own self-perspective, keeps him from seeing accurately what is taking place. When he reacts in defensiveness and anger, he is failing the test of criticism. He has not separated the merits or demerits of ideas from an attack on himself. He may also fail the test of criticism by being dismissive of it as an "attack of Satan" when it is not an attack of Satan.

- The test of recurrent sins or "besetting sins" -- Heb. 12:1 KJV Sinful bad habits are challenges that must be met with the Word, prayer, and a faith-filled plan to release the grace of overcoming. Distancing oneself from the person we used to be, radically avoiding the "feeding factors" of failure, and renewing our minds in the person that we are in Christ, are all vital to passing the test of recurrent sin. Philemon 6 NASU. Fundamental to passing this test is answering biblically the question, "Who am I?" Am I the person that keeps failing or am I who God says I am?

- The test of offence and forgiveness and reconciliation -- 2 Cor. 5:19 says, "…he has committed to us the message of reconciliation." The relationships that leaders have amongst themselves, must mirror the mission they have of reconciliation. No one gets through life without offence and the necessity of forgiveness and reconciliation. Taking those difficult, pride-abasing steps is so necessary and so right. The wholeness of the church depends on it and the standard of leadership is nothing without it. Loving those who once wounded you, is only possible if you actually forgive and reconcile. Some of the greatest offences that take place, take place behind closed doors among leaders. Shocking, contradictory, and brutal things sometimes take place. Ps. 55:12-14. Deciding that no matter what comes your way, you decide you will not let it pollute your spirit with bitterness and anger.

You will never be satisfied with any attempt you make to understand the "why" of offence…so you will just take the opportunity to rise above it, forgive, and live in love. Some may walk away from you but that is their decision…your heart is to go on loving even those who have greatly wounded or abused you. To fail this test is fatal to your life and ministry. Matt 5:44-45 KJV says, "But I say unto you, Love your enemies, bless them that curse you, do good to them that hate you, and pray for them which despitefully use you, and persecute you; That ye may be the children of your Father which is in heaven…." Rom. 12:21 says, "Do not be overcome by evil, but overcome evil with good."

Leaders are regularly "tested and approved."

- The test of weariness – Gal. 6:9-10. Every leader faces the test of weariness as human strength is gone and the potential of discouragement comes with exhaustion. In this test, we face the necessity of learning how to avail ourselves of His strength so that we can continue in leadership. Physical tiredness is simply a result of labouring throughout a day. Mental, physical, and spiritual exhaustion come when we encounter unceasing difficulty, unrelenting circumstances, delayed breakthrough and negativity of various kinds. Getting the "word that sustains the weary" is vital. Isa. 50:4. The schedule of responsibilities and tasks seems overwhelming. The seeming lack of inner motivation and desire, robs us of the "push" to continue. Thoughts of resignation appear like a welcome relief to the on-going pressure. The pressure to make a stress-based decision without hearing from God is great. Rev 2:3 says "You have persevered and have endured hardships for my name, and have not grown weary." The times of refreshing come from the Presence of the Lord. Acts 3:19 NKJV.

- The test of pride – 2 Chron. 26:16. Leaders are given responsibility which comes with authority. Success at what they do gives them greater influence. Greater influence leads to greater responsibility and authority and the process goes on. The challenge for leaders is to remain humble, remembering where they got all the "stuff" that has made them "successful." 1 Cor. 4:7. God loves to exalt the humble and they do well as long as, in their "new place," they still remember who got them there and why. He is also fully capable of humbling those who exalt themselves. Dan. 4:37. Isa. 26:12 says, "…all that **we** have accomplished, **you** have done for us."

- The test of purity – purity of thought life, purity of motive, and purity of disposition are great tests every leader faces. Rom. 12:17; 2 Cor. 8:21; Heb. 4:13; I John 3:3. Purity in the whole of Scripture is something done both by the Holy Spirit and the specific acts of the believer based on a heart revelation of the need. Ps. 24:4, 5 NASU; Ps. 51:10; 1 John 3:2, 3. Living a lifestyle of beholding Him, we discover, in His reflected glory, the need to remove or purge some things that are not absolutely pure. 2 Cor. 3:18 ESV. Our conscience and the Holy Spirit inform our decisions regarding purity, not what others do or don't do.

- The test of family life -- leaders are always endeavouring to mature themselves, mature their own family and bring maturity to other believers in the family of God. This three-fold task demands dependence upon God. To neglect family life and fail to see the opportunities to develop the maturity that is provided through facing problems with faith, is to lose one's qualification and the right to lead, at least temporarily. 1 Tim. 3:4-5 NLT. Your first "pastoral role" is your family. You don't successfully "father" or "mother" others in the family of God if you don't live successfully in those roles in your own family.

- The test of submission – wives to husbands, husbands to God and church leaders, children to parents--all of these and more, are the "places" of submission and

Leaders are regularly "tested and approved."

yielding, developing the character of humility and faith in the lives of leaders. When wives rule their husbands and children rule their parents and leaders fail to yield to their leaders, the family and the leader become a liability and not an asset. Heb. 13:7, 17. Learning to yield is a basic lesson of spiritual maturity. Without the right attitude of yielding to authority figures, the would-be leader cancels his opportunity to lead. He expects others to yield to his authority— thus he must yield to his authority. Submission does not devalue, it enables progression and relationship.

- The test of correction and adjustment -- any leader who fails the test of correction and adjustment makes himself unusable for leadership. Heb. 12:5-11 NASU. So many leaders enter into the "adolescent stage" of leadership development and, like teenagers, rebel against the authorities in their lives, "run away from home" and start their own church or ministry, building on their rebellion. It is a mark of maturity to submit to others even when you believe you are right and they are wrong, just as a wife is to submit to her husband when she believes he is in error in his judgment. Adjustment is not a devaluing of another but an enabling of them to be better and do better. John 15:2.

- The test of passion and zeal -- Rom 12:11 says, "Never be lacking in zeal, but keep your spiritual fervour, serving the Lord." Ps. 69:9; Prov. 23:17; Sometimes leaders simply "coast" through the days, depending on their maturity, history, experience, capability, gifts and knowledge. They lose the zeal that is inspired by a fresh hearing from the Lord.

- The test of loss…death or departure of others near and dear to the leader. Every leader faces the loss of someone that has become a precious friend in their journey. Changes can include death, ministry changes, illness, sinful failures leading to dismissal, and the call to another place. The leader is profoundly thankful for the blessing others have been in his life, is gracious in their departure and looks to God to replace them in His time with another precious fellow-soldier, mentor or spiritual father. Acts 8:2, 6-8. The Early Church suffered great losses but continued to expand and increase because its leaders did not stop when loss took place.

- The test of modelling – the constant consciousness of recognising that you don't live merely for yourself but others, who observe you and take their cue from you, as to how to live, whether good or bad. 2 Cor. 8:21; 1 Tim. 4:12. Beyond what most leaders realise, those they lead are examining, weighing and judging everything about them—from their appearance to their tone of voice. Living in a "glass house," leaders learn to lean on Jesus for their power to exhibit Him in all ways. Rom. 12:17.

- The test of delay – the leader learns to wait for God's appointed time for some things to be manifested as Abraham did. Manifestation is sometimes not the

Leaders are regularly "tested and approved."

immediate that the leader desires, but in the grand redemption scheme, always "on time" ("the fullness of time). Hab. 2:3; Heb. 10:37-39. The test of delay is a test of persevering faith. Maintaining your daily focus on Him and what He has said, and declaring that His word is faithful and true, will anchor your soul through the time of waiting. Becoming negative, faithless, doubtful and sceptical will cancel the blessings that only *persevering faith* can bring. Heb. 6:12; Ps. 105:19 NKJV. What are you doing while "waiting" for promises to manifest? Are you still being fruitful while you wait? Gen. 41:52. Saul did not pass the test of waiting and it cost him. 1 Sam. 13:8-13. Declare aloud the promises and praise Him "until".... 2 Cor. 4:13.

- The test of disappointment -- Ps. 62:5 KJV. When circumstances don't turn out like we planned and hoped, we can get disappointed. At times, this seems a great contradiction, as we may have been resting our plans in faith in His promises. However, life in God goes according to His plans and we are challenged to get up and believe Him again when disappointing news has come. No one can afford to "camp" at disappointment, regardless of whether they can figure out why things turned out as they did. Get up, get on, and get over it! God is not dead and neither is His great plan for you! Your unanswered questions are not your god. You make them your "god" if you halt forward progress insisting on your questions being satisfactorily answered before trusting again.

- The test of time pressure -- only the wisdom of God can enable the leader to deal with the test of time pressure. 2 Cor. 1:8 says, "...we were under great pressure...." The pressure to meet deadlines is constant and of greater measure in some seasons. In these times, the leader reveals the level of wisdom he has and the fruit of the Spirit he has in operation. Becoming negative, critical and selfishly demanding of others, creates a difficult working environment and stifles the ability to accomplish all that needs to be done. Encouraging others with words of enablement and getting the wisdom as to how to do the tasks on time, is vital in this test. 2 Cor. 11:28.

- The test of faith...the trial of your faith. 1 Peter 1:7 KJV says, "That the **trial of your faith**, being much more precious than of gold that perisheth, though it be tried with fire, might be found unto praise and honour and glory at the appearing of Jesus Christ...." Luke 22:31-32.

There is a sense in which all the tests that we face as leaders, are tests of faith because our faith is tested as to whether or not we will continue to lead God's people in grace and favour. We choose to discover and receive more of Him in a test or we choose to allow discouragement to take us out of our place in His great purposes. When we cannot see the way ahead or the way out or the way through, we can opt to surrender to the pressures and quit our calling to serve. Open your mouth against your "Goliath" and speak from your amazing faith

Leaders are regularly "tested and approved."

to your "giant" like David did and you are well on your way to defeating what threatens your progress.

- The test of spiritual opposition…there is an enemy who comes to steal, kill and destroy. John 10:10. God has allowed him that opportunity but He has given you the resources to win, when you face demonic opposition. Recognising this test is essential to passing it. 1 Thes. 2:17-20-3:1-8 ESV; Acts 20:19; 1 John 4:1-3; Rev. 2:10; 1 John 3:8. When great attacks come against you in the public domain, don't give in to the temptation to defend yourself. Let your Master defend you and be at peace. He will give you grace in the trial and in the end, reward you double for your trouble.

- The test of change…responsibilities, roles, new frontiers of service, physical hardships – 2 Cor. 11:26-28. Everything changes in life. Embracing change is vital to maintaining a progressive and zealous life. To resist change is normal, but to resist change finally, is to signal the end of powerful leadership. The Early Church faced unending changes. From the outpouring of the Holy Spirit, great numerical increase, opposition, restructuring, sending out ministries, expansion, global recognition, and governmental persecution, the Church had to accommodate consistently, a changing world and their own progression. When it *settled down*, it declined. It became hardly recognisable from what it had been.

- The test of distraction. To be distracted is to lose focus on one thing and become focussed on another. We can be subtly lured away from our focus on Jesus and His great plan by Satan or by earthly pursuits. Heb. 12:2 NASU tells us that we are "fixing our eyes on Jesus." Luke 10:40; Prov. 4:5, 27. This test is subtle and has its entrance into our minds in the "camouflage of legitimate pursuit." Heb. 2:1 says, "We must pay the most careful attention, to what we have heard, so that we do not *drift* away." One godly man with a wonderful family gradually drifted away from spiritual vitality and lost his marriage and family in the pursuit of mountain climbing. No one would have ever predicted this happening. A legitimate desire became the consuming passion, justified and embraced, to great loss.

- The test of personal danger – Luke 8:23; 2 Cor. 11:26. (Eight times the word, "danger" is used in this one verse). More and more leaders are faced with the implications of a bold and committed declaration of the Word of God. Knowing that our lives are held in His hands, we set our hearts and our faces to embrace the extreme with our powerful weapon of faith expressed in great boldness.

- The test of failure…recovery, discovery, and new plateaus of enablement. Acts 15:37-38; 2 Tim. 4:11; 2 Cor. 6:2-11. No leader can afford to camp at failure. Living a resurrected life means there is a new beginning in Divine enablement to the leader who will rise and take "hold of the plough" again. Forgiveness, mercy,

Leaders are regularly "tested and approved."

and new beginnings in grace and new-found wisdom, cause the road ahead to beckon to us. This test also involves giving others who have had great failures a new place to start having repented. We offer them the same grace that is offered to us to bury the past and step into favour and great fruitfulness.

- The test of great achievement and accomplishment – Nebuchadnezzar is a great example of someone who failed the test of achievement and accomplishment. Self-exaltation based on the expansion of one's ministry is a great temptation or test. Many leaders have succeeded, only to fail, as their accomplished goals have led them to become a person others secretly dislike due to the blindness of their own self-importance, self-congratulation, and self-promotion. Isa. 26:12 says, "…all that **we have accomplished** *you have done for us.*" This is a great balancing verse helping us to maintain right perspective about our partnership with Him.

- The test of what we have built – 1 Cor. 3:12-15. One man who led a church of 6000 members saw it decline to 300 when testing came. There is fruit and there is fruit that *remains*. John 15:16 NLT; Matt. 7:25. What is not securely built will not remain when tests come. It will be blown over. Wise leaders build with The Rock on The Rock. Prov. 24:3, 4.

- The test of contradiction – Heb. 12:3 KJV. Sometimes leaders face tests that fly in the face of what they know of God and the Word. They are tests of "contradiction" that they undergo, just as Christ did. He was the Innocent One, killed as a criminal. We hold on to Christ or we submit to the discouragement of reason that refuses to be submitted to Him. Sometimes we may have prayed for someone who eventually passed away. The Early Church faced and passed this test. Stephen, a great evangelist, was stoned. Right after that, the miraculous resumed and a great harvest continued to pour into the Church. Interestingly, no one raised him from the dead.

The test of contradiction can come in many different forms. It can be that you didn't get what others have received…yet. It could be that the word you received didn't come to pass…yet. It could be that circumstances are so opposite to what you believe. In all these things and more, God's plan has not been cancelled and He still holds the door of great opportunity and blessing open to you as long as you hold on to your faith. Without your faith, you are destined to live in disappointment and frustration. Passing this test is vital to progressing in your spiritual life and walk as a person, as well as a leader. At some point you will need to "say" to your disappointment (aloud is best), "disappointment, you can go now. You are dismissed." Then get up and get on with your life of faith believing Him again for He cannot lie and He cannot fail, regardless of our perceptions.

One man felt that he truly believed and had faith that his son-in-law would be healed. He had prophecies. The son-in-law died. This apparent contradiction

Leaders are regularly "tested and approved."

became a great wrestling match. Many questions arose within him. After a period of time, he had to lay his mind "on the altar" and hear God to go forward with his life even if the questions remained unanswered. Because we don't understand, it doesn't mean that we should quit or back away from believing, doing the miraculous, or living in faith. We press into Him. So many great miracle workers have had disappointing losses. They could have quit. They didn't.

- The test of spiritual/physical attack against your family. Norvel Hayes daughter had the Devil appear to her and say, "I am going to kill you because that is the only way I can get at your Dad." Norvel prayed about this. God said to him, "how long will you let the Devil attack your daughter?" The head of the house has authority to establish his home in security, health and safety and must do so. Matt. 8:14-15.

- The test of false accusation. False accusation is different from the normal criticism that leaders receive. It is an accusation of alleged motive, alleged behaviour, or alleged words that are false. The fact that they are false may only be ultimately known by yourself and God, who knows all things, but it is nevertheless false. It is in this test, that the leader learns Who his Vindicator is. Mark 15:3-5; Luke 23:2; 1 Pet. 2:12; Rev. 12:10. Jesus, Joseph, and Paul, were all falsely accused. How did they handle this test? One pastor was falsely accused of the rape of a young woman. He was arrested and put in a cell. However, it was discovered that her story was totally false and he was released. It was a great test, however, for him and his family and his congregation.

Churches Face Tests
Every congregation that pursues God's Presence and purpose will face tests. The tests are, as they are with individuals, both internal and external. Discernment, wisdom, faith and endurance are vital to walk through the "time of testing." Every wise leader will discern what is happening and step into their personal part in maintaining unity and accessing grace to make the test into a triumph. Acts 8:1-4; 9:31; Acts 12:1, 5; Acts 15:1-3, 6, 22, 30, 31. Prayer, faith-filled discussion amongst leaders, Satan-shattering praise and worship, wise decisions, and the exercise of spiritual authority are all vital strategies for leaders whose congregation is undergoing a test. The seasonal great trials that test a local church, demand a quality of leadership that enables the church to gain and not to lose from those seasons. Fire should only consume restrictions as in the case of the three Hebrew children.

Passing the Tests – Leading the Way
Leaders, who are always under observation and scrutiny by those they are leading, whether family members or church members, are meant to pass all the tests they face. This potential legacy of success reveals both the possibility and the encouragement to those that follow, to do the same. Satan would use every test that you face, to get you to quit your leadership role, for you influence others to also pursue his loss.

Leaders are regularly "tested and approved."

Heb. 13:7 says, "Remember your leaders, who spoke the word of God to you. Consider the outcome of their way of life and imitate their faith."

Passing the tests requires:

God knows the tests you are undergoing and has promised grace to enable you to pass each and every test you go through. Consider Joseph of whom Acts 7:9, 10 says, "…But God was with him and rescued him from all his troubles. He gave Joseph wisdom and enabled him to gain the goodwill of Pharoah King of Egypt; so Pharoah made him ruler over Egypt and all his palace." Receive the following wisdom to pass your tests:

1. Maintain your focus on Jesus. Heb. 12:2 NASU. He enables you to maintain faith during the trial. Tests tend to make us self-focussed. When you become self-focussed you operate unwittingly out of your own strength. The hardest tests are the longest tests. Only as you stay focused on Jesus, the Finisher, will your faith enable you to endure.

2. Maintain communication with those around you and over you. Ecc. 4:10. Sometimes leaders "pull back" from others and live in the "shell" of their own world while they attempt to handle the test they are undergoing. This gives their followers the wrong message and also their fellow-leaders.

3. Examine in quietness, what is "going through you" and take the steps to anchor your thought life in faith and the Word. What is "going through you" is what you are "going through!" Rom. 12:1-2. Discern the nature of the test and prepare yourself inwardly to win! Isa. 49:2-4.

4. Maintain your Bible-based confession about everything. 2 Cor. 4:13; 1 Tim. 6:12. One of the greatest challenges of faith that a leader faces is to hold on to his positive, faith-filled confession and not surrender to the temptation to give an "evil report" of his circumstances. Num. 13:32; 14:6-9.

5. "Slam the door" on any activity that is enabling you to "check out" of the trial in your mind. Rom. 13:14 NKJV.

6. Live in a worship atmosphere, not a worldly one. There is no solace or solution in this world's system or activities. "…worship…in the wilderness." Ex. 7:16; 2 Cor. 3:18 ESV; Heb. 12:28; Eph. 5:19. Paul and Silas sang in the prison. Acts 16:25; Hab. 3:17-19.

7. Keep living for God and others. 2 Cor. 5:15. The unselfish lifestyle of constantly serving others is a statement of faith that you are trusting Him to "take you to the next level." Your circumstantial breakthrough is coming. You simply need to live as though it is—busy about your Father's business, you are certain that He is taking care of your "stuff" while you are carrying out His continuing mission.

Leaders are regularly "tested and approved."

8. Listen for all the messages that enable you to endure, capture any insight or instruction that He is giving or make any changes that He is desiring. Job. 29:3; 1 Kings 19:12-15; Isa. 30:21.

How You Know You Are Not Passing the Test
There are certain evidences that we are not passing the tests that we face. Israel revealed those evidences.

- Complaining -- Phil. 2:14-15; Num. 11:1. Leaders, like those who are not leaders, can complain for a host of reasons. This means that they have failed to see their circumstances from God's point of view. If you are going to complain, complain to God and then listen to what He has to say. You will have to get back to faith and a right confession.

- Disobedience -- Num. 14:22-23 says, "…not one of those who saw my glory and the signs I performed in Egypt and in the wilderness but who **disobeyed** me and tested me ten times — not one of them will ever see the land I promised on oath to their ancestors. No-one who has treated me with contempt will ever see it." To choose to not finish your life mission is disobedience. Acts 26:19.

- Shrinking back -- Heb. 10:39; Rev. 12:11. Leaders can "pull back" inwardly from the Lord, from other leaders, from family, from the vision and from doing their tasks with excellence, simply because they have lost heart.

- Quitting – John 6:66. Leaders are meant to endure for a lifetime, not quit. Ps. 78:9 says, "The men of Ephraim, though armed with bows, **turned back** on the day of battle." Isa. 26:3-4 TMV says, "People with their minds set on You, You keep completely whole, steady on their feet, because they keep at it and don't quit. Depend on GOD and keep at it because in the LORD GOD you have a sure thing."

- Blaming others -- Ps. 15:3 TMV. When leaders blame others they have lost perspective on who the real enemy is and have descended to a fleshly and satanic level in their perspective and possibly their words. Hosea 4:4 TMV. Adam started the "blame game" in the Garden after his failure. Own your own failures, let others own theirs, and recognise Satan's attempt to distract you from vital issues.

- Allowing discouragement – Deut. 1:21; Josh. 10:25; Rom. 14:23. Whatever is not of faith, is sin, according to the Scriptures. We must recognise discouragement and deal with it. Wrong thoughts stimulate wrong emotions that can lead to wrong decisions. Deal with the thoughts that have come into the mind by replacing them with the liberating truth of what He has spoken about your circumstances.

Leaders are regularly "tested and approved."

- Not getting up after failure -- Prov. 24:16. Every leader makes mistakes, and has failures...but the real leader rises in fresh grace to succeed with wisdom. Micah 7:8. God is a god of resurrection and new beginnings. Learn from the failure, bury by forgiveness and repentance, what took place, and get on with unmerited favour to new places of victory and advance!

- Comparison -- Sometimes leaders who question why they are not getting the results they hoped for, look around and begin to compare their situation, church, programme or themselves with others they think are having more success. Gal. 6:4-5.

Summary

The essence of a testing is this: what is going *through you* is what you are really going through. Tests have two parts: an external part and an internal part. Most believers tend to focus on the outward or external circumstances when testing comes. They ask God to change the circumstances. God will change circumstances, however, He is interested more in what is going on, on the inside of the believer. Heb. 11:29 tells us that Israel passed *through* the Red Sea. However, the Red Sea *passed through* them in their thoughts and feelings before they passed through it. Get the inside straightened out with faith, forgiveness, strength, the Word, right believing, right confession, rejoicing and insight. Your test, the one designed for you, you are now winning! James 1:12 says, "Blessed is the one who perseveres under trial, that person will receive the crown of life that the Lord has promised to those that love Him." Maintain your inner life, for that is your life. Eph. 3:16.

Application

In a small group discuss which tests of the tests mentioned above you have undergone. Share how you responded initially and how you finally passed. Listen carefully to the stories of the others so you can benefit from their life experience. Pray together for everyone in the group regarding the tests they are currently facing.

Leaders are regularly "tested and approved."

Test Scriptures

1 Cor. 1:8-9
"He will **keep you firm to the end**, so that you will be blameless on the day of our Lord Jesus Christ. God **is faithful**, who has called you into fellowship with his Son, Jesus Christ **our Lord**."

Matt. 7:25
"The rain came down, the streams rose, and the winds blew and beat against that house; yet it did not fall, because it had its **foundation on the rock**."

Gen. 22:1
"Some time later **God tested Abraham**. He said to him, 'Abraham!' 'Here I am,' he replied."

Heb. 11:17
"By faith Abraham, **when God tested him**, offered Isaac as a sacrifice."

Ex. 15:23-25
"When they came to Marah, they could not drink its water because it was bitter. (That is why the place is called Marah.) So the people grumbled against Moses, saying, 'What are we to drink?' Then Moses cried out to the Lord, and the Lord showed him a piece of wood. He threw it into the water, and the water became fit to drink. There the Lord issued a ruling and instruction for them, and **there He tested them**."

Ex. 16:4
"Then the Lord said to Moses, 'I will rain down bread from heaven for you. The people are to go out each day and gather enough for that day. **In this way I will test them** and see whether they will follow my instructions.'"

Ex. 20:20
"Moses said to the people, 'Do not be afraid. **God has come to test you**, so that the fear of God will be with you to keep you from sinning.'

Jer. 6:27
'**I have made you a tester of metals and my people the ore**, that you may observe and **test** their ways.'

Ps. 17:3
"Though you probe my heart, and though you examine me at night **and test me**, you will find that I have planned no evil; my mouth has not transgressed."

Ps. 66:10-14
"**For you, O God, tested us; you refined us like silver.** You brought us into prison and laid burdens on our backs. You let people ride over our heads; we went through

Leaders are regularly "tested and approved."

fire and water, but you brought us to a place of abundance. I will come to your temple with burnt offerings and fulfil my vows to you — vows my lips promised and my mouth spoke when I was in trouble."

Isa. 28:16
"So this is what the Sovereign Lord says: 'See, I lay a stone in Zion, **a tested stone**, a precious cornerstone for a sure foundation; the one who relies on it will never be stricken with panic."

Luke 22:28
"You are those who have stood by me **in my trials**."

Jer. 12:3
"Yet you know me, Lord; you see me and **test my thoughts about you**."

Luke 8:13
"Those on the rocky ground are the ones who receive the word with joy when they hear it, but they have no root. They believe for a while, but in **the time of testing** they fall away."

1 Thes. 2:4
"On the contrary, we speak as those approved by God to be entrusted with the gospel. We are not trying to please people but **God, who tests our hearts**."

1 Peter 4:12
"Dear friends, do not be surprised at the fiery ordeal that has come on you **to test you**, as though something strange were happening to you."

Rev. 3:10-11 NASU
'Because you have kept the word of My perseverance, I also will keep you from **the hour of testing**, that *hour* which is about **to come upon the whole world, to test those who dwell on the earth**."

Deut. 8:2-5
"Remember how the Lord your God led you all the way in the wilderness these forty years, to humble you and **to test you in order to know what was in your heart**, whether or not you would keep his commands. He humbled you, causing you to hunger and then feeding you with manna, which neither you nor your ancestors had known, to teach you that man does not live on bread alone but on every word that comes from the mouth of the Lord. Your clothes did not wear out and your feet did not swell during these forty years. Know then in your heart that as a man disciplines his son, so the Lord your God disciplines you."

Deut. 13:3
"The Lord your God is **testing you to find out whether you love him with all your heart** and with all your soul."

Leaders are regularly "tested and approved."

Judg. 2:22
"I will use them **to test Israel** and see whether they will keep the way of the Lord and walk in it as their ancestors did."

Judg. 3:1-4
"These are the nations the Lord left **to test all those Israelites** who had not experienced any of the wars in Canaan (he did this only to teach warfare to the descendants of the Israelites who had not had previous battle experience): the five rulers of the Philistines, all the Canaanites, the Sidonians, and the Hivites living in the Lebanon mountains from Mount Baal Hermon to Lebo Hamath. They were left **to test the Israelites to see whether they would obey the Lord's commands**, which he had given their ancestors through Moses."

1 Chron. 29:17
"I know, my God, that **you test the heart and are pleased with integrity**. All these things I have given willingly and with honest intent. And now I have seen with joy how willingly your people who are here have given to you."

2 Chron. 32:31
"But when envoys were sent by the rulers of Babylon to ask him about the miraculous sign that had occurred in the land, **God left him to test him and to know everything that was in his heart**."

James 1:3
"…because you know that the **testing of your faith** produces perseverance."

James 1:12
"Blessed is the one who perseveres under trial, because having **stood the test**, that person will receive the crown of life that the Lord has promised to those who love him."

Prov. 17:3
"The crucible for silver and the furnace for gold, but **the Lord tests the heart**."

Ex. 14:15
"Then the Lord said to Moses, 'Why are you crying out to me? Tell the Israelites to **move on**.'

Phil. 2:25-27
"…Epaphroditus, my brother, co-worker and fellow soldier, who is also your messenger, whom you sent to take care of my needs. For he longs for all of you and is distressed because you heard he was ill. Indeed he was ill, and almost died. But God had mercy on him, and not on him only but also on me, to spare me sorrow upon sorrow."

Est. 4:8-14
"He also gave him a copy of the text of the edict for their annihilation, which had been published in Susa, to show to Esther and explain it to her, and he told him to

Leaders are regularly "tested and approved."

instruct her to go into the king's presence to beg for mercy and plead with him for her people. Hathak went back and reported to Esther what Mordecai had said. Then she instructed him to say to Mordecai, 'All the king's officials and the people of the royal provinces know that for any man or woman who approaches the king in the inner court without being summoned the king has but one law: that they be put to death unless the king extends the gold sceptre to them and spares their lives. But thirty days have passed since I was called to go to the king.' When Esther's words were reported to Mordecai, he sent back this answer: 'Do not think that because you are in the king's house you alone of all the Jews will escape. For if you remain silent at this time, relief and deliverance for the Jews will arise from another place, but you and your father's family will perish. And who knows but that **you have come to your royal position for such a time as this?**"

2 Cor. 8:2
"**In the midst of a very severe trial**, their overflowing joy and their extreme poverty welled up in rich generosity."

John 6:5-6
"When Jesus looked up and saw a great crowd coming towards him, he said to Philip, 'Where shall we buy bread for these people to eat?' He asked this only **to test him**, for he already had in mind what he was going to do."

Matt. 10:9-10
'Do not get any gold or silver or copper to take with you in your belts—no bag for the journey or extra shirt or sandals or a staff, for the worker is worth his keep."

Prov. 27:21 NCV
"A hot furnace tests silver and gold, and **people are tested by the praise they receive**."

3 John 9
"I wrote to the church, but Diotrephes, who loves to be first, will not welcome us."

Acts 6:1
"In those days when the number of disciples was increasing, the Hellenistic Jews among them **complained against** the Hebraic Jews because their widows were being overlooked in the daily distribution of food."

Acts 11:2
"So when Peter went up to Jerusalem, the circumcised believers **criticised him**...."

1 Peter 4:14
"If **you are insulted** because of the name of Christ, you are blessed, for the Spirit of glory and of God rests on you."

Leaders are regularly "tested and approved."

Heb. 12:1 KJV
"Wherefore seeing we also are compassed about with so great a cloud of witnesses, let us lay aside every weight, and the sin which doth **so easily beset us**, and let us run with patience the race that is set before us...."

Philemon 6 NASU
"...*and I pray* that the fellowship of your faith may become effective **through the knowledge of every good thing which is in you** for Christ's sake."

Ps. 55:12-16
"If an enemy were insulting me, I could endure it; if a foe were rising against me, I could hide. But it is you, a man like myself, **my companion, my close friend**, with whom I once enjoyed sweet fellowship at the house of God, as we walked about among the worshippers. Let death take my enemies by surprise; let them go down alive to the realm of the dead, for evil finds lodging among them. As for me, I call to God, and the LORD saves me...."

Gal 6:9-10
"Let us **not become weary** in doing good, for at the proper time we will reap a harvest if we do not give up. Therefore, as we have opportunity, let us do good to all people, especially to those who belong to the family of believers."

Isa. 50:4
"The Sovereign Lord has given me a well-instructed tongue, to know **the word that sustains the weary**. He wakens me morning by morning, wakens my ear to listen like one being instructed."

2 Chron. 26:16
"But after Uzziah became powerful, **his pride led to his downfall**. He was unfaithful to the Lord his God, and entered the temple of the Lord to burn incense on the altar of incense."

1 Cor. 4:7
"For who makes you different from anyone else? **What do you have that you did not receive?** And if you did receive it, why do you boast as though you did not?"

Dan. 4:37
"...those who walk in pride **he is able to humble**."

Rom. 12:17
"Do not repay anyone evil for evil. Be careful to **do what is right in the eyes of everyone**."

2 Cor. 8:21
"For we are taking pains to do what is right, not only **in the eyes of the Lord but also in the eyes of men**."

Leaders are regularly "tested and approved."

Heb. 4:13
"Nothing in all creation is hidden from God's sight. Everything is uncovered and laid bare before the eyes of him to whom we must give account."

1 John 3:3
"All who have this hope in him **purify themselves**, just as he is pure."

Ps. 24:4-5 NASU
"He who has clean hands and a pure heart, who has not lifted up his soul to falsehood and has not sworn deceitfully. He shall receive a blessing from the Lord and righteousness from the God of his salvation."

Ps. 51:10
"Create in me a pure heart, O God, and renew a steadfast spirit within me."

1 John 3:2-3
"Dear friends, now we are children of God, and what we will be has not yet been made known. But we know that when Christ appears, we shall be like him, for we shall see him as he is. All who have this hope in him purify themselves, just as he is pure."

2 Cor. 3:18 ESV
"And we all, with unveiled face, beholding the glory of the Lord, **are being transformed into the same image** from one degree of glory to another. For this comes from the Lord who is the Spirit."

1 Tim. 3:4-5 NLT
"He must **manage his own family well**, having **children who respect and obey him.** For if a man cannot manage his own household, how can he take care of God's church?)"

Heb. 13:7, 17 ESV
"Remember your leaders, who spoke the word of God to you. Consider the outcome of their way of life and imitate their faith." **Obey your leaders and submit to them**, for they are keeping watch over your souls, as those who will have to give an account. Let them do this with joy and not with groaning, for that would be of no advantage to you."

Heb. 12:5-11 NASU
"And have you forgotten the exhortation that addresses you as sons? "My son, do not regard lightly **the discipline of the Lord**, nor be weary when reproved by him. For the Lord **disciplines the one he loves**, and chastises every son whom he receives." **It is for discipline that you have to endure**. God is treating you as sons. For what son is there whom his father does not discipline? If you are left **without discipline**, in which all have participated, then you are illegitimate children and not sons. Besides this, we have had earthly fathers who **disciplined us** and we respected them. Shall we not much more be subject to the Father of spirits and live? For they disciplined us

Leaders are regularly "tested and approved."

for a short time as it seemed best to them, but **he disciplines us for our good**, that we may share his holiness. For the moment all **discipline seems painful** rather than pleasant, but later it yields the peaceful fruit of righteousness to those who **have been trained by it.**"

John 15:2
"He cuts off every branch in me **that bears no fruit**, while every branch that does bear fruit he prunes so that it will be even more fruitful."

Ps. 69:9
"…for **zeal for your house consumes me**, and the insults of those who insult you fall on me."

Prov. 23:17
"Do not let your heart envy sinners, but always **be zealous for the fear of the Lord.**"

Acts 8:2; 6-8
"Godly men buried Stephen and **mourned deeply** for him…when the crowds heard Philip and saw the signs he performed, they all paid close attention to what he said. For with shrieks, impure spirits came out of many, and many who **were paralysed or lame were healed. So there was great joy in that city.**"

2 Cor. 8:21
"For we are taking pains to do what is right, not only **in the eyes of the Lord but also in the eyes of man.**"

1 Tim. 4:12
"Don't let anyone look down on you because you are young, but set an example for the believers in speech, in conduct, in love, in faith and in purity."

Rom. 12:17
"Do not repay anyone evil for evil. Be careful to **do what is right in the eyes of everyone.**"

Hab. 2:3
"For the revelation awaits **an appointed time**; it speaks of the end and will not prove false. Though it linger, wait for it; it will certainly come and will not delay."

Heb. 10:37-39
"For 'in just a very little while, He who is coming will come and **will not delay.**' And, 'But my righteous one will live by faith. And I take no pleasure in the one who shrinks back.' But we do not belong to those who shrink back and are destroyed, but to those who have faith and are saved."

Leaders are regularly "tested and approved."

Heb. 6:12
"We do not want you to become lazy, but to imitate those who **through faith and patience inherit what has been promised**."

Ps.105:19 NKJV
"**Until the time** that his word came to pass, the word of **the Lord tested him**."

Gen. 41:52
"The second son he named Ephraim and said, 'It is because **God has made me fruitful in the land of my suffering**.'

1 Sam. 13:8-13
"He waited for seven days, the time set by Samuel; but Samuel did not come to Gilgal, and Saul's men began to scatter. So he said, 'Bring me the burnt offering and the fellowship offerings.' And Saul offered up the burnt offering. Just as he finished making the offering, Samuel arrived, and Saul went out to greet him. 'What have you done?' asked Samuel. Saul replied, 'When I saw that the men were scattering, and that you did not come at the set time, and that the Philistines were assembling at Michmash,' I thought, "Now the Philistines will come down against me at Gilgal, and I have not sought the Lord's favour." So I felt compelled to offer the burnt offering.' 'You have done a foolish thing,' Samuel said. 'You have not kept the command the Lord your God gave you; if you had, he would have established your kingdom over Israel for all time.'

2 Cor. 4:13
"It is written: 'I believed; therefore I have spoken.' Since we have that same spirit of faith we also believe and therefore speak…."

Ps. 62:5 KJV
"My soul, wait thou only upon God; for **my expectation is from him**."

2 Cor. 11:28
"Besides everything else, **I face daily the pressure** of my concern for all the churches."

Luke 22:31-32
'Simon, Simon, Satan has asked **to sift all of you as wheat**. But I have prayed for you, Simon, that **your faith may not fail**. And when you have turned back, strengthen your brothers.'

John 10:10
"The thief comes only to **steal and kill and destroy**; I have come that they may have life, and have it to the full."

1 Thes. 2:17-20 ESV
"But since **we were torn away from you**, brothers, for a short time, in person not in heart, we endeavored the more eagerly and with great desire to see you face to face,

Leaders are regularly "tested and approved."

because we wanted to come to you—I, Paul, again and again—but Satan hindered us. For what is our hope or joy or crown of boasting before our Lord Jesus at his coming? Is it not you? For you are our glory and joy."

1 Thes. 3:1-8 ESV
"Therefore when we could bear it no longer, we were willing to be left behind at Athens alone, and we sent Timothy, our brother and God's coworker in the gospel of Christ, to establish and exhort you in your faith, that **no one be moved by these afflictions.** For you yourselves **know that we are destined for this**. For when we were with you, we kept telling you beforehand that **we were to suffer affliction**, just as it has come to pass, and just as you know. For this reason, when I could bear it no longer, I sent to learn about your faith, for fear that somehow the tempter had tempted you and our labor would be in vain. But now that Timothy has come to us from you, and has brought us the good news of your faith and love and reported that you always remember us kindly and long to see us, as we long to see you—for this reason, brothers, **in all our distress and affliction we have been comforted about you through your faith**. For now we live, if you are standing fast in the Lord."

Acts 20:19
"I served the Lord with great humility and with tears and in the midst of **severe testing by the plots of my Jewish opponents**."

1 John 4:1-3
"Dear friends, do not believe every spirit, but **test the spirits** to see whether they are from God, because many false prophets have gone out into the world. This is how you can recognise the Spirit of God: every spirit that acknowledges that Jesus Christ has come in the flesh is from God, but every spirit that does not acknowledge Jesus is not from God. This is the spirit of the antichrist, which you have heard is coming and even now is already in the world."

Rev. 2:10
"Do not be afraid of what you are about to suffer. I tell you, the devil will put some of you in **prison to test you**, and you will suffer persecution for ten days. Be faithful, even to the point of death, and I will give you **your victor's crown**."

1 John 3:8
"...The **reason the Son of God appeared** was to destroy the devil's work."

1 Cor. 11:26-28
"I have been constantly on the move. I have been **in danger** from rivers, **in danger** from bandits, **in danger** from my fellow Jews, **in danger** from Gentiles; **in danger** in the city, **in danger** in the country, **in danger** at sea; and **in danger** from false believers. I have laboured and toiled and have often gone without sleep; I have known hunger and thirst and have often gone without food; I have been cold and naked. Besides everything else, I face daily the pressure of my concern for all the churches."

Leaders are regularly "tested and approved."

Luke 10:40
"But Martha was distracted by all the preparations that had to be made. She came to him and asked, 'Lord, don't you care that my sister has left me to do the work by myself? Tell her to help me!'

Prov. 4:5, 27
"Get wisdom, get understanding; do not forget my words or turn away from them… Do not turn to the right or the left; keep your foot from evil."

Luke 8:23
"As they sailed, he fell asleep. A squall came down on the lake, so that the boat was being swamped, and they were in great danger."

2 Cor. 11:26-28
"I have been constantly on the move. I have been **in danger** from rivers, **in danger** from bandits, **in danger** from my fellow Jews, **in danger** from Gentiles; **in danger** in the city, **in danger** in the country, **in danger** at sea; and **in danger** from false believers."

Acts 15:37-38
"Barnabas wanted to take John, also called Mark, with them. but Paul did not think it wise to take him, because **he had deserted them** in Pamphylia and had not continued with them in the work."

2 Tim 4:11
"Get Mark and bring him with you, **because he is helpful to me in my ministry**."

2 Cor. 6:2-11
"For he says, 'In the time of my favour I heard you, and in the day of salvation I helped you." I tell you, now is the time of God's favour, now is the day of salvation. We put no stumbling-block in anyone's path, so that our ministry will not be discredited. Rather, as servants of God we commend ourselves in every way: in great endurance; in troubles, hardships and distresses; in beatings, imprisonments and riots; in hard work, sleepless nights and hunger; in purity, understanding, patience and kindness; in the Holy Spirit and in sincere love; in truthful speech and in the power of God; with weapons of righteousness in the right hand and in the left; through glory and dishonour, bad report and good report; genuine, yet regarded as impostors; known, yet regarded as unknown; dying, and **yet we live on**; beaten, and yet not killed; sorrowful, yet always rejoicing; poor, yet making many rich; having nothing, and yet possessing everything. We have spoken freely to you, Corinthians, and opened wide our hearts to you.'

1 Cor. 3:12-15
"If anyone builds on this foundation using gold, silver, costly stones, wood, hay or straw, their work will be shown for what it is, because the Day will bring it to light. It will be revealed with fire, and **the fire will test the quality of each person's work**. If what has been built survives, the builder will receive his reward. If it is burned up,

Leaders are regularly "tested and approved."

the builder will suffer loss but yet will be saved--but only as one escaping through the flames."

John 15:16 NLT
"You didn't choose me. I chose you. **I appointed you to go and produce lasting fruit**, so that the Father will give you whatever you ask for, using my name."

Matt 7:25
"The rain came down, the streams rose, and the winds blew and beat against that house; yet it did not fall, because it had its **foundation on the rock**."

Prov. 24:3-4
"By wisdom a house is built, and through understanding it is established; through knowledge its rooms are filled with rare and beautiful treasures."

Heb. 12:3 KJV
"For consider him that **endured such contradiction** of sinners against himself, lest ye be wearied and faint in your minds."

Matt. 8:14-15
"When Jesus came into Peter's house, he saw Peter's mother-in-law lying in bed with a fever. He touched her hand and the fever left her, and she got up and began to wait on him."

Mark 15:3-5
"The chief priests **accused him of many things**. So again Pilate asked him, 'Aren't you going to answer? See **how many things they are accusing you of.' But Jesus still made no reply**, and Pilate was amazed."

Luke 23:2
"And they began **to accuse him**, saying, 'We have found this man subverting our nation. He opposes payment of taxes to Caesar and claims to be Messiah, a king.'

1 Peter 2:12
"Live such good lives among the pagans that, though **they accuse you** of doing wrong, they may see your good deeds and glorify God on the day he visits us."

Rev. 12:10
"Then I heard a loud voice in heaven say: "Now have come the salvation and the power and the kingdom of our God, and the authority of his Christ. For **the accuser of our brothers and sisters, who accuses them** before our God day and night, has been hurled down."

Acts 8:1-4
"And Saul approved of their killing him. On that day a great persecution broke out against the church in Jerusalem, and all except the apostles were scattered throughout

Leaders are regularly "tested and approved."

Judea and Samaria. Godly men buried Stephen and mourned deeply for him. But Saul began to destroy the church. Going from house to house, **he dragged off both men and women and put them in prison**. Those who had been scattered preached the word wherever they went."

Acts 9:31
"Then the church throughout Judea, Galilee and Samaria enjoyed a time of peace and was strengthened. Living in the fear of the Lord and encouraged by the Holy Spirit, it increased in numbers."

Acts 12:1, 5
"It was about this time that King Herod **arrested some** who belonged to the church, **intending to persecute** them. So Peter was kept in prison, but the church was earnestly praying to God for him."

Acts 15:1-3
"Certain people came down from Judea to Antioch and were teaching the brothers: 'Unless you are circumcised, according to the custom taught by Moses, you cannot be saved.' This brought Paul and Barnabas into **sharp dispute and debate** with them. So Paul and Barnabas were appointed, along with some other believers, to go up to Jerusalem to see the apostles and elders about this question. The church sent them on their way, and as they travelled through Phoenicia and Samaria, they told how the Gentiles had been converted. This news made all the believers very glad."

Acts 15:6, 22, 30, 31
"The apostles and elders met to consider this question…Then the apostles and elders, with the whole church, decided to choose some of their own men and send them to Antioch with Paul and Barnabas. They chose Judas (called Barsabbas) and Silas, two men who were leaders among the believers."…so the men were sent off and went down to Antioch, where they gathered the church together and delivered the letter. The people read it and were glad for its encouraging message."

Heb. 12:2 NASU
"…fixing our eyes on Jesus, the author and perfecter of faith, who for the joy set before him endured the cross, despising the shame, and has sat down at the right hand of the throne of God."

Eccl. 4:10
"If either of them falls down, one can help the other up. But pity anyone who falls and has no-one to help them up!"

Rom. 12:1-2
"Therefore, I urge you, brothers and sisters, in view of God's mercy, to offer your bodies as a living sacrifice, holy and pleasing to God — this is your true and proper worship. Do not conform to the pattern of this world, but be transformed by the

Leaders are regularly "tested and approved."

renewing of your mind. Then you will be able to test and approve what God's will is — his good, pleasing and perfect will."

Isa. 49:2-4
"He made my mouth like a sharpened sword, in the shadow of his hand he hid me; he made me into a polished arrow and concealed me in his quiver. He said to me, 'You are my servant, Israel, in whom I will display my splendour.' But I said, '**I have laboured to in vain; I have spent my strength for nothing at all**. Yet what is due to me is in the Lord's hand, and my reward is with my God.'

Phil. 2:14-15
"**Do everything without grumbling or arguing**, so that you may become blameless and pure, 'children of God without fault in a crooked and depraved generation,' then you will shine among them like stars in the universe."

Num. 11:1
"Now the people **complained** about their hardships in the hearing of the Lord, and when he heard them his anger was aroused. Then fire from the Lord burned among them and consumed some of the outskirts of the camp."

Acts 26:19
'So then, King Agrippa, I was not **disobedient to the vision** from heaven.'

Heb. 10:39
"But we do not belong to **those who shrink back** and are destroyed, but to those who have faith and are saved."

Rev 12:11
"They triumphed over him by the blood of the Lamb and by the word of their testimony; they did not love their lives so much as to **shrink from death**."

John 6:66
"From this time many of his **disciples turned back** and no longer followed him."

Ps 15:3 TMV
"Don't hurt your friend, **don't blame** your neighbour...."

Hos. 4:4 TMV
"But don't look for **someone to blame**. No finger pointing! You, priest, are the one in the dock"

Deut. 1:21
'See, the Lord your God has given you the land. Go up and take possession of it as the Lord, the God of your ancestors, told you. Do not be afraid; **do not be discouraged**.'

Leaders are regularly "tested and approved."

Josh. 10:25
"Joshua said to them, 'Do not be afraid; **do not be discouraged**. Be strong and courageous. This is what the Lord will do to all the enemies you are going to fight.'

Rom. 14:23
"…and everything that does not come from faith is sin."

Prov. 24:16
"…for though the righteous falls seven times, **he rises again**, but the wicked stumble when calamity comes."

Mic. 7:8 NKJV
"Do not rejoice over me, my enemy; **When I fall, I will arise**; When I sit in darkness, The LORD *will be* a light to me."

Gal. 6:4-5
"Each one should test his own actions. They can take pride in themselves alone, **without comparing themselves to someone else**, for each one should carry his own load."

Eph. 3:16
"I pray that out of his glorious riches he may strengthen you with power through his Spirit in your inner being…."

Leaders are regularly "tested and approved."

The Leader and.....

Lifelong Friendships

Introduction
Christianity is relationship. It is a dynamic, personal, intimate relationship with God as our Heavenly Father, our closest Friend, and our lover. No leader can expect to sustain healthy, effective, and exemplary leadership without embracing relationship. One pastor's wife was heard to say seriously of her husband in a public meeting, "My husband loves the ministry, he just doesn't like people." Her poverty of understanding of the real nature of ministry was quite dramatic. The structure of the godhead is relational. The basis of our relationship to God is love, a term of intimacy and commitment. The place where we "flesh-out" our understanding and ability in relationships is in our families and among our friends. If we have shallow relationships with friends and family, we are not ready yet to model the loving, accepting, gracious, relationship that is the core of Christian living, to others. Eph. 5:1-2. Paul spoke of his "dear friend, Luke" in Col. 4:14. Do you have any "dear friends" that walk closely with you in the journey?

Often leaders can be in the company of other people and even other leaders for years and never form any deep bonds that are the foundations of lifelong friendships. They work with others but never *mesh* or *merge* with others. They have retained their individuality in a level of separating independence. Even though they are *with* others, they fundamentally live alone. I was recently told a story of a middle-aged pastor of a large, "successful" congregation that hung himself. Everyone speculated why he did something so irrational to his beliefs. The question that came to my mind was, "Where were his friends?" Had he made any deep personal friendships that he could comfortably and confidentially share his life? Was he walking the "lonely road" that some have taught is just the way leadership has to be? Great notoriety has destroyed many lives as the most important option of all the options that are opened up through notoriety, is not taken up—intimacy with God and other lifelong friends.

Relationships With Other Leaders
Some people demand that others be like them in order to develop any significant relationship. Others hide themselves and in so doing, they fail to mirror the heart-disclosing nature of Christ. John 15:15; Phil. 1:8; 2 Cor. 6:12-13. Leaders are meant to live in the "real world." The reality that comes to a leader through knowable relationships is the world out of which a leader leads. The transparency of intimacy gives authenticity and wisdom to the leader he or she would otherwise not have. It provides the message to followers that the leader is "real" and has a genuine connection with their lives. No leader can truly be a biblical leader without embracing relationships of intimacy

Leaders develop lifelong friendships—great treasures of life.

and longevity. The Cross of Christ is the supreme statement of how much God values relationships. Leaders are meant to reflect that value, both in their publicly-observable relationships as well as in their private lives.

In 1 Thess. 2:8 NASU Paul reveals this "real" type of transparency as he says, "Having so fond an affection for you, we were well-pleased to **impart to you not only the gospel of God but also our own lives**, because you had become very dear to us." Many leaders are willing to open the Word to others but **not their lives**. Being honest and humble about one's failings and mistakes, being willing to talk about the 'hard' places and openness to personal questions helps others to see the "gospel in operation" in the life of the leader.

The Bible couples various people together in Christian relationships other than marriage. Specific names and details are given to us to inspire the reality of deep and lifelong friendships with others, both in the work of ministry and apart from it. The New Testament reveals that the relationships of the Body of Christ are referred to in "family" terms, "brothers," "sisters," "fathers" and "mothers." 1 Tim. 5:1-2; Rom. 16:14-15. This speaks of the purity of motivation and the affection that everyone is to have for fellow believers. Leaders are meant to model this way of relating to others.

The Bible speaks of close friendships. Deut. 13:6; Prov. 17:17; Prov. 18:24; Prov. 27:10; Philemon 1.

- Paul and Silas are mentioned together 17 times in the New Testament.

- Paul and Barnabas are mentioned 15 times together in the New Testament.

- Paul and Timothy are mentioned 9 times together in the New Testament.

The Bible records that these men walked through life together and faced together, hazards and hardships, successes and accomplishments. Their life experience welded them together as they mutually sought to fulfill the same mission—extend the Kingdom and build with Him, His Church.

The Great Treasure of Lifelong Friendships
Paul, the Apostle, had numerous friends that he laboured with throughout his lifetime. From the beginning he had Priscilla and Aquila, who took him "under their wings" and mentored him and with whom he walked as dear friends. Others formed close, lifelong friendships with him. We build a great resource of friendship, accountability and blessing as we sow into friendship with others.

- Fellow-workers – Priscilla and Aquila, who risked their lives for me -- Rom. 16:3-4, Urbanus -- Rom. 16:9; Timothy -- Rom. 16:21; Epaphroditus -- Phil. 2:25; Titus -- 2 Cor. 8:23; Clement -- Phil. 4:3;

Leaders develop lifelong friendships—great treasures of life.

- "Dear friends" – Epenetus -- Rom. 16:5; Stachys -- Rom. 16:9; Persis -- Rom. 16:12; Luke -- Col. 4:14; Philemon -- Philemon. 1; Gaius -- 3 John 1.

How could Paul have developed so many close and wonderful friends? He lived sowing love into relationships with his fellow leaders and those he met. He, no doubt, did not expect instant intimacy and trust but sowed his love and life "with no strings attached," expecting nothing. He allowed intimacy and friendship and self-disclosure to develop. What will you develop, in terms of close and intimate friends, over your lifetime?

Developing Lifelong Friendships
The story of Jonathan and David's relationship is a great documentation of the principles of friendship necessary to develop and sustain a lifelong bond. Thirty-two times they are spoken of in the same chapter as the narrative of their friendship unfolds. Their exemplary friendship was formed in the most unique circumstances. We gain from this that God uses the unique design of our lives to connect us with people in His great purposes that we may have never chosen. The following are fundamental principles of friendship, that pursued and shared, become foundations for developing lifelong friendships.

- Friendship as believers is both spirit and soul. It is a spiritual relationship, having at its core, spiritual matters and in addition, earthly matters. 1 Sam. 18:1.

- Friendship affords protection from the unwarranted attacks of others by providing an objective sanctuary and refuge. 1 Sam. 18:2; 19:1-3 NLT.

- Friendship involves a covenant or commitment either spoken or unspoken but mutually assumed. 1 Sam. 18:3.

- Deep friendship involves accepting and honouring the place the other has in your life and in the larger scheme of things. 1 Sam. 18:4.

- Friends defend the positive reputation of each other in front of others. 1 Sam. 19:4-7. They also act as mediators or intercessors.

- Friends have honest, humble disclosure between them. 1 Sam. 20:1, 8. The great struggles of life are easier to win when we receive the targeted wisdom, love and encouragement of lifelong friends.

- Friends serve one another. 1 Sam. 20:4.

- Friends have each other's "back." 1 Sam. 20:9.

- Friendships are covenants that endure through the generations. 1 Sam. 20:14-17, 23. David looked after Jonathan's family after Jonathan had died. 2 Sam. 9:6; 21:7. 1 Sam 20:42 says, "Jonathan said to David, 'Go in peace, **for we have**

Leaders develop lifelong friendships—great treasures of life.

sworn friendship with each other in the name of the Lord, saying, "The Lord is witness between you and me, and between your descendants and my descendants forever."'

Potential Toxic Relationships
Some believers unwittingly seek to develop relationships that end up suffocating others by their possessive, obsessive and manipulative efforts. They so desperately want the attention and affirmation of others, especially leaders, that they approach them in ways that are quite oppressive. Attempts to adjust their approach are often met with anger and denial of any wrongdoing or misplaced approaches. When honest confrontation has taken place and there is no change in the obsessive approach to a leader, the leader must graciously seek to minimise the attempts to control his time and attention. To fail to do this is to the detriment of his ability to help others. Such persons can be used by Satan to harass and oppress a leader so as to make him ineffective.

Building Solid Friendships
There are principles of building relationships. To utilise them is to have the best relational life. To ignore them is to violate them and suffer. Here are some tips for general friendship development.

1. Look to love people. Love everyone, and don't necessarily set out to "make friends." This tends to create awkwardness as people may discern that that is what is happening. However, to have friends you must show yourself friendly or take a friendly, welcoming approach to other people. Prov. 18:24 KJV. Let your basic heart motivation be to love others and let that be initially evidenced by your friendliness.

2. Always move toward others in social situations. Don't wait for them to come toward you. Introduce yourself and take a positive interest in them. This is love in action right at the very beginning. God's love is a "first-loving" initiator.

3. Smile whenever you meet people. It helps relax them and it helps you to relax as well. Your smile puts the face of God on your face. Ps. 80:7 TMV says, "… smile your blessing smile."

4. Structure your life to be with people more than to be on your own. Don't consider yourself a leader if you live a secluded life. Live connecting with people. This is truly living a life of love, as Jesus came to "give His life a ransom for many" and so do we. Look for ways to serve and help others. Do all that you do with "no strings attached." You are not loving and giving and serving to gain something for yourself but a better life for others. 2 Cor. 5:15. Your agenda is always to be a blessing to others.

5. Don't be suspicious about what others may be thinking. This is a terribly destructive practice. Speculation is most often wrong. It is a human and feeble

Leaders develop lifelong friendships—great treasures of life.

attempt at negative prophecy that unwittingly invites Satan's input. Wrong thoughts lead to wrong conclusions, which lead to wrong decisions and wrong judgments, and wrong words and the wrong results. Relate to others on the basis of what they actually say to you. If they express appreciation for you or something you have done, accept it graciously and believe that it was genuine. To do otherwise is to make them a liar and a hypocrite. 1 Chron. 19:1-4 tells us that David's pure motive was misjudged. We should **not** have a perspective that is skeptical, cynical, judgmental or critical. Love believes. 1 Cor. 13:7. The leader is one who begins by believing others. He does not live with a suspicious mind-set, for that is evil.

6. If someone criticises you, take it, and ask the Lord how you can use that to be a better person. Don't hold grudges. Don't examine the vessel that offered the criticism for their flaws. Don't judge the value or merits of their criticism by the negative impressions you may have of the person who was criticising you. God uses donkeys to adjust prophets.

7. Don't allow yourself one moment of self-pity or depression. That is self-preoccupation and is utterly destructive and sinful. Forget about yourself and abandon yourself to others. That is really fun!

8. Allow some relationships that are **not** based on your helping some other person who is desperate spiritually or someone with whom you find yourself always pouring out your own troubles to. Relate to some simply on a peer level, anticipating just having fun and fellowship with them.

9. Learn to take a joke on yourself and laugh at yourself. Don't be fragile, over-sensitive and way too serious.

10. Surprise people with little blessings. Many kindnesses, stacked up over time, are a powerful message. Don't wait for or expect thanks…just do it because it is right.

11. Be a thankful and a grateful person. Express appreciation for all that others do for you. Selfish people take and are not thankful.

12. Pray for God's help in loving others with His love. Loving is always right though not always easy. He has poured His love into your heart that it might pour through you. That outpouring through you cleanses you and brings wholeness to others. Rom. 5:5.

13. Immediately forgive others and ignore provocation. Be a peacemaker. If you find yourself in anger and resentment and unforgiveness, go and seek reconciliation immediately. Remember as you go to reconcile, that the two things that sabotage your success in reconciliation most often are: 1) **choice of words** and 2) **tone of voice**. Pray until you have peace and have in yourself

Leaders develop lifelong friendships—great treasures of life.

resolved *to go in peace to make peace*. Be humble, forgiving, and determined that you are going to come away loving and free along with the other person. Do your very best. Easily ask to be forgiven for any offences others think you caused whether you think you caused it or not. Determine that you will go toward all others on the planet lovingly regardless of how they may have treated you or any attitude of animosity they may display.

14. Recognise the Divine purpose and design in the connection you have with your current fellow leaders. God has placed them in your life and you in their lives. Seek to develop loving, caring relationships with them. Some of those relationships will develop and those friends will walk with you all the days of your life and you with them, even with changing circumstances.

15. Don't get caught in the trap of taking up another's offence. Prov. 26.17 ESV. All too often, believers fall into the trap of *listening* to someone else's offence and then take up sides with them against the one who caused the offence. This is foolish and forbidden. At the first sign of an offence someone says they have, you interrupt them and tell them they need to go to the other person…that you don't want to know about it. This practice can save several friendships.

16. If you are friendless, in your own mind, suspect that the difficulty is with you and not all "the others." Often those who do not believe they have friends suspect the difficulty is with others who are just not "relational" or genuinely friendly. Friendless leaders cast others in the dim light of "rejecting them" and justify their loneliness, resentment and anger. They sometimes accuse all "the others" of being in a clique having established their network of friends and have padlocked the door so that no other can enter the sanctuary of intimacy they enjoy with others. All of these attitudes point to the need for counselling and help to rid the "friendless" person of the rejection syndrome and become a whole, healthy, friend-rich person. Hurting people unwittingly build walls. Whole people open doors. These two instinctive dynamics are mutually exclusive—you cannot build walls and open doors at the same time. Fear is self-protecting and love is self-giving.

17. Allow your friends, no matter how close, the freedom to develop other close friends without threatening any loss in your love and approach to them. You don't own them or have exclusive right to their heart, attention, time or interest. A healthy relationship is a relationship that allows others to share what you have found to be such a blessing. Trying to own, control, or scare others off is selfish and destructive.

Summary

Don't go through the remainder of your life as a leader without developing friendships of love, transparency and selflessness. Your survival depends on people knowing you and loving you. Too many so-called strong men and women have lived independent

Leaders develop lifelong friendships—great treasures of life.

of deep and lasting friendships and have lived to pay a price they wouldn't have paid had they had the safety and spiritual provision of deep, lifelong friendships.

Application

1. Decide and follow through with efforts to invite other leaders to your home or out for a meal. Decide to get to know them better and allow them to get to know you better. Make this a part of your on-going lifestyle.

2. Pray regularly for other members on the leadership team. Send them cards, texts, emails of encouragement. Bless them in as many ways as you can. Loving others, you make your world good and theirs as well.

3. Reach out to newcomers and people who seem to be struggling. Engage them in conversation to see how you can be an encouragement to them. Invite some of these people to your home for a meal. Bless them and do for them whatever God tells you to do.

4. In a small group, discuss what challenges each one faces in making a life of hospitality and connecting with other leaders and how these challenges are overcome. Some may have come from family backgrounds that were not particularly hospitable. Some may feel embarrassed about their accommodation. Some may have financial issues.

5. Purchase and read the book, "An Apple for the Road," by Pam Spinosi. Note especially the chapter entitled, "Comfy in the Cluster."

6. Purchase and read the book, "Quality Friendship" by Gary Inrig.

Leaders develop lifelong friendships—great treasures of life.

Lifelong Friendship Scriptures

Eph. 5:1-2
"Follow God's example, therefore, as dearly loved children and **live a life of love**, just as Christ loved us and gave himself up for us as a fragrant offering and sacrifice to God."

Col. 4:14
"Our **dear friend Luke**, the doctor, and Demas send greetings."

John 15:15
"I no longer call you servants, because a servant does not know his master's business. Instead, I have called you **friends, for everything that I learned from my Father I have made known to you**."

Phil. 1:8
"God can testify how I long for all of you **with the affection** of Christ Jesus."

2 Cor. 6:12-13
"We are **not withholding our affection** from you, but you are withholding yours from us. As a fair exchange — I speak as to my children — **open wide your hearts** also."

1 Tim. 5:1-2
"Do not rebuke an older man harshly, but exhort him as if he were **your father**. Treat younger men **as brothers**, older women **as mothers**, and younger women **as sisters**, with absolute purity."

Rom. 16:14-15
"Greet Asyncritus, Phlegon, Hermes, Patrobas, Hermas and **the other brothers and sisters** with them. Greet Philologus, Julia, Nereus and **his sister**, and Olympas and all the Lord's people with them.

Deut. 13:6
"If your very own brother, or your son or daughter, or the wife you love, or **your closest friend** secretly entices you…."

Prov. 17:17
"A **friend loves at all times**, and a brother is born for a time of adversity."

Prov. 18:24
"…there is **a friend who sticks closer than a brother**."

Prov. 27:10
"**Do not forsake your friend** or a friend of your family, and do not go to your relative's house when disaster strikes you — better a neighbour nearby than a relative far away."

Leaders develop lifelong friendships—great treasures of life.

Philemon 1
"Paul, a prisoner of Christ Jesus, and Timothy our brother, To Philemon **our dear friend** and fellow-worker...."

Rom. 16:3-4
"Greet Priscilla and Aquila, my **fellow-workers** in Christ Jesus. **They risked their lives for me**. Not only I but all the churches of the Gentiles are grateful to them."

Rom. 16:9
"Greet Urbanus, our **fellow worker** in Christ, and my dear friend Stachys."

Rom. 16:21
"Timothy, **my co-worker**, sends his greetings to you, as do Lucius, Jason and Sosipater, my fellow Jews."

Phil. 2:25
"But I think it is necessary to send back to you Epaphroditus, **my brother, co-worker and fellow soldier**, who is also your messenger, whom you sent to take care of my needs."

2 Cor. 8:23
"As for Titus, he is **my partner and fellow-worker** among you; as for our brothers, they are representatives of the churches and an honour to Christ."

Phil. 4:3
"Yes, and I ask you, my true companion, help these women since they have contended at my side in the cause of the gospel, along with Clement and the rest of my **co-workers**, whose names are in the book of life."

Rom. 16:5
"Greet also the church that meets at their house. Greet **my dear friend** Epenetus, who was the first convert to Christ in the province of Asia."

Rom. 16:9
"Greet Urbanus, our fellow worker in Christ, and my **dear friend Stachys**."

Rom. 16:12
"Greet **my dear friend Persis**, another woman who has worked very hard in the Lord."

Col. 4:14
"Our **dear friend Luke**, the doctor, and Demas send greetings."

Philemon 1
"Paul, a prisoner of Christ Jesus, and Timothy our brother, To Philemon our **dear friend** and fellow worker...."

3 John 1
"The elder, To my dear friend Gaius, **whom I love** in the truth."

Leaders develop lifelong friendships—great treasures of life.

1 Sam. 18:1
"After David had finished talking with Saul, Jonathan became **one in spirit with David, and he loved him as himself**."

1 Sam. 18:2
"From that day Saul kept David with him and did not let him return home to his family."

1 Sam. 19:1-3 NLT
"Saul now urged his servants and his son Jonathan to assassinate David. But Jonathan, **because of his close friendship with David**, told him what his father was planning. "Tomorrow morning," he warned him, "you must find a hiding place out in the fields. I'll ask my father to go out there with me, and I'll talk to him about you. Then I'll tell you everything I can find out."

1 Sam. 18:3
"And **Jonathan made a covenant with David** because he loved him as himself."

1 Sam. 18:4
"Jonathan took off the robe he was wearing and gave it to David, along with his tunic, and even his sword, his bow and his belt."

1 Sam 19:4-7
"Jonathan **spoke well of David to Saul** his father and said to him, 'Let not the king do wrong to his servant David; he has not wronged you, and what he has done has benefited you greatly. He took his life in his hands when he killed the Philistine. The Lord won a great victory for all Israel, and you saw it and were glad. Why then would you do wrong to an innocent man like David by killing him for no reason?' Saul listened to Jonathan and took this oath: 'As surely as the Lord lives, David will not be put to death.' So Jonathan called David and **told him the whole conversation**. He brought him to Saul, and David was with Saul as before."

1 Sam. 20:1, 8
"Then David fled from Naioth at Ramah and went to Jonathan and asked, 'What have I done? What is my crime? How have I wronged your father, that he is trying to kill me?' As for you, show kindness to your servant, for you have brought him into a covenant with you before the Lord. If I am guilty, then kill me yourself! Why hand me over to your father?'

1 Sam. 20:4
"Jonathan said to David, 'Whatever you want me to do, I'll do for you.'

1 Sam. 20:9
'Never!' Jonathan said. 'If I had the least inkling that my father was determined to harm you, wouldn't I tell you?'

Leaders develop lifelong friendships—great treasures of life.

1 Sam. 20:14-17, 23
"But show me unfailing kindness like that the Lord's kindness as long as I live, so that I may not be killed, and do not ever cut off your kindness from my family — not even when the Lord has cut off every one of David's enemies from the face of the earth.' So Jonathan made a covenant with the house of David, saying, 'May the Lord call David's enemies to account.' And Jonathan made David reaffirm his oath out of love for him, because he loved him as he loved himself….and about the matter you and I discussed — remember, the Lord is witness between you and me for ever.'

2 Sam. 9:6
"When Mephibosheth son of Jonathan, the son of Saul, came to David, he bowed down to pay him honour. David said, 'Mephibosheth!' 'At your service,' he replied."

2 Sam. 21:7
"The king spared Mephibosheth son of Jonathan, the son of Saul, because of the oath before the Lord between David and Jonathan son of Saul."

Prov. 18:24 KJV
"A man that hath friends **must shew himself friendly**: and there is a friend that sticketh closer than a brother."

2 Cor. 5:15
"And he died for all, that those who live should **no longer live for themselves** but for him who died for them and was raised again."

1 Chron. 19:1-4
"In the course of time, Nahash king of the Ammonites died, and his son succeeded him as king. David thought, 'I will show kindness to Hanun son of Nahash, because his father showed kindness to me.' So David sent a delegation to express his sympathy to Hanun concerning his father. When David's envoys came to Hanun in the land of the Ammonites to express sympathy to him, the Ammonite commanders said to Hanun, 'Do you think David is honouring your father by sending envoys to you to express sympathy? Haven't his envoys come to you to explore and spy out the country and overthrow it?' So Hanun seized David's envoys, shaved them, cut off their garments at the buttocks, and sent them away."

1 Cor. 13:7
"It always protects, **always trusts**, always hopes, always perseveres."

Rom. 5:5
"And hope does not put us to shame, because **God's love has been poured out into our hearts** through the Holy Spirit, who has been given to us."

Prov. 26:17 ESV
"**Whoever meddles in a quarrel not his own** is like one who takes a passing dog by the ears."

Leaders develop lifelong friendships—great treasures of life.

The Leader and.....

Work

Introduction
In a world where the work ethic is poor or non-existent, leaders must be diligent, energetic and exemplary workers. Prov. 24:30-34 NLT says, "I walked by the field of a **lazy person**, the vineyard of one with no common sense. I saw that it was overgrown with nettles. It was covered with weeds, and its walls were broken down. Then, as I looked and thought about it, I learned this lesson: A little extra sleep, a little more slumber, a little folding of the hands to rest—then poverty will pounce on you like a bandit; scarcity will attack you like an armed robber."

Often leaders can assess their work load by comparison with others. Comparison rarely, if ever, is a good means of measurement, as we would most often compare ourselves with one extreme or the other and miss out what God is really requiring of us personally. The leader who is thinking he is doing way more than others compares himself with those he perceives are doing less. The leader who believes he is doing so little compares himself with those who are doing so much more without regard to any legitimate reasons why they might be doing more. Luke 10:40.

Paul says of himself, "I have been constantly on the move. I have been in danger from rivers, in danger from bandits, in danger from my fellow Jews, in danger from Gentiles; in danger in the city, in danger in the country, in danger at sea; and in danger from false believers. **I have laboured and toiled and have often gone without sleep**; I have known hunger and thirst and have often gone without food; I have been cold and naked. Besides everything else, I face daily the pressure of my concern for all the churches." 2 Cor. 11:26-28.

1 Cor. 15:58 says, "…Always give yourselves **fully to the work** of the Lord, because you know that your **labour** in the Lord is not in vain." Applying yourself to the tasks that are assigned to you is a labour that has eternal reward as it is done "unto Him." It is not measured completely in this life with our natural eyes, but by Him, from His eternal perspective. Prov. 18:9.

Jesus had a "completion" mentality. John 17:4; John 4:34. He called his assignment from the Father, "work." John 5:17; John 9:4. We, too, must have a "work" and "completion" mentality. We must have clear understanding of the work that we are to do and then an attitude and a performance that is characterised by **faithfulness, diligence, application and completion**. Acts 13:2; Acts 13:25; Acts 14:26; Acts 15:38; Acts 20:35; Rom. 16:12; 1 Cor. 4:12; 1 Cor. 16:16. Often men and women who retire from employment, whether it

Leaders work hard, rest when they should, and finish their mission.

is paid ministry or secular employment, struggle unwittingly, thinking their "work" is over. From Heaven's perspective they have simply changed from one form or avenue of life-contribution to another. If they do not find that "work" that enables them to finish "their course," they decline spiritually, physically, and mentally, in ways that God never intended. Their daily and weekly schedule may be more relaxed, but their life purpose has not been fulfilled until they breathe their last breath. Ex. 40:33 says, "…and so Moses **finished the work**."

Work/Rest Cycle
The natural life cycle for man was established in Creation. Man was to work, then rest. However, sin changed all that. Man, apart from Christ, discovers that often in the time slot that he has chosen to rest, he does find himself refreshed and ready to take on the cycle of work. When work multiplies to an overwhelming level, he often attempts to sleep but finds that he rests even less. Rest, in the Bible, is more than the sleep that renews our body. It is a place where stress, anxiety, pressure, and weariness of soul are replaced with peace, strength and fresh inner energy. Eph. 3:16. The pressure of schedule subsides and a fresh perspective filled with faith and creativity arises.

The leader must learn to make a "place of rest" in his inner life during the day and the week. He **must learn how to renew his soul and body** while the battle and the pressure is on-going. If you don't learn to rest well, you won't work well.

Jesus said in Matt. 11:29-30, "Take my yoke upon you and learn from me, for I am gentle and humble in heart, and you will find rest for your souls. For my yoke is easy and my burden is light.' Intimacy with the Lord brings rest and peace, releasing the leader from the stresses and strains of human-effort based living.

Jer. 31:25 says, 'I will refresh the weary and satisfy the faint.'

Gal. 6:9 "Let us **not become weary** in doing good, for at the proper time we will reap a harvest if we do not give up."

There are seasons of added responsibility and activity. Those seasons can wear away the strength of the inner man and make the leader vulnerable to negativity and discouragement. No leader can afford to allow this to happen. Recognising the necessity of inner renewal, he must pause to "mount up into the Presence" and "recharge his batteries." Singing, worship, quiet meditation, verbal declarations of Scripture, and prayer, all provide the on-the-job relief that we need when they are filled with faith. "Rest" is another word for faith. Heb. 4:9-11. 1 Peter 5:7 says, "…casting all your care upon Him, for He cares for you." (NKJV). The weights that weigh us down inwardly must be released to Him who is capable of carrying them all. Our focus must return to the One who is our strength in order to carry on. Isa 40:31 says, "But those who wait on the Lord shall **renew their strength**; They shall mount up with wings like eagles, They shall run and **not be weary**, they shall walk and not faint." NKJV Ps. 63:1-7.

Leaders work hard, rest when they should, and finish their mission.

Sometimes, leaders think that sitting in front of the television, "vegging out," as the saying goes, helps them to recharge or rest. However, there is rarely any renewal to the inner man and thus no real re-energising of the physical body. It is simply taking the mental focus away from the "work-stress" and a massaging of the emotions. The definition of amusement is: not thinking. Not thinking about something can seem to be restful, but in reality, that is not the substantial rest that the leader requires to take up his responsibilities with vitality and fresh wisdom. There may be nothing wrong with a given television programme but let us not delude ourselves into thinking that watching it will help us find rest in our souls, invigorate our bodies, and provide the strength that only joy and rejoicing can bring.

One very valuable tool available to the Spirit-baptised believer is the facility of speaking in tongues. Jude 20 says, "…**building yourselves up** on your most holy faith, praying in the Holy Spirit…." (NKJV). The Holy Spirit quickens your mortal body, renews your spirit-man and brings creative wisdom to your mind. The net effect of all this is peace and strength. Many believers and leaders underestimate the power of praying in tongues to regenerate their inner man, release peace and give fresh steps of direction.

Joy is also a powerful tool or avenue for releasing strength into the physical body, the mind and the spirit. Joy comes through celebration. It isn't necessarily feeling that all the circumstances in your life are aligned as you would have them. Make time to celebrate the good things, the victories and the blessings He has brought. Nehemiah 8:10-12 says, "Nehemiah said, 'Go and enjoy choice food and sweet drinks, and send some to those who have nothing prepared. This day is holy to our Lord. Do not grieve, for **the joy of the Lord is your strength**.' The Levites calmed all the people, saying, 'Be still, for this is a holy day. Do not grieve.' Then all the people went away to eat and drink, to send portions of food and **to celebrate with great joy**….' Joyless leaders become weary and faint-hearted on the journey. Ps. 81:1. Ruth 4:15 says, "He will renew your life and sustain you." Ps. 103:5.

Fellowship also renews the inner man. Prov. 27:9 TMV says, "Just as lotions and fragrance give sensual delight, a sweet friendship refreshes the soul." When leaders are continually weary, they can often isolate themselves from the 'refreshing' that comes from true Christian fellowship. True Christian fellowship is profoundly based in spiritual things although natural things are not taboo, of course. But it is the spiritual exchange between believers that brings insight, relief to the soul, and a burden-lifting rise to the spirit-man. Prov. 16:24 says, "Gracious words are a honeycomb, sweet to the soul and healing to the bones."

A time away to seek and wait on the Lord is a valuable tool that renews and refreshes. Jesus said in Mark 6:31-32, "Then, because so many people were coming and going that they did not even have a chance to eat, he said to them, 'Come with me by yourselves to a quiet place and get some rest.' So they went away by themselves in a boat to a solitary place."

Leaders work hard, rest when they should, and finish their mission.

Rehearsing the favour of God that is on your life is also a means of rest. Reminding yourself that you live in favour and under favour, helps to 'kindle' your faith again to release that favour. Meditating in the Scriptures that speak of God's favour on your life helps to remind you that your life success is built on His favour not your superhuman effort. Neh. 5:19; Ps. 5:12; Ps. 30:5; 2 Cor. 6:2.

Application

1. Keep a diary of your daily schedule in fifteen minute segments beginning from when you arise to when you go to bed. Do this for three weeks. List what you did for all your waking hours. After three weeks read over what you have written and examine how you have spent your time. Evaluate the changes you may need to make. Set those changes in motion.

2. Assess your regular energy levels. Are you always tired? What are the reasons for being consistently weary? Are you getting enough physical exercise? Are you sleeping deep sleep consistently? Are you eating a healthy diet in sufficient quantities? Are you carrying spiritual, mental and emotional burdens that Christ never meant you to carry that are "wearing you out?" Are you worrying about some things? Deal with them in the Word, faith and prayer. Seek counsel if necessary.

3. Are you having a consistent annual holiday? Do you make it physically and mentally relaxing and spiritual refreshing?

4. Are you working too long hours? Do you need to exercise your faith for a new job?

5. Do you get regularly refreshed through the fellowship you have with other Christian friends?

6. Do you have your own "solitary place" of rest? Do you use it regularly?

Leaders work hard, rest when they should, and finish their mission.

Work Scriptures

Luke 10:40
"But Martha was distracted by all the preparations that had to be made. She came to him and asked, 'Lord, don't you care that my sister has left me **to do the work by myself?** Tell her to help me!'

Prov. 18:9
"One who is slack in his work is brother to one who destroys."

John 17:4
"I have brought you glory on earth **by finishing the work** you gave me to do."

John 4:34
'My food,' said Jesus, 'is to do the will of him who sent me and **to finish his work.'**

John 5:17
"In his defence Jesus said to them, 'My Father is always at his **work** to this very day, and I, too, **am working.'**

John 9:4
"As long as it is day, **we must do the works** of him who sent me."

Acts 13:2
'Set apart for me Barnabas and Saul **for the work** to which I have called them.'

Acts 13:25
"As John was **completing his work**, he said: 'Who do you suppose I am?'

Acts 14:26
"From Attalia they sailed back to Antioch, where they had been committed to the grace of God for **the work they had now completed**."

Acts 15:38
"…Paul did not think it wise to take him, because he had deserted them in Pamphylia and **had not continued with them in the work**."

Acts 20:35
"In everything I did, I showed you that by **this kind of hard work** we must help the weak…."

Rom. 16:12
"Greet Tryphena and Tryphosa, those **women who work hard** in the Lord."

1 Cor. 4:12
"We **work hard** with our own hands."

Leaders work hard, rest when they should, and finish their mission.

1 Cor. 16:16
"…to submit to such people and to everyone who **joins in the work, and labours** at it."

Eph. 3:16
"I pray that out of his glorious riches he may **strengthen you with power** through his Spirit **in your inner being**.…"

Heb. 4:9-11
"There remains, then, a Sabbath-rest for the people of God; for anyone who enters God's rest also **rests from** their works, just as God did from his. Let us, therefore, make every effort **to enter that rest**, so that no-one will perish by following their example of disobedience."

Ps. 63:1-7
"You God, are my God, earnestly I seek you; I thirst for you, my whole being longs for you, in a dry and parched land where there is no water. I have seen you in the sanctuary and beheld your power and your glory. Because your love is better than life, my lips will glorify you. I will praise you as long as I live, and in your name I will lift up my hands. I will be satisfied as with the richest of foods; with singing lips my mouth will praise you. On my bed I remember you; I think of you through the watches of the night. Because you are my help, I sing in the shadow of your wings."

Ps. 81:1
"Sing for joy to God our strength; shout aloud to the God of Jacob!"

Ps. 103:5
"…who satisfies your desires with good things so that **your youth is renewed** like the eagle's."

Neh. 5:19
"**Remember me with favour**, my God, for all I have done for these people."

Ps. 5:12
"Surely, LORD, you bless the righteous; **you surround them with your favour** as with a shield."

Ps. 30:5
"For his anger lasts only a moment, but **his favour lasts a lifetime**; weeping may stay for the night, but **rejoicing comes in the morning**."

2 Cor. 6:2
"For he says, 'In the time of my favour I heard you, and in the day of salvation I helped you.' I tell you, **now is the time of God's favour**, now is the day of salvation."

Leaders work hard, rest when they should, and finish their mission.

The Leader and.....

Health

Leaders only endure as long as they have their health. If their health breaks, they can no longer lead. This is a major area of Satan's attack on leaders. He can do so much more damage limitation to his own kingdom, if he knocks out a leader, through attacks on their physical body. When leaders are younger, they tend to give less consideration to their physical health, simply assuming they will be healthy and get over any minor issues that arise. When leaders get older, they become more conscious of their physical health as the tendencies toward a more sedentary lifestyle, slower metabolism and poor dietary habits take their toll.

Too many leaders die prematurely or are forced to relinquish their role in leadership because of health reasons—some of which are satanic attacks and others which are poor lifestyle habits. Many widows are heard to say, "My husband died before his time." It is certain that Satan wants to take you out of action and your health is one way he can accomplish his mission. John 10:10. The leader must learn how to walk in Divine health. The leader learns to take decisions that are based in Divine wisdom from a Divine Creator, and in Divine power, conquering every spiritual attempt to bring sickness on the leader.

Solomon said, "My son, pay attention to what I say; turn your ear to my words. Do not let them out of your sight, keep them within your heart; for they are life to those who find them and **health to one's whole body**." Prov. 4:20-22. There is wisdom for walking in health.

Leaders do not generally expect to get sick or incapacitated in any way, but it does sometimes happen, as Satan attacks your body. God expects us to look after our bodies, which is His temple, in which we live, respecting it as such. 1 Cor. 6:19, 20. When you are young, you face the tendency of subscribing to modern life and the things of this world and live as though your body will never age. Sometimes, carelessness allows a person to eat anything, go without adequate sleep, fail to hydrate sufficiently, and get very little heart-racing, exercise. Sustained over time, the body wears away faster than it should and becomes susceptible naturally to diseases and infections. The natural immunity level from disease and illness is lowered. If the leader looks at his body like an automobile, he knows he will have to treat it in specific ways to maintain both its longevity and its full performance.

There are three dimensions of approaching our health: the preventive, the restorative and appropriating Divine health. If a leader takes no steps to establish good health

Leaders learn the secret of lifelong, Divine health.

habits, he can fully expect that the abuse of his body will have an impact at some point. The leader, who influences others, will want to take care of the temple that he and God live in together. 1 Cor. 6:19-20 says, "Do you not know that your bodies are the temples of the Holy Spirit, who is in you, whom you have received from God? You are not your own; you were bought with a price. Therefore honour God with your bodies."

Preventive methods means wearing the "shield of faith" to quench the fiery dart of sickness that would attack your body. Under a lesser covenant the Bible says in Deut. 7:15, "The Lord will keep you from every disease." As it is His will for you to walk in Divine health (3 John 2 NKJV), you must live believing, that no sickness can take up residence in your body and inwardly resist all attempts of that satanic attack just as you would resist satanic attacks against your mind. 2 Cor. 10:3-5. Establishing this "ground of believing" as a rock-hard foundation of your core of inner beliefs, you will walk in Divine health.

Accepting and accommodating, unwittingly, the possibilities of getting any illness, opens the door to getting some sickness or illness. Satan still attacks. He uses any notion of believing, to provide access to your body, from the "negative form of faith" that you have unwittingly allowed. Get back to a biblical position of total health in your body. Get yourself healed of *every* condition that you have accommodated. Then anchor your health in a well-established faith that you walk in, every day, as He walked…in health. "Whoever says He abides in Him ought to walk in the same way as he walked." 1 John 2:6 ESV. The Healthy One has been united with you in spirit and you are one. 1 Cor. 6:17.

Diet
Modern food processing and preparation is done with so many chemicals that the leader will definitely want to pray in faith over his food and sanctify it and believe that if he unwittingly eats any deadly thing it will not hurt him. Matt. 16:18; 1 Tim. 4:3-5 NKJ.

Consumption
Overweight and obesity diminish your quality of life and your life span and open you to many other diseases. To fail to address this in the power of the Holy Spirit and self-discipline, is to slowly drift toward a state of physical health you do not want to ever come. Most people who smoke cigarettes are taking another step every day towards life-shortening and painful diseases. Leaders who don't stop and discover how to live victoriously over overeating, set themselves up for the same scenario. Live with respect for the "temple" in which you live, for it belongs to Him.

Exercise
Paul said that bodily exercise profits little. 1 Tim. 4:8. It places into perspective, the lower priority that bodily exercise has, in the focus of our lives. However, it does profit some profit and that profit enables all the other more important pursuits we have to be maintained. If my body becomes weak and sickly, I will not be able to function as

God intended. My unique contribution to the Body of Christ and my Kingdom mission will suffer. People who get some physical exercise tend to sleep better and people who sleep better function better. Living in a very sedentary world, where most work is not physically strenuous, we must, as leaders, take care of the temple we live in so that it functions at its best.

Sleep
Prov. 3:21-24 NASU says, "My son, keep **sound wisdom** and discretion, so they will be life for your soul, and adornment to your neck. Then you will walk in your way securely, and your foot will not stumble; when you lie down, you will not be afraid; when you lie down, your **sleep will be sweet**." There is an old saying, "Day is for working and night is for sleeping." You can only violate this law of work and rest before it takes its toll on every area of your life as a leader. If you are tired all the time you become more "body-conscious" rather than spiritually alert. It may be that you are not getting adequate sleep or what is called deep (rem or rapid eye movement sleep) sleep. Your waking/sleeping schedule needs to be examined and altered. Often leaders make excuses to themselves saying, "I am a night person..." or "I am a morning person...." Using this as an excuse, they justify their tiredness, their sense of overwork, or being late to commitments and responsibilities.

Changing their waking/sleeping pattern is not easy, but necessary, if they are to succeed. Your natural inclinations are meant to serve you, not subjugate you. Buy a new medium/firm bed, force yourself to get to bed early and arise early. Make your body conform to what makes for the best lifestyle. It takes approximately 8 weeks to accomplish this task. It will serve you all the days of your life.

This also requires a look at how you handle your work load and your perspective on the issues you face. Weariness of mind also can destroy your sleep effort if you are worried and fearful. Ps. 4:8; Ps. 127:2. Insomnia or inability to sleep in our time is most often caused by worry, television, video games, lack of physical exercise and unrelenting pressures. All of these do not allow the body to relax and sleep to overtake you. Deal with them all. Claim the promises of the Word of God concerning sleep and rest like a baby.

Sabbath
God meant every believer to live in the principle and practice of Sabbath rest. It is both a principle of faith-based living and a lifestyle practice. The term, "Sabbath," is mentioned 163 times in the Bible—108 times in the Old Testament and 55 times in the New Testament. Chapters three and four of the book of Hebrews make it clear that the fundamental truth connected to Sabbath-rest, is the rest that is defined as faith, in what God has said and done. It is further illustrated in the historical revelation of the beginning of Sabbath and how it was to be practiced. God worked six days and rested from work on the seventh day. He established this principle as a law for Israel to observe under the Law of Moses as well. Work, then, cease from work, and rest. The Sabbath was a principle that flowed through their entire lives. The land had to

Leaders learn the secret of lifelong, Divine health.

have a Sabbath from being tilled for produce. The animals that were used in tilling the land also enjoyed the Sabbath. When Israel was supernaturally fed by God in the wilderness with manna, they could only gather it for six days…then they rested from gathering it on the seventh. Ex. 16:23-26. God's people were required to trust Him to supply and accomplish during the Sabbath because He had ordained it. When they refused to honour the Sabbath principle they went into captivity. In the end, they had to remain there as long as 70 years as they had not observed the Sabbath for the appropriate number of years. Dan. 9:2.

There are two apparently conflicting instincts in man—his need for rest and his desire to work or labour to accomplish. God intended that man be dependent upon Him. He requires Him to work but then make a space (Sabbath) to rest and cease from his labours and rest. He was to celebrate God's goodness, relax and be renewed. This practice demanded faith in God. It is still the same today. Men rush to and fro today in the busiest time in human history. Believers can easily get caught up in the world's system of busyness and hurry and make no time for rest. They may be saying to themselves that they have very legitimate reasons for a lifestyle that is slowly "killing them" and their families. Their marriages and families suffer and they begin to break apart in themselves from lack of Sabbath. They become susceptible to disease and to discouragement and to temptation unnecessarily. One pastor of a large congregation required all of his elders to have two days off each week. If they failed to do this they were fired. Heb. 4:4-11; Isa. 40:28-31 NKJV.

The fundamental principle and practice of *Sabbath-rest* in our lives is vital to our expression of faith and our continued success. There is always more work than time. Thus the One who is in charge of all things must be given the opportunity to accomplish what we are not meant to accomplish. He has so many ways of getting things done that need to be done and getting what is most important, done at the right time.

Visiting a believer who was hospitalised for a "breakdown" I asked him, "What is the Lord saying to you?" He spoke without hesitation. He said, "I told the Lord the long list of things I was doing." The Lord said to me, "Did I tell you to do those things?" I said, "No." The man concluded he had worn himself out by doing things very passionately that he had no grace for doing. He quit those things and began to wait on the Lord for exactly what to do. We can simply be "too busy" or be doing things sincerely that we were not meant to be doing. We can also fail to have a life-schedule that schedules the necessity of rest for our body, mind and spirit.

A pastor of a congregation of 22,000 members in his message, "Five mistakes I have made in my life and Ministry," listed not resting adequately enough. Leaders with a good work ethic are often prone to this kind of mistake. You are your best for all others when you look after yourself wisely and biblically. 1 Tim. 4:16 NKJ; Mark 6:31-32 says, "Then, because so many people were coming and going that they did not even have a chance to eat, he said to them, 'Come with me by yourselves to a quiet place and get

---

Leaders learn the secret of lifelong, Divine health.

some rest." So they went away by themselves in a boat to a solitary place.' Your body and mind can get very weary, wear away, and dilute your effectiveness. How are you practising "Sabbath" in terms of your body, soul and spirit?

Aging

There are diseases associated with old age: diabetes, arthritis, bowel and digestive tract issues, osteoporosis, memory loss, strength loss, mental acuity lessened, heart disease, shortness of breath, macular degeneration, and many others. Every symptom of these issues must be vigorously resisted. Your body was made to be like His body with the quickening Spirit of God in you! Rom. 8:11 ESV. Moses, Caleb, Joshua and many others under a lesser covenant had none of the common health struggles related to old age.

Ruth 4:15
"He will renew your life and **sustain you in your old age.**"

Prov. 3:7-8
"Do not be wise in your own eyes; fear the Lord and shun evil. This will bring **health to your body and nourishment to your bones.**"

Eph. 6:2-3
'Honour your father and mother' — which is the first commandment with a promise— 'that it may go well with you and that **you may enjoy long life on the earth**.'

Appropriating Your Own Healing

There are two primary ways to get healed and they both involve faith. One may be termed, "faith healing" where the believer appropriates by faith what God has spoken. The other may be termed, "gift healing," where someone else operates in healing and speaks and/or touches the believer and healing manifests. Both involve faith on the part of both parties (with the exception of those incapable of exercising faith i.e. those dead, in a coma, or not conscious). The following provides a combination of both means.

Every believer needs to know how to get healed and then sustain that healing. As every benefit that Christ's death has secured for the believer is only manifested by faith, it is vital to always be growing your faith. 2 Thess. 1:3. Don't try to analyse your perceived level of faith and get into confusion and despair over whether you had "enough" faith or not but simply go after what you **know** will make the difference in your physical condition—overcoming faith. 1 John 5:4; Mt. 9:22; Acts 3:16; Luke 8:50. Take the following "medicine" for your condition as the Great Physician's prescription for your healing:

1. **Get** the promises of healing deep into your spirit and mind by *hearing them* over and over and *meditating* on them. Ask God in your meditation to take them by revelation deep into your spirit and mind that faith would rise through the hearing of His voice from the Word. Rom. 10:17 NKJV; Ps. 103:3; Ps. 107:20, 21;

Leaders learn the secret of lifelong, Divine health.

Isa. 53:5; Jer. 30:17; Matt. 4:23-24; Matt. 8:8, 13 NASU; Matt. 9:35; Matt. 10:1; Matt. 12:15; Mk. 6:13; Luke 8:50; Matt. 8:17; 3 John 2 NKJV.

One young woman who suffered from seizures, and that had had extensive tests that were inconclusive, decided deep in herself, that she would relentlessly pursue her healing through the developing of her faith. She ordered some cds of Kenneth Hagin's healing promises that were the promises of healing from the Scripture. She listened to them night and day and even at night had them playing in her room while she slept. After a short while, all of her symptoms disappeared and she was totally healed. The Word spoken had done its perfect work of producing her miracle cure. This "hearing-of-faith" saturation produced the faith that healed her!

2. **Create** the atmosphere of faith by making your home and entire habitat, a place of worship and praise. Acts 2:28; Ps. 22:3 KJV; 1 John 3:19. Let the worship music and the spoken Word fill the atmosphere of your home and car and all other spaces where you live. Print the Word and put it where you will see it. Sing praises. Rejoice in the Lord. Believe His manifest Presence brings His Reward to your body and life. Heb. 11:6. Many people have been healed as they have communed with the Lord in worship. His Presence cannot come without His power. Receive what He brings when you sense He has come.

3. **Speak with commanding authority** the Word of healing over your own body, in specific terms, releasing the power of your faith-filled words just as you did in salvation. Rom. 10:8-10 NASU. The word of faith is in you! 1 Thes. 2:13. The Word is in you and is working in you even as you believe. Prov. 12:18; Luke 7:7; 1 Tim. 6:12. Your words are powerful to affect your own physical body! 1 Thes. 2:13.

4. **Take** communion every day and as often as you are prompted, believing that you are taking into the "temple" what cleanses and restores it. John 6:54-57. You are partaking of eternal life and blessing. Read five times the two books, "The Miracle Meal," by David Oyedepo and "The Meal that Heals," by Perry Stone.

5. **Call** yourself **healed** according to the Word of God. Rom. 4:17-21 ASV. Abraham continued to introduce himself as "Abraham," ("father of many nations") until what God had spoken, manifested in a miracle. "Against all…Abraham believed." Rom. 4:18. What is in you, in faith and power, is far greater than all that is against you. Arise and let that "mighty power" that is within you, work its awesome work as you speak and believe! Ps. 30:2.

6. **Get** to any place in the world where healing is taking place and present yourself in faith to be healed. Make any and all effort to get to such a place, believing that you have an appointment to get healed and that as soon as hands are laid on you and words are spoken, you will immediately feel the power flowing

Leaders learn the secret of lifelong, Divine health.

into your body making you one hundred percent whole! If you are unable to travel, find out who is doing healing and make all efforts to get them to come to you. If they cannot come, get someone else who is healing people to come… but get it done! John 5:1-7. There is a "pool of Bethesda" today where you can be healed! It may be in your bedroom, at your local church, or in some other city—but get there!

One man tells a story of an evangelist who was getting ready to pray for a blind woman. He asked her to close her eyes and say what she saw. She did. Then she opened her eyes. He told her, "I didn't say open your eyes. Now close your eyes and tell me what you see." She closed her eyes. Then she said, "I see myself seeing." He said, "Now open your eyes." She did and she saw perfectly. If you are to live in a better place in God, in a Word-described place, you need to "see it." Mark 11:24; Heb. 11:3, 7 ESV.

7. **Regardless** of the duration of symptoms, do **not** allow yourself to fall into the trap of doing some autopsy on your spiritual life, looking for some secret sin that you think delays or prevents your healing. After an initial examination of whether you hold any unforgiveness or bitterness against anyone and if so, forgiving that person, get on with believing. 1 Cor. 11:28-31 ESV. It is true that bitterness, resentment, anger and unforgiveness can prevent your healing but deal with it and deal with it quickly. Then **do not** go looking for something else. This leads to despair and failure and is Satan's trap to prevent your success. Keep on point, mission and focus. Heb. 12:2 NASU. You don't have to be a "perfect person" to appropriate healing. Most of the people healed under Jesus' ministry did not know Him as Saviour yet and many healed today do not know Him as Saviour. Some never turn to Him as Saviour, even though they experienced His unwarranted, unearned, unmerited favour in the healing of their bodies. Isa. 57:17-19; Acts 10:38.

8. **Keep** your healing by realising that the same Devil who brought the sickness the first time, will try to bring it back. When any symptoms occur, speak aloud to the Devil and declare you *were healed* and you *are healed*! Tell him to "get off your body" and then get on with your life ignoring any of the lying symptoms that say you are wearing a "vacancy here" sign! Phil. 3:16.

Appropriating Your Own Divine Health
There is no biblical record that Jesus ever suffered a cold, flu, or sickness of any kind. He did not undergo "burn out" as a result of the load of ministry and mission that He carried. This is the goal of the leader—to live as He lived, appropriating Divine health and finishing his or her course in strength. 1 John 2:6 ESV.

Most leaders fully expect to be ill at numerous times in their lives especially as they age, but this is not God's will. 3 John 2. Deut. 34:7 KJV says, "And Moses was an hundred and twenty years old when he died: his eye was not dim, nor his natural

Leaders learn the secret of lifelong, Divine health.

force abated." Joshua 14:10-11. If those under a lesser covenant could walk in Divine health, then leaders under a greater covenant can walk in Divine health. Ps. 105:37 NKJV. Deut. 29:5. Billy Graham says, "No one tells you how to live the last 35 years of your life after retirement." He goes on to suggest how this is to be done. Leaders always think ahead and live different from this world's way of thinking and living.

- Plan on getting older without losing your health. Don't plan on getting any impairments associated with aging. Job 29:19-20 TMV says, "A life deep-rooted and well-watered, a life limber and dew-fresh, my soul suffused with glory and **my body robust** until the day I die."

- Plan on having financial blessing in your latter years. Don't plan on just 'getting by' on a dubious government pension. Believe you will finish with a legacy to leave financially. Prov. 13:22.

- Plan on having great friendships in your latter years. Don't plan on living the last years of your life lonely. Live a lifestyle of loving and the sustaining of relationships and you will not outlive all the relationships you have made. Eph. 5:1-2. Relationships are the great treasures you make and carry through the years of your life. Don't end up "bankrupt" because you just "ministered" but did not make deep friendships *on the way.*

- Plan on being productive and fruitful in your old age--not watching all the younger people accomplish for the Lord. Ps. 92:12-14. Don't grow old in your prophetic delivery. Often older leaders unwittingly and unconsciously "sit down" on the inside and do not allow the "push" of the prophetic to come forth with passion and power. Maintain the "fire" of His passion in preaching and the prophetic delivery.

- Look after your soul. Emotions, following your thought life, have a great impact on your health. The worrier, the stressed leader, the anxious or fearful, all suffer needlessly in the health of their bodies. Prov. 14:30 says, "A heart at peace gives life to the body, but envy rots the bones." What you can't fix in your own human ability, **must** be exchanged for His ability to fulfil His promises. Carrying what you cannot fix that distresses you, will kill you prematurely. Matt. 11:29-30. God never meant your latter years to be full of anything other than "Caleb" type energy and passion. If you are not laughing so much and at full rest in yourself, you need some of the fresh medicine of Heaven--joy. Neh. 8:10; Ps. 81:1.

- Take communion every day in your home, believing that it is a "miracle meal." 1 Cor. 11:24-26; John 6:54-57. Believe that you are taking into yourself the very life of Christ and in so doing ingest the health of Heaven and all of its power. Jesus gave us the example to follow, defined its significance and let us partake of something so amazing and so powerful we should never neglect it. Many

Leaders learn the secret of lifelong, Divine health.

great men and women of God took communion every day in their homes and lived without the sicknesses that are common, right up until they went "home."

A leader makes a plan to be healthy or he automatically falls into the "default position" of sickness and disease. It becomes an instinctive thing to say, "A senior moment," or "just a reminder that I am not as young as I used to be…." It is easy to slip into a frame of mind that has more faith for weakness, fragility, disease, and decay in old age by simply accepting that this is the "norm" for all people. Joint replacements, arthritis, weakness, deafness, sight loss, and other age-related conditions are not exceptions to the full and abundant life that Jesus died to bring. Stop accepting the world's perspective on aging and get the one described in the Bible. Isa. 46:4 says, "Even to your old age and grey hairs I am he, I am he who will sustain you. I have made you and I will carry you; I will sustain you and I will rescue you."

Application

- Have a group discussion on what others have found to be challenging in maintaining their health and what some have discovered as keys to maintain good health.

- Have fellow team members heal you of any ailments including those that are longstanding.

- Read the book, "The Miracle Meal" by David Oyedepo.

- Read the book, "The Meal that Heals" by Perry Stone. Decide how you will apply the revelation you receive from the book into your lifestyle.

- Read the book, "Becoming A Man of Unwavering Faith," by John Osteen. This book will give you key insights and inspiration regarding your healing. It is authored by Joel Osteen's father.

- Read "Your Body's Many Cries For Water," by F. Batmanghelidj. Decide on how much water you intend to take, on a regular basis, to assist your healthy lifestyle.

Leaders learn the secret of lifelong, Divine health.

Health Scriptures

John 10:10
"The thief comes only to steal and kill and destroy; I have come that they may have life, and have it to the full."

1 Cor. 6:19-20
"Do you not know that your bodies are temples of the Holy Spirit, who is in you, whom you have received from God? You are not your own; you were bought at a price. Therefore honour God with your bodies."

3 John 2-3 NKJV
"Beloved, I pray that you may prosper in all things and be in health, just as your soul prospers."

2 Cor. 10:3-5
"For though we live in the world, we do not wage war as the world does. The weapons we fight with are not the weapons of the world. On the contrary, they have divine power to demolish strongholds. We demolish arguments and every pretension that sets itself up against the knowledge of God, and we take captive every thought to make it obedient to Christ."

1 Cor. 6:17 NKJV
"But whoever is united with the Lord is one with him in spirit."

Matt. 16:18
"And I tell you that you are Peter, and on this rock I will build my church, and the gates of Hades will not overcome it."

1 Tim. 4:3-5 NKJV
"They forbid people to marry and order them to abstain from certain foods, which God created to be received with thanksgiving by those who believe and who know the truth. For everything God created is good, and nothing is to be rejected if it is received with thanksgiving, because it is consecrated by the word of God and prayer."

1 John 2:6 ESV
"…whoever says he abides in him ought to walk in the same way in which he walked."

1 Cor. 6:17 NKJV
"But whoever is united with the Lord is one with him in spirit."

1 Cor. 9:27
"No, I strike a blow to my body and make it my slave so that after I have preached to others, I myself will not be disqualified for the prize."

Leaders learn the secret of lifelong, Divine health.

1 Tim. 4:8
"For **physical training is of some value**, but godliness has value for all things, holding promise for both the present life and the life to come."

Ps 4:8
"I will lie down and **sleep in peace**, for you alone, O Lord, make me dwell in safety."

Ps 127:2
"In vain you rise early and stay up late, toiling for food to eat — for he **grants sleep** to those he loves."

Ex. 16:23-26
"He said to them, "This is what the Lord commanded: 'Tomorrow is to be a day of rest, a holy Sabbath to the Lord. So bake what you want to bake and boil what you want to boil. Save whatever is left and keep it until morning.'" So they saved it until morning, as Moses commanded, and it did not stink or get maggots in it. "Eat it today," Moses said, "because today is a Sabbath to the Lord. You will not find any of it on the ground today. **Six days you are to gather it, but on the seventh day, the Sabbath, there will not be any**."

Dan. 9:2
"I, Daniel, understood from the Scriptures, according to the word of the Lord given to Jeremiah the prophet that the desolation of Jerusalem would **last seventy years**."

Heb. 4:4-11
"For somewhere he has spoken about the seventh day in these words: "And on the seventh day **God rested from all his work**." And again in the passage above he says, "They shall never enter my rest." It still remains that some will enter that rest, and those who formerly had the gospel preached to them did not go in, because of their disobedience. Therefore God again set a certain day, calling it Today, when a long time later he spoke through David, as was said before: "Today, if you hear his voice, do not harden your hearts." For if Joshua had given them rest, God would not have spoken later about another day. There remains, then, a Sabbath-rest for the people of God; for anyone who enters God's rest also **rests from his own work**, just as God did from his. Let us, therefore, make every effort to enter that rest, so that no-one will fall by following their example of disobedience."

Isa 40:28-31 NKJV
"Have you not known? Have you not heard? The everlasting God, the Lord, The Creator of the ends of the earth, neither faints nor is weary. His understanding is unsearchable. He gives power to the weak, And to *those who have* no might He increases strength. Even the youths shall faint and be weary, and the young men shall utterly fall, but **those who wait on the Lord shall renew *their* strength**; they shall mount up with wings like eagles, they shall run and not be weary, they shall walk and not faint."

Leaders learn the secret of lifelong, Divine health.

1 Tim. 4:16 NKJV
"Take heed to yourself and to the doctrine. Continue in them, for in doing this you will save both yourself and those who hear you."

Rom. 8:11 ESV
"If the Spirit of him who raised Jesus from the dead dwells in you, he who raised Christ Jesus from the dead **will also give life to your mortal bodies through his Spirit** who dwells in you."

2 Thess. 1:3
"We ought always to thank God for you, brothers and sisters, and rightly so, because **your faith is growing more and more**, and the love all of you have for one another is increasing."

1 John 5:4
"This is the **victory that has overcome** the world, even **our faith**."

Matt. 9:22
"Jesus turned and saw her. 'Take heart, daughter,' he said, '**your faith has healed you**.' And the woman was healed at that moment."

Acts 3:16
"**By faith in the name of Jesus**, this man whom you see and know was made strong. It is Jesus' name and **the faith that comes through him** that has completely healed him, as you can all see."

Luke 8:50
"Hearing this, Jesus said to Jairus, 'Don't be afraid; **just believe, and she will be healed**.'

Rom. 10:17 NKJV
"So then **faith *comes* by hearing**, and hearing by the word of God."

Ps. 103:3
"…who forgives all your sins and **heals all your diseases**…."

Ps. 107:20, 21
"He **sent out his word and healed them**; he rescued them from the grave. **Let them give thanks to the Lord** for his unfailing love and his wonderful deeds for mankind."

Isa. 53:5
"But he was pierced for our transgressions, he was crushed for our iniquities; the punishment that brought us peace was on him, and **by his wounds we are healed**."

Jer. 30:17
"But **I will restore you to health** and heal your wounds,' declares the Lord…."

Leaders learn the secret of lifelong, Divine health.

Matt. 4:23-24
"Jesus went throughout Galilee, teaching in their synagogues, proclaiming the good news of the kingdom, and **healing every disease and illness** among the people. News about him spread all over Syria, and people brought to him **all who were ill with various diseases, those suffering severe pain, the demon-possessed, those having seizures, and the paralysed; and he healed them.**"

Matt. 8:8
"The centurion replied, 'Lord, I do not deserve to have you come under my roof. But just **say the word, and my servant will be healed.**"

Matt. 8:13 NASU
"And Jesus said to the centurion, 'Go! **It shall be done for you as you believed.**' And the servant was healed that very moment."

Matt. 9:35
"Jesus went through all the towns and villages, teaching in their synagogues, proclaiming the good news of the kingdom and **healing every disease and illness.**"

Matt. 10:1
"He called his twelve disciples to him and gave them authority to drive out impure spirits and **to heal every disease and illness.**"

Matt. 12:15
"Aware of this, Jesus withdrew from that place. A large crowd followed him, and **he healed all who were ill....**"

Mark 6:13
"They drove out many demons and **anointed with oil many people and healed them.**"

Luke 8:50
"Hearing this, Jesus said to Jairus, 'Don't be afraid; **just believe**, and **she will be healed.**'

Matt. 8:17
'He **took up our infirmities and bore our diseases.**'

3 John 2-3 NKJV
"Beloved, I pray that you may prosper in all things and **be in health**, just as your soul prospers."

Acts 2:28
"You have made known to me the paths of life; **you will fill me with joy in your presence.**'

Leaders learn the secret of lifelong, Divine health.

Ps. 22:3 KJV
"But thou art holy, O thou that inhabitest the praises of Israel."

1 John 3:19
"This is how we know that we belong to the truth, and how **we set our hearts at rest in His Presence:**"

Heb. 11:6
"And without faith it is impossible to please God, because anyone who comes to him must believe that he exists and that **He rewards** those who earnestly seek him."

Rom. 10:8-10 NASU
"But what does it say? *"the word is near you, **in your mouth and in your heart**"*— that is, the **word of faith** which we are preaching, that if you **confess with your mouth** Jesus *as* Lord, and **believe in your heart** that God raised Him from the dead, you will be saved; for **with the heart a person believes**, resulting in righteousness, and **with the mouth he confesses**, resulting in salvation."

1 Thess. 2:13
"And we also thank God continually because, when you received the word of God, which you heard from us, you accepted it not as a human word, but as it actually is, the word of God, **which is indeed at work in you who believe.**"

Prov. 12:18
"…the **tongue** of the wise **brings healing**."

Luke 7:7
"But **say the word**, and my servant **will be healed**."

1 Tim. 6:12
"Fight the good fight of the faith. Take hold of the eternal life to which you were called when you made **your good confession** in the presence of many witnesses."

1 Thes. 2:13
"…the word of God, which is indeed **at work in you who believe.**"

John 6:54-57
"Whoever eats my flesh and drinks my blood has eternal life, and I will raise them up at the last day. For my flesh is real food and my blood is real drink. Whoever eats my flesh and drinks my blood remains in me, and I in them. Just as the living Father sent me and I live because of the Father, so **the one who feeds on me will live** because of me."

Rom. 4:17-21 ASV
"(as it is written, A father of many nations have I made thee) before him whom he believed, (even) God, who giveth life to the dead, and **calleth the things that are not,**

Leaders learn the secret of lifelong, Divine health.

as though they were. Who in hope believed against hope, to the end that he might become a father of many nations, according to that which had been spoken, So shall thy seed be. And without being weakened in faith he considered his own body now as good as dead (he being about a hundred years old), and the deadness of Sarah's womb; yet, looking unto the promise of God, he wavered not through unbelief, but waxed strong through faith, giving glory to God, and being fully assured that what he had promised, he was able also to perform."

Rom. 4:18
"**Against all** hope, **Abraham** in hope **believed**...."

Ps. 30:2
"O Lord my God, I called to you for help, and **you healed me**."

John 5:1-7
"Some time later, Jesus went up to Jerusalem for one of the Jewish festivals. Now there is in Jerusalem near the Sheep Gate a pool, which in Aramaic is called Bethesda and which is surrounded by five covered colonnades. Here a great number of disabled people used to lie — the blind, the lame, the paralysed. One who was there had been an invalid for thirty-eight years. When Jesus saw him lying there and learned that he had been in this condition for a long time, he asked him, 'Do you want to get well?' 'Sir,' the invalid replied, 'I have no-one to help me into the pool when the water is stirred. While I am trying to get in, someone else goes down ahead of me.'

Mark 11:24
"Therefore I tell you, whatever you ask for in prayer, **believe that you have received it**, and it will be yours."

Heb. 11:3-7 ESV
"By faith we understand that the universe was created by the word of God, so that what is seen was not made out of things that are visible. By faith Abel offered to God a more acceptable sacrifice than Cain, through which he was commended as righteous, God commending him by accepting his gifts. And through his faith, though he died, he still speaks. By faith Enoch was taken up so that he should not see death, and he was not found, because God had taken him. Now before he was taken he was commended as having pleased God. And without faith it is impossible to please him, for whoever would draw near to God must believe that he exists and that he rewards those who seek him. By faith Noah, being warned by God concerning events as yet unseen, in reverent fear constructed an ark for the saving of his household. By this he condemned the world and became an heir of the righteousness that comes by faith."

1 Cor. 11:28-31 ESV
"Whoever, therefore, eats the bread or drinks the cup of the Lord in an unworthy manner will be guilty of profaning the body and blood of the Lord. Let a person examine himself, then, and so eat of the bread and drink of the cup. For anyone who

Leaders learn the secret of lifelong, Divine health.

eats and drinks without discerning the body eats and drinks judgment on himself. That is why many of you are weak and ill, and some have died. But if we judged ourselves truly, we would not be judged."

Heb. 12:2 NASU
"…**fixing our eyes on Jesus**, the author and perfecter of faith…."

Isa. 57:17-19
"I was enraged by his sinful greed; I punished him, and hid my face in anger, yet he kept on in his wilful ways. I have seen his ways, but I will heal him; I will guide him and restore comfort to him, creating praise on the lips of the mourners in Israel. Peace, peace, to those far and near," says the Lord. "And I will heal them."

Acts 10:38
"…how God anointed Jesus of Nazareth with the Holy Spirit and power, and how he went around doing good and **healing all who were under the power of the devil**…."

Phil. 3:16
"Only let us live up to what we have already attained."

1 John 2:6 ESV
"…whoever says he abides in him ought to walk in the same way in which he walked."

3 John 2
"Dear friend, I pray that you may **enjoy good health** and that all may go well with you, even as your soul is getting along well."

Josh 14:10-11
"Now then, just as the Lord promised, he has kept me alive for forty-five years since the time he said this to Moses, while Israel moved about in the desert. So here I am today, eighty-five years old! **I am still as strong today as the day Moses sent me out**; I'm just as vigorous to go out to battle now as I was then."

Ps 105:37 NKJV
"He also brought them out with silver and gold, and *there was* **none feeble among His tribes**."

Deut. 29:5
"During the forty years that I led you through the desert, **your clothes did not wear out, nor did the sandals on your feet**."

Ps 92:12-14
"The righteous will flourish like a palm tree, they will grow like a cedar of Lebanon; planted in the house of the Lord, they will flourish in the courts of our God. **They will still bear fruit in old age, they will stay fresh and green**…."

Leaders learn the secret of lifelong, Divine health.

Matt 11:29-30

"Take my yoke upon you and learn from me, for I am gentle and humble in heart, and you will find rest for your souls. For my yoke is easy and my burden is light."

Neh. 8:10

"…for the **joy of the Lord is your strength**."

Ps 81:1

"Sing for joy to God our strength; shout aloud to the God of Jacob!"

1 Cor. 11:24-26

"…and when he had given thanks, he broke it and said, "This is my body, which is for you; do this in remembrance of me." In the same way, after supper he took the cup, saying, "This cup is the new covenant in my blood; do this, whenever you drink it, in remembrance of me." For **whenever you eat this bread and drink this cup**, you proclaim the Lord's death until he comes."

John 6:54-57

"Whoever eats my flesh and drinks my blood has eternal life, and I will raise him up at the last day. For my flesh is real food and my blood is real drink. Whoever eats my flesh and drinks my blood remains in me, and I in him. Just as the living Father sent me and I live because of the Father, so **the one who feeds on me will live because of me**."

Leaders learn the secret of lifelong, Divine health.

The Leader and.....

Lust

Introduction
Lust is defined as: any desire that requires fulfillment outside the boundaries of righteous living. Every believer has legitimate desires in himself, given by God, in the creation of mankind. One definition of sin (of which there are several) is the decision, pursuit and experience of desires, outside the boundaries God has commanded. In the Garden of Eden, Adam and Eve had a legitimate desire for food that they could consume. However, their desire found expression outside the commanded boundaries of God's word to them when they ate of the forbidden tree. It was a legitimate desire for food, that when wrongly expressed, corrupted their nature and gave them what the Bible calls "evil desires" or desires for things outside the boundaries God has set. It was the legitimate desire for food that the Last Adam (1 Cor. 15:45) faced in temptation, in the desert. In the passage in Matt. 4:3, Satan offered Christ the opportunity to fulfill His own human needs with the unauthorised use of power. Jesus, hungry from fasting, was tempted to use His gifts to supernaturally feed Himself, rather than in faith-dependence on His Father.

Man becomes an idolater when he chooses to pursue desires forbidden by God. Col. 3:5.
The old nature, the person I used to be, was a nature characterised by lusts or desires outside the boundaries God has intended. Eph. 2:3 TLB. 1 John 2:15-17 tells us that as believers we are not to return to a love of those things that characterised our former life. There is the possibility of having our lives "polluted by the world." James 1:27; James 4:4.

Desires, Thoughts, Emotions, and Decisions
Desires, whether good or evil, move us toward decisions, good or bad. If you focus or get a "fix on" a particular desire or want, you will eventually move inwardly toward that thing. If you continue in that focus, you will make some decisions regarding that focus. Proverbs 11:6 says, "The righteousness of the upright delivers them, but the unfaithful are trapped by evil desires."

Evil desires thrive in secret before they manifest in public. There are two kinds of a secret life...one that blesses and builds you and one that shames you...pursuing the first, we will help ourselves "wear" our new identity in Christ. 2 Cor. 4:2 says, "Rather, we have renounced **secret and shameful ways;** we do not use deception, nor do we distort the word of God. On the contrary, by setting forth the truth plainly we commend ourselves to every man's conscience in the sight of God."

Leaders discern the power of lust and choose to live safe.

Kinds of Lusts, Unlawful Desires or Desires Outside Godly Boundaries

Lust, mentioned 31 times in Scripture, is defined as: longing for what is forbidden. Sometimes leaders might think that lust is something that the "wicked" are involved in and nothing to do with themselves. However, the Bible is fundamentally written to believers, some of which, will grow up to be good leaders. There are several types of lust that leaders face:

1. Lust for power over people, position, or public adoration -- The pursuing of what only God is to give you, in self-centred ways, is morally wrong. God has designed you to be powerful. God has given you a spiritual position and God is in charge of promotion. God's affirmation is sufficient. To look for ways to manipulate others and circumstances for your advantage in order to gain power, position, and public adoration is to fail in trusting God and to surrender to an evil desire of self-promotion. Matt. 23:12. This lust is not a "looking to serve out of loving" but a using of serving and other means to gain promotion.

2. Lust for material things -- lust is an unlawful desire or a desire outside of the boundaries. God wants us to enjoy things. 1 Tim. 6:17. To allow or make them a prevailing consciousness is to be more aware of "things" than God. 1 John 2:15 NKJV; Col. 3:2. All of the things that God provides are also meant to be used to bless others. If our natural desires for things is not coupled with a generosity that will allow them all to be given away, we are living in the lust of material things. The material is to serve the eternal.

3. Lust for sexual experience outside of marriage. 1 Cor. 6:18. Desire for a sexual experience is in itself a holy, God-given desire to be expressed righteously *inside the boundary* of marriage alone. The intent to pursue and experience that desire outside of marriage is an unlawful pursuit and experience, forbidden by God. Sin is cruel, selfish, destructive, and alienating. Our new nature, that we to put on, hates sin and loves purity. Believing God for a spouse if you do not have the 'gift of celibacy' and maintaining intimacy in your marriage, if you have a spouse, are vital ways of addressing a legitimate desire. 1 Cor. 7:2-5, 7, 9.

4. Lust for something or someone who does not belong to you – Solomon lusted for a woman who was someone else's wife. 2 Sam. 11:2-4. Achan lusted for riches not to be taken. Joshua 7:20, 21. Sometimes believers may be tempted with desire for another person that can never truly belong to them in a righteous marriage relationship.

5. Lust for affection and attention from others that compulsively drives one outside the boundaries. 2 Cor. 5:15. Often believers who have experienced rejection and not fully recovered from it, discover they have a fruitless pursuit for the attention they never received. When they solicit attention, praise and affirmation, it never truly satisfies their need for a healthy sense of self-worth or self-valuing. Such a lust for the attention and affirmation of others makes

Leaders discern the power of lust and choose to live safe.

such a person a socially awkward person. Sometimes this "addiction" to the praise of others requires help from others to break.

Conquering Lust – Rom 8:12, 13 NLT and Rom. 8:1-9
There are three dimensions of life that must be addressed to have victory over lust. They are:

1. Nature.

2. Desires.

3. Thoughts.

Every believer has been given a new **nature**. It is the Christ-nature. This nature is characterised by desires and thoughts consistent with Christ's holy nature. Rom. 8:5 NASU tells us that our "mind-set" or what we set our minds on, releases the old nature of selfish, sinful living or the new nature of Christ-centred, selfless living. The old nature of carnal, selfish living has within it, sinful **desires**. When *we set our minds on* the things of this world, things outside the boundaries of holy living, or selfish things, we prompt the emergence of the old nature, its desires and subsequently its behaviour.

If you choose to saturate your mind with earthly, sinful, self-indulgent things, you can be sure you will eventually succumb to the desires of the nature you have stirred up. Setting your mind on the things of Heaven, godly things, matters of the Kingdom, loving others, etc., you release the desires of that new nature that is fundamentally who you are as a new creation in Christ. Col. 3:2 says, *"Set your minds on things above, not on earthly things."*

Eph. 4:19 speaks of two words that are keys to conquering lust: sensitivity and sensuality. Cultivating sensitivity to the Holy Spirit, you develop a **discernment** and a **power to deny** all sensuality. Rom. 8:12, 13 NLT. If you cultivate sensuality, you lose your sensitivity to the Holy Spirit. These two things are mutually exclusive. You cannot feed one, without losing the other. The wise leader learns what accentuates their own sense life and makes them vulnerable to lust, which has to do with satisfying the senses outside the boundaries of righteousness. Ps. 101:3. Prayer, worship, reading the Word, living for God and others, exercising faith, being about your Father's business, meditating in the Scripture, fellowshipping with other believers on spiritual matters, speaking in tongues, and cutting out of your schedule the activities that are the slippery slope of decline, are all biblical means for stamping out the old nature's ability to influence your inner life.

Triggers are what we do that seems legitimate, but in the end, feed the earthly, carnal nature and release its thoughts and desires…Rom. 8:5, 13 ESV. You cannot immerse yourself in the filth of this world and not be affected by it. It stirs, prompts or triggers the old nature with its desires and thoughts. One of the great dangers of

Leaders discern the power of lust and choose to live safe.

our time is the entertainment world. In the desire for legitimate entertainment, we are sometimes placed in a position of having to accommodate illegitimate aspects of legitimate activity, if we are to "enjoy" some legitimate activity. It is this compromise that de-sensitises the leader's spirit and dulls the conscience. When the old nature is stimulated, the allurements of sin rise to greater strength in the mind. Every leader has to discern the unique and particular "triggers" that Satan uses to dilute his spiritual strength. When Samson lost his covenant strength, they took his eyes out. This physical removal of his eyes was but a symbol of the spiritual blindness that had led him to this place. We cannot afford to be "blind" to the "Philistine" spirit of lust. Rom. 13:14 NLT says, "…don't let yourself think twice about **ways** to indulge your evil desires."

Temptation
Temptation happens…Vital to a leader's success is the understanding of the God-appointed test of temptation. God never tempts anyone (James 1:3) but the Holy Spirit will lead us to a place where our lives are tested by temptation. God placed Adam and Eve in the Garden and allowed Satan to be there as well. He tested them by placing them in location with The Tempter. He also led His own Son into the desert to be tested by the very same Tempter. He had Divine purpose in allowing the test. God allows us to be tested because He trusts us to pass the test using the Divine nature within us and the speaking of the Word to Satan. In so doing we are, as His sons, like The Son, who passed all the tests. We are meant to be conformed in our lifestyle and ways to the image of His Son. Rom. 8:29. Standing in the deep conviction of our identity, we exercise authority over Satan and retain our integrity. What Satan offers is simply "not who we are!"

We know that Satan is using all the evil of this world in an attempt to dig up the "old man," that we used to be, to seduce us. In all of the three major temptations of Christ we discover they are prefaced with an identity question. The first two actually state, "If you are the Son of God…." The last one begins with the assumption, "deny who you are and worship me." Leaders recognise the clever, devious, subtle nature of Satan's temptation attempts. Without immersing yourself in the understanding of who you are and living with Spirit-consciousness (Rom. 8:12, 13 NLT), the leader will succumb to temptation.

Knowing who you are in Christ and *discerning what is really happening,* are vital to the leader's victory over temptation. Sometimes repetitive failure in a specific temptation has become so consistent, that it is vital to sit down and ask God in meditation and prayer: What are the initial lies that I have listened to and accepted? What are any rationalisations or excuses I have made that open the door to failure? Then we must seek out the truth in the Word of God that exposes those lies. Meditating in those lie-exposing truths strengthens the conscience, commits the truth to memory and activates discernment at the beginning of the temptation. You become spiritually aware of what is "on offer" and what Satan is attempting. Habits are often things we do without total awareness of what we are doing. You probably don't remember

Leaders discern the power of lust and choose to live safe.

which shoe you put on first today. The Word and the Spirit make you aware of what is going on at the outset so you can make deliberate changes to your thought life and behaviour.

Temptation is an offer from the "spirit of disobedience" or an evil spirit plying our old nature with an opportunity to disobey God's Word and ways. Eph. 2:2 speaks of "…the spirit who is now at work in those who are disobedient." What Satan used to do with us when we had his nature of selfishness, sensuality and rebellion, he still attempts to do even after we have received a new nature, new desires and new thoughts. He **especially** seeks to send a seducing spirit to the life and mind of a leader, for the leader is a greater prize for him to capture. Temptation, as in the tempting of Christ, comes as a voice-thought into the mind.

Several years ago we rented facilities for church services. Sometimes we had to wait for the previous users to leave before we could enter to set up for service. On this particular day, I stood at the doorway, holding some equipment while an attractive, buxom woman dressed in a "catsuit" with more of her out than in, stood guard at the door, not allowing us to enter. She engaged me in conversation. Immediately my mind was filled with the "why" of this situation. Why did I have to converse with this woman while I was trying to do His work? Why did she have to be dressed like she was? Why was she insistent on talking to me when I really wanted to get past her and get on to worshipping the Lord? Why was it so difficult to see past her sexually provocative appearance and converse with her? All of these why questions agonised my mind instead of the realisation that this was a test He had allowed, so that I might access His Divine nature and speak to this woman about her soul. I failed to do what was best because I was mired in the "whys" and the frustration of having to face this distressing situation.

God led Jesus by the Spirit into the desert to be tested with temptation to show two primary things: (1) only by the Divine nature are we able to choose righteousness consistently and (2) we repel the work of temptation by specific means. The following are some aspects of temptation.

1. Jesus was led by the Spirit into the **desert** to be tested. Matt. 4:1.

2. Jesus was taken to the highest point of the **temple** in Jerusalem. Matt. 4:5.

3. Jesus was taken to a very **high mountain** to view the **splendour** of the kingdoms **of this world**. Matt. 4:8.

These are primary **places** or **settings** of temptation revealing the context of some of the temptations that leaders face. They represent:

1. The place of **desire** unfulfilled. The "desert" is a barren place. Desires that are frustrated, unfulfilled, or disappointed can beckon or call a person to choose some illegal, sinful method of pursuit. James 1:14. A desire, no matter how

Leaders discern the power of lust and choose to live safe.

legitimate, becomes evil when satisfying it is sought outside God-ordained boundaries and methods. A young woman may have a legitimate desire for a husband. It becomes an evil desire when it entices her to pursue a husband outside of God-ordained commands. A man may have a desire for promotion but his desire becomes evil when he uses manipulation or scheming to gain it for himself.

What danger there is in frustration, disappointment and discouragement as it is in those "places," the desires of the flesh (the person I used to be) come rising to the surface. It is in this "desert" that the leader must draw upon the Divine nature (2 Pet. 1:2-4) and recognise the "messages" being sent to the brain as sourced in Satan, this world, and the flesh. He must also do as Christ did and **address Satan aloud verbally.** Matt. 4:4, 7, 10.

Whenever temptation arises, (the thoughts, desires and feelings), recognise immediately that it is Satan injecting those thoughts, arousing the old person that you used to be and speak aloud as Jesus did, "Away from me, Satan!" Matt. 4:10. Identifying the source, speaking to the spirit behind what is happening, you then **choose to set** your mind on something entirely wholesome and good. You also declare, "that is not who I am, Satan, get off my mind, now!" Some believers get confused about what is happening. They suspect that those thoughts are sourced in themselves and thus they are an evil person. If this were not so, they think, they wouldn't have or keep having these thoughts. It is, however, Satan that is injecting those thoughts to stir up the desires of the carnal, previous person I used to be. I am not, in my new nature in Christ, trying to sabotage my own success.

2. The place of **spiritual accomplishment**. The holy city of Jerusalem and the highest point of the temple, represent a height of spiritual accomplishment. When God has partnered with you and you have seen some great level of achievement or blessing, it is in that "place," that you can unwittingly surrender to the temptation to believe wrongly about your partnership. The lack of alertness and being on your guard against pride and spiritual danger, makes you vulnerable to Satanic plots. It is often in the hours *after* a glorious service, mission success, or revival meetings that Satan comes to draw us into his trap when our "guard is down." Many great men and women have fallen into shame and sin right after some great spiritual "high" of success or campaign.

The very same Satan who has suffered the ravages of your success is the one who still waits for an opportunity to inject the subtle life-destroying, slow-acting poison of self-ballooning, self-importance into your mind. He is as 1 Tim. 4:1 refers to, as a "seducing spirit." For Satan, any kind of seduction will suffice—whether a compromise on what is visual or verbal or behavioural, he is happy to offer the enticement. We choose to rehearse that the great anointing

Leaders discern the power of lust and choose to live safe.

we carry is Him. 1 Cor. 4:7. Isa. 26:12 says, "…all that we have accomplished, **you** have done for us."

3. The place of **splendour**. This world's system offers a magnetism clothed in Satanic camouflage that is so subtle. Every person is drawn to splendour. To fail to discern correctly the enticements of this world, is to become a prisoner of them and the one who directs their entry into your life. Power, position, money, acclaim, glamour, adulation, and great possessions all speak. They all beckon to the old person I used to be. The imagination is filled with "seeing yourself" in some context that is "high and lifted up." It is no use thinking "I am not like others. I am not tempted by what others are tempted by." Christ's great temptations are recorded in the Bible for a reason that includes your life. All flesh is the same. In the right context, Satan has a trap that is "tailor-made" just for you. Some dimension of splendour, unique to your own makeup, will beckon to you. You can unwittingly surrender to self-worship. This splendour includes the "glory of things (possessions)," the hallucinogenic of fame, or the acclaim of achievement.

Nebuchadnezzar suffered from this "splendour" temptation. God may allow you great personal wealth. God may allow you an amazing scope of international recognition. God may enable great achievement. All of the glory goes to Him, however. 1 Cor. 4:7. If you surrender to this particular test of temptation you can suffer great pain and loss. **Your greatest possession is Him**. **Your greatest reputation is His reputation**. Be like Jesus and don't seek to enlarge your reputation even through some rationalised means. Phil. 2:7 NKJV. The glory of your greatest accomplishments belongs to the One who chose to partner with you. Whatever He gives, use it to bring even more glory to Him. You don't need to announce your great ministry and always seek to "dial down" any attempts by others to do so. Let God trumpet what He wants to do through you. Let Him be your "PR" man. Prov. 27:2. Otherwise, you can unwittingly promote self-exaltation.

When believers soak their inner lives with the "splendour" of this world through the sources of media that provide this well-painted splendour, they enlarge the desires of the flesh (the person I used to be). They make themselves more vulnerable to failing in this temptation test. We are meant to learn that we can enjoy **things** but things do not provide lasting fulfillment. 1 Tim. 6:17. Relax. God wants you to enjoy things. Don't let them or the lack of them, define you. Solomon discovered that great and glorious possessions only provide a temporary "Wow!" and that feeling is soon gone like a vapour.

Discerning and Overcoming
Accessing the Divine nature is a Holy Spirit lifestyle. Gal. 5:16-26. God leads us to the "test of temptation" that we might pass the test and choose Him and what is righteous and holy. 1 Cor. 10:13. The way of escape that God has provide has various means.

Leaders discern the power of lust and choose to live safe.

- You may have to flee a certain setting like Joseph did. Gen. 39:9; 2 Tim. 2:22. Sometimes the "flight" or distancing we need to take is from realms of pursuit that cause us to live more in our soul and this world than the more obvious areas of temptation. Physical locations may obviously need our "flight," but subtle temptations and dilutions of our sensitivity also need some radical action. We must guard our sensitivity of conscience by taking specific steps toward purity that are related to the unique tendencies of compromise connected to our previous nature. Examine what appeals to your particular old nature and take a decision to **hate** that especially.

- It is choosing to leave even the **proximity** of any evil opportunity as Joseph did. Gen. 39:9. We must be spiritually alert and aware of potential situations that are dangerous for our flesh. We must build a lifestyle **away** or distant from these physical or figurative "locations." Whatever the activities are, that are connected to this subtle pathway to failure, must be forsaken and become prohibited territory. No rationalisation or excuse can be accepted in your mind, lest you deceive yourself and fail. Sometimes believers wonder why they only seem to fail to make good relationships when they choose to pursue those they met while clubbing.

How often, in this evil world, believers can unwittingly allow their minds to be filled, *innocently* they think, with all kinds of evil. What is pure? Why choose to mix pure with impure? We can't leave this world until our appointed time but we can choose how much of it we allow into our inner life. This is a great challenge with television, movies, music, internet and other sources of media produced by the prince of the power of the air with his agenda. 2 Tim. 3:13; Ps. 101:3. The Holy Spirit will help you to make **specific steps** to insure your own personal success.

Lust, in the Scripture, is most often connected to the eyes and heart. What we look at feeds one nature or another, our true identity or the one that is supposed to be dead and buried. So many Scriptures teach us that the most common *door* for awakening unlawful desires comes from *what we look at*. Preserving purity begins with decisions regarding what we look at. Hab. 1:13 says, "Your eyes are too pure to look on evil; you cannot tolerate wrong." Num. 15:39; Job 31:1; Ezek. 6:9; 1 John 2:16. Col. 3:5 says we are to put the behaviour of the old nature **to death**. This means we must make every effort to extinguish every aspect of its attempted appearance in our lives.

The eyes awaken the heart in a unique and powerful way—powerful for good or evil. Often believers fail to realise that what their eyes behold, for the most part, cannot but stimulate the nature that is connected to what they are looking at.

One minister became curious about the realms of occultic evil. He set himself to study them and pursue specific locations where these things were practised. After a few

Leaders discern the power of lust and choose to live safe.

years he left the ministry and joined the occultic realm. There is a cause and effect relationship between what we allow or pursue and where we end up.

Application

1. Make a list of Satanic temptations that come to you from time to time. Divide them into categories e.g. relationships, activities, opportunities, goals and accomplishments. Write out the lie Satan tells you e.g. "you must defend yourself, you are weak in this area, you can get ahead if you will but…, you need to make sure others know how great, talented, or capable you are, these activities are okay even though they are the trail to illegitimate pursuits." Find the Scriptures that expose these lies. Meditate in them.

2. Write out any of the rationalisations you have told yourself to justify what has been done that is wrong and "nail" them for what they are—well-packaged lies.

3. Spend some more time in renewing your identity and in speaking in tongues every day. Satan is out to attack you every day and wear away your spiritual stamina and sensitivity. Becoming more of who you are, you will be empowered to discern and decide in keeping with who you are.

4. In small groups discuss the following questions:

    - How does Satan use the media to draw the believer into sin?

    - What steps should a believer and leader take to minimise the risk of becoming anaesthetised to evil (an insensitive conscience)?

    - How is comparison with what others do and "get away with," a faulty approach for dealing with the hidden power of lust or sin?

Leaders discern the power of lust and choose to live safe.

Lust Scriptures

1 Cor. 15:45
"So it is written: "The first man Adam became a living being"; **the last Adam**, a life-giving spirit."

Matt. 4:3
"The tempter came to him and said, "If you are the Son of God, tell these stones to become bread."

Col. 3:5
"Put to death, therefore, whatever belongs to your earthly nature: sexual immorality, impurity, lust, evil desires and greed, which is idolatry."

Eph. 2:3 TLB
"All of us used to be just as they are, our lives expressing the evil within us, doing every wicked thing that our **passions** or our evil **thoughts** might lead us into. We started out bad, being born with evil **natures**...."

1 John 2:15-17
"Do not love the world or anything in the world. If anyone loves the world, the love of the Father is not in him. For everything in the world — the **cravings of sinful man**, the **lust** of his eyes and the boasting of what he has and does — comes not from the Father but from the world. The world and its desires pass away, but the man who does the will of God lives for ever."

James 1:27
"...keep oneself from being **polluted by the world**."

James 4:4
"You adulterous people, don't you know that **friendship with the world** is hatred towards God? Anyone who chooses to be a friend of the world becomes an enemy of God."

Matt. 23:12
"For whoever **exalts himself** will be humbled, and whoever humbles himself will be exalted."

1 Tim. 6:17
"Command those who are rich in this present world not to be arrogant nor to put their hope in wealth, which is so uncertain, but to put their hope in God, who **richly provides us with everything for our enjoyment**."

1 John 2:15-16 NKJV
"Do not love the world or **the things in the world**. If anyone loves the world, the love of the Father is not in him."

Leaders discern the power of lust and choose to live safe.

Col. 3:2
"**Set your minds** on things above, not on earthly things."

1 Cor. 6:18
"**Flee from sexual immorality**. All other sins a man commits are outside his body, but he who sins sexually sins against his own body."

1 Cor. 7:2-5, 7, 9
"But since there is so much immorality, each man should have his own wife, and each woman her own husband. The husband should fulfil his marital duty to his wife, and likewise the wife to her husband. The wife's body does not belong to her alone but also to her husband. In the same way, the husband's body does not belong to him alone but also to his wife. Do not deprive each other except by mutual consent and for a time, so that you may devote yourselves to prayer. Then come together again so that Satan will not tempt you because of your lack of self-control….I wish that all men were as I am. But each man has his own gift from God; one has this gift, another has that…but if they cannot control themselves, they should marry, for it is better to marry than to burn with passion."

2 Sam. 11:2-4
"One evening David got up from his bed and walked around on the roof of the palace. From the roof **he saw a woman bathing**. The woman was very beautiful, and David sent someone to find out about her. The man said, "Isn't this Bathsheba, the daughter of Eliam and the wife of Uriah the Hittite?" Then David sent messengers to get her. She came to him, and **he slept with her**. (She had purified herself from her uncleanness.) Then she went back home."

Josh. 7:20-21
"Achan replied, "It is true! I have sinned against the Lord, the God of Israel. This is what I have done: **When I saw** in the plunder a beautiful robe from Babylonia, two hundred shekels of silver and a wedge of gold weighing fifty shekels, I coveted them and took them. They are hidden in the ground inside my tent, with the silver underneath."

2 Cor. 5:15
"And he died for all, that those who live should **no longer live for themselves** but for him who died for them and was raised again."

1 Cor. 6:18
"**Flee** from sexual immorality. All other sins a man commits are outside his body, but he who sins sexually sins against his own body."

Rom. 8:12, 13 NLT
"Therefore, dear brothers and sisters, you **have no obligation to do what your sinful nature urges you to do**. For if you live by its dictates, you will die. But if **through the power of the Spirit you put to death the deeds of your sinful nature**, you will live."

Leaders discern the power of lust and choose to live safe.

Rom 8:1-9
"Therefore, there is now no condemnation for those who are in Christ Jesus, because through Christ Jesus the law of the Spirit of life set me free from the law of sin and death. For what the law was powerless to do in that it was weakened by the sinful nature, God did by sending his own Son in the likeness of sinful man to be a sin offering. And so he condemned sin in sinful man, in order that the righteous requirements of the law might be fully met in us, who do not live according to the sinful nature but according to the Spirit. Those who live according to the sinful nature have their minds set on what that nature desires; but those who live in accordance with the Spirit have their minds set on what the Spirit desires. The mind of sinful man is death, but the mind controlled by the Spirit is life and peace; the sinful mind is hostile to God. It does not submit to God's law, nor can it do so. Those controlled by the sinful nature cannot please God. You, however, are controlled not by the sinful nature but by the Spirit, if the Spirit of God lives in you. And if anyone does not have the Spirit of Christ, he does not belong to Christ."

Eph. 4:19
"Having lost all **sensitivity**, they have given themselves over to **sensuality** so as to indulge in every kind of impurity, with a continual lust for more."

Ps. 101:3
"I will set before my eyes no vile thing. The deeds of faithless men I hate; they shall not cling to me."

Rom 8:5-6, 13 ESV
"For those who live according to the flesh **set their minds on** the things of the flesh, but those who live according to the Spirit **set their minds on** the things of the Spirit… For if you live according to the flesh you will die, but if by the Spirit you put to death **the deeds** of the body, you will live."

Matt. 4:1
"Then Jesus was led by the Spirit into the desert to be **tempted by the devil**."

Matt. 4:5
"Then the devil took him to the holy city and had him stand on the **highest point of the temple.**

Matt. 4:8
"Again, the devil took him to **a very high mountain** and showed him all the **kingdoms of the world** and their **splendour**."

James 1:14
"…but each one is tempted when, by his own evil **desire**, he is dragged away and enticed."

Leaders discern the power of lust and choose to live safe.

2 Peter 1:2-4

"Grace and peace be yours in abundance through the knowledge of God and of Jesus our Lord. His divine power has given us everything we need for life and godliness through our knowledge of him who called us by his own glory and goodness. Through these he has given us his very great and precious promises, so that through them you may **participate in the divine nature** and escape the corruption in the world caused by evil desires."

Matt. 4:4, 7, 10

"Jesus **answered**, "It is written: 'Man does not live on bread alone, but on every word that comes from the mouth of God.'" …Jesus **answered** him, "It is also written: 'Do not put the Lord your God to the test.'"…Again, the devil took him to a very high mountain and showed him all the kingdoms of the world and their splendour. "All this I will give you," he said, "if you will bow down and worship me." **Jesus said to him**, "Away from me, Satan! For it is written: 'Worship the Lord your God, and serve him only.'"

1 Tim. 4:1 KJV

"Now the Spirit speaketh expressly, that in the latter times some shall depart from the faith, giving heed **to seducing spirits**, and doctrines of devils…."

1 Cor. 4:7

"What do you have that you did not receive? And if you did receive it, why do you boast as though you did not receive it?"

Phil. 2:7 NKJV

"…but **made himself nothing**, taking the very nature of a servant, being made in human likeness."

Prov. 27:2

"**Let another praise you**, and not your own mouth; someone else, and **not your own lips**."

1 Tim. 6:17

"God, who richly provides us with **everything for our enjoyment**.

Gal 5:16-26

"So I say, live by the Spirit, and you will not gratify the desires of the sinful nature. For the sinful nature desires what is contrary to the Spirit, and the Spirit what is contrary to the sinful nature. They are in conflict with each other, so that you do not do what you want. But if you are led by the Spirit, you are not under law. The acts of the sinful nature are obvious: sexual immorality, impurity and debauchery; idolatry and witchcraft; hatred, discord, jealousy, fits of rage, selfish ambition, dissensions, factions and envy; drunkenness, orgies, and the like. I warn you, as I did before, that those who live like this will not inherit the kingdom of God. But the fruit of the Spirit is love, joy, peace, patience, kindness, goodness, faithfulness, gentleness and self-control.

Leaders discern the power of lust and choose to live safe.

Against such things there is no law. Those who belong to Christ Jesus have crucified the sinful nature with its passions and desires. Since we live by the Spirit, let us keep in step with the Spirit. Let us not become conceited, provoking and envying each other."

1 Cor. 10:13
"No temptation has overtaken you except what is common to mankind. And God is faithful; he will not let you be tempted beyond what you can bear. But when you are tempted, he will also provide a way out so that you can endure it."

Gen 39:9
"No-one is greater in this house than I am. My master has withheld nothing from me except you, because **you are his wife**. How then could I do such a wicked thing and sin against God?"

2 Tim 2:22
"Flee the evil desires of youth, and pursue righteousness, faith, love and peace, along with those who call on the Lord out of a pure heart."

2 Tim 3:13
"…while evil men and impostors will go from bad to worse, deceiving and being deceived."

Ps. 101:3
"I will **set before my eyes no vile thing**. The deeds of faithless men I hate; they shall not cling to me."

Num. 15:39
"You will have these tassels to look at and so you will remember all the commands of the Lord, that you may obey them and not prostitute yourselves by going after **the lusts of your own hearts and eyes**."

Job 31:1
"I made a **covenant with my eyes not to look lustfully at a girl**."

Ezek. 6:9
"Then in the nations where they have been carried captive, those who escape will remember me — how I have been grieved by their adulterous hearts, which have turned away from me, and **by their eyes, which have lusted** after their idols. They will loathe themselves for the evil they have done and for all their detestable practices."

1 John 2:16
"For everything in the world — the cravings of sinful man, **the lust of his eyes** and the boasting of what he has and does — comes not from the Father but from the world."

Leaders discern the power of lust and choose to live safe.

The Leader and.....

Identity

Introduction
Only God can define correctly what He has made and is making. When men and women allow their history, the words of others, or themselves, to define themselves, they take the road to failure, disappointment and loss. God speaks into the life of a leader to answer the most basic question that arises in a leader's mind, "Who am I?"

This question is also tied to the same question that Saul asked on the road to Damascus, "Lord, who are you?" Acts 9:5. One of definitions of who the Lord is, is that of Creator. Since the Lord is The Creator and our Creator, He has ultimate right to designate who we are. We cannot afford to allow experience, others, or even ourselves to define who we are. Isa. 45:9-10; Isa. 64:8. He defines who we are in His Word. He also speaks to us, as we behold Him, in loving devotion, the revelation of who we really are.

Satan suggested that man was other than what God had made him to be in the Garden and used the same ploy with Christ in the temptation when he said, "**If you are the Son of God….**" Matt. 4:6. If the leader at any time allows himself a definition of himself that is not how God has defined him, he steps into "holes and traps" designed to nullify his effectiveness and ruin his mission accomplishment. Satan is the great thief of rightful identity. *His intent is to distort your self-perception.* Apart from God, men and women often perceive and define themselves by what others say, what they think about themselves, or the person reflected in the treatment they have received. The woman, raped three times, can often believe she is no good, rubbish, permanently soiled, and never to be wanted and cherished. She now defines herself in this way and reaps the life that comes from that definition.

Who Am I?
A lot of self-image psychology today is used by believers to bolster their confidence in themselves so they might "feel" better about themselves. However, the God who made us, and wants us to "feel" good about what He has made, wants us, even more, to fulfill the mission He has uniquely designed for us which will actually confirm those good feelings. There is no point "feeling" good about yourself, if your life does not evidence that very value of goodness that He has designed. Thus the feelings of inadequacy, lack, inferiority and worthlessness are all powerful emotional signals to press into the definition and design the Maker has for us all. To endeavour to change the feelings without subscribing to the Divine lifestyle design is futile and potentially self-deceptive.

Leaders discover their true, God-made identity and live exclusively in whom He has made them.

You may attempt to persuade a man sleeping rough on the streets that he is a valuable and worthwhile person. He will not ultimately succeed emotionally in this new-found definition until he takes the steps of repentance and responsibility and accountability for that definition. He has value, simply because he exists. Rom. 5:8.

His value is not determined by his lifestyle but he will only truly believe and realise his value, when he adopts the lifestyle his Creator has designed. If he unwittingly rejects Creator design, (and thus the Creator), he will never "feel" good about himself. His struggle with his notions concerning himself are confirmed by what he has done and hasn't done, in his mind. Repentance then enables him to jettison those corroborating thoughts and emotions by having them "sent away" through God's forgiveness. Having been forgiven, he can now live differently. The message that plays in his mind regarding his past failures can now be ended, as he takes up the favour that God has now given him for a new life by the exercise of his faith. Rom. 5:2.

A man who had significant failures as a husband, father, employee, neighbour, believer, and friend and had fallen into alcohol addiction came to see me. He confessed all of his failures and then announced that he actually knew the answer to all of his difficulties. I said, "What is the answer?" He said that his fundamental issue was that he did not love himself enough. He had heard this and *believed* this was the way forward. I asked him, "If love is caring more about others than yourself, who were you really loving when you did not go to work and you lost your job? Who were you really caring about when you neglected your wife and kids? Was it them or yourself?" He said, "I guess it was myself."

The important question in this instance is, "which self are we talking about?" If you cling to the "old self" of who you used to be, before you came to Christ, you will live *selfishly and sinfully.* James 1:23-27.

Modern life for those of this world can be defined as the "attempt to find and sustain the highest level of positive emotions." Thus it is self-focussed and self-centred. The Christian life is, at its base, a relationship with Christ accompanied by a lifestyle of faith that pleases Him. **As a result** of this relationship and lifestyle, we have "righteousness, peace and joy…**in** the Holy Spirit." Rom. 14:17. It is a totally unselfish lifestyle. 2 Cor. 5:15. Sin and guilt destroy your true *sense of identity* but not your identity. Your identity in Christ cannot be destroyed as it has been made by God to be eternal. It is how He sees what He has made.

Thus, the fundamental issue is not helping others to "feel" good about themselves but to adopt the view of themselves that their Creator has designed. Having agreed with God about who they are, they can get on with living out that design, with the power to live out the design that goes with accepting that design. You actually can be who God made you to be because He has released power to become who you really are in the new creation design. There is the new life of who you are in your new nature.

Leaders discover their true, God-made identity and live exclusively in whom He has made them.

"Therefore, if any anyone is **in Christ**, he is a new creation; the old things have passed away, behold, all things have become new." 2 Cor. 5:17 NKJV. This is God's statement. It is accepted by faith, as the brand new believer has had very little experience "being" this "new" person. A believer is not the "old" trying to become the "new." He *is* the "new person." Recognising the "old" from time to time, he rejects it as, "that's not the person that I am." John 1:12 KJV says, "…But as many as received him, to them gave He power **to become the sons** of God…." We became "sons of God" like unto His Son, Jesus, and we have been given power **to fully express** what and who we are. Gal. 3:26; 4:5-6.

Gideon and Nebuchadnezzar – Judges 6; Dan. 4:30, 36.
Gideon and Nebuchadnezzar both reveal two ends of the spectrum of individuals who did not have the Divine definition of themselves. They did not see themselves as God saw them. Gideon, self-deprecating and fearful, hid from his enemies and sought a low-profile lifestyle of self-preservation like many today. Nebuchadnezzar, self-promoting and self-congratulating, sought to publicise his accomplishments and pursued a high-profile lifestyle of self-exaltation.

What God has said about me is the person I am, regardless of how I feel or what others have said about me. Others can both criticise and praise me in a way that leads me to believe that I am someone that I am not. Everyone has faults and failings, talents and graces, but not one of them fully defines that person. God related to all the great men and women of the Bible as He saw them as He had made them. Ps. 139:16. The public today would not necessarily relate to those men and women as God has related to them. What God has said about me is what provides the most basic definition of who I am. What has He said?

Moses struggled with the mission God had called him to because he believed it was not "him." He resisted God's call because he felt inadequate and incapable. Ex. 4:10-17. Feelings of inadequacy and incapacity are initially **judgments we make about ourselves**. They stand in the way of our obedience. They are not valid or legitimate judgments. We unwittingly resist our own progression and development when we allow them to be legitimate reasons for refusing to do what He has given us to do. Moses was promised that God would "**help him and teach him**." Ex. 4:15. This process is the developmental process that leaders undergo throughout their whole lifetime. God actually got angry with Moses for stalling His programme with his own illegitimate reasoning. God took a man **hidden** in the bulrushes, **hidden** in the palace, **hidden** in the desert and **hidden** from *himself* and made him into a great leader.

Past experiences, statements made about you, parental training, and the lies of Satan, are often the layers of false identity that must be "peeled off" to reveal the amazing, wonderful, loved, powerful and capable person that you are. This is the process of leadership development. You never are greatly effective in bringing others into a true knowledge of themselves if you have not embraced the "peeling process" and begun to store and believe what is true about yourself. You have no right to cling deliberately

---

Leaders discover their true, God-made identity and live exclusively in whom He has made them.

or subconsciously to a definition of yourself that God has not given. Col 3:9-10 says, "…you have **taken off your old self** with its practices and have **put on the new self**, which is being renewed in knowledge in **the image of its Creator**." What is that "new self" that you are to "put on?" It begins with embracing the following:

A New Creation -- 2 Cor. 5:17 NKJV

1. A new order of being – flesh is flesh, spirit is spirit – 1 Cor. 6:17; Gal 5 not after the flesh but after the spirit – biological life vs eternal life John 6:57-63

2. A new focus – self and things vs Christ and people – Col 3:1-2, Heb. 12:2 NASU

3. A new location – earth vs heaven (under vs above) Eph. 2:6.

4. A new name – flesh or birth name vs Christ's Name (identity and power) Acts 2:38; Ps. 111:9; Prov. 30:4.

5. A new mission – serving selfish pursuits vs serving God and others 2 Cor. 5:15

6. A new family – earth family vs heavenly family Eph. 3:15; Ps. 68:6

7. A new destiny – Hell vs Heaven Luke 16:22-23; 2 Thes. 1:8-9; 2 Pet. 3:13; John 14:2-3

8. A new legacy – things vs Christ Col. 2:6; Acts 20:32; Col. 1:12

9. A new father – the Devil vs God John 8:42-44; John 20:17 Satan influenced vs God-possessed

10. A new relationship to the Devil – subject *to* vs ruling *over* Eph. 2:1-3; Luke 10:19;

11. A new power level – weak vs strong Eph. 6:10; 2 Tim. 1:7 KJV

12. A new nature – selfish nature vs Divine nature 2 Pet. 1:3-4 ESV; 2 Cor. 5:17 NKJV; 2 Cor. 5:15.

13. A new union – the world vs Christ Luke 16:8 ("…people of this world…") 1 Cor. 6:17.

14. A new resource – self and this world vs God and Heaven 2 Cor. 1:9; 2 Cor. 3:5

15. A new template for living – this world vs kingdom of Heaven Rom. 12:2 "be not conformed to this world…", fashion, "cool", what's politically correct, the moral compass of this world's "modern" thinking vs. cultivating the fruit of the Spirit

16. A new relationship to your body – user vs respect for the temple 1 Cor. 6:19-20

Leaders discover their true, God-made identity and live exclusively in whom He has made them.

Being "In Christ"
We often may think of Christ as someone so different from ourselves and unwittingly focus on who we used to be, not who *we have become* by grace. Col. 3:3; Gal. 2:20. Often the things we say to ourselves and to others, are not accurate descriptions of who we are **in Christ** but the "dead carcass" of a person buried in water baptism. Our self-perceived identity is mistaken and uninformed biblically. We may live more in the consciousness of weakness, inability, and self-doubt than in the consciousness of the "new person" we have become in Christ. Little power, abiding character issues and scant fruitfulness are signs of living in the "wrong person." 1 John 2:6 ESV.

We must learn to recognise and say to ourselves, "that is not the person that I am." I am all that God says I am for I am *in Him*. John 14:20. Things or activities that dilute or diminish our consciousness of who we are in Christ must be distanced from us lest we live *in* and *out of,* the wrong "person." How much of you is Christ in your life expression? Only your Creator can correctly and legitimately define who you are. It must come to you as a revelation—something given to you from God. Jesus asked Peter in Matt. 16:13 KJV, "Whom do men say that I am?" Peter answered correctly. Jesus' response was that this correct identification was not earth-based but a *revelation* from Heaven. He then went on to say who Simon Bar-Jonas was...now to be called Peter. From that day Peter was to live out his name. Even though he was to slip and fail at the crucifixion, he still was Peter, as God sees us as He has made us. We are not to define ourselves by our failures as He does not define us by our failures. Peter went on to be the spokesman on the day of Pentecost and to be used by God to write a portion of the New Testament.

Who You Are Not – The False View of Yourself – The View of Self to be Rejected
There are many voices that Satan uses to affect your thinking and project the false notion of who you are. It is vital that you discern these voices that "play in the mind." They are often so recurrent, that believers can simply think they are just the way I think and thus the "way I am." You would never do anything to sabotage your own success. Your Heavenly Father would never do anything to sabotage your success. The only such source of the thought patterns mentioned below, is Satan. Satan would *never* want you to discern what he is doing and then move into your true identity, as that threatens his kingdom and his limiting efforts in your life. The following are thoughts, feelings, and self-judgments inspired by Satan to subtly prevent the God-made *you* from emerging:

- Inadequate
- Fearful
- Incapable
- Discouraged
- Addicted
- Ignorant
- Not spiritual enough
- Not smart enough

Leaders discover their true, God-made identity and live exclusively in whom He has made them.

- Not educated enough
- Not talented
- Unable to hear God
- Not attractive
- Missing out
- Not desirable
- Unredeemable
- Unable to recover from loss
- Cancelled destiny
- Different, in a negative sense, from others
- Not wanted
- Rejected

All of the above are *spiritually illegal* for you to hold or think continually. They are fundamentally not the "you" that He has made. God does not make "junk" or defective people in new creation.

Also, you are not, in totality, what you do. Some people define themselves totally by what they do and when they cannot do that any longer or no longer have the opportunity to do it, they are adrift mentally, emotionally and sometimes spiritually in life. What you do comes out of who He has made you to *be*. What He has made you to *be* is always much larger than any particular role you have.

Below are three primary occasions in which your identity development is greatly threatened by Satan who does not want you to ever fully become who you are:

1. New Birth – even as Christ's birth was threatened by Herod's edict to kill all the male babies. Matt. 2:16. Believers, newly born, receive great attacks so that their new-found-faith never really gets a chance to be established.

2. Baptism – Satan comes to destroy the emerging person released at baptism just as he sought to destroy Christ just after His baptism. Matt. 3:16-4:11. After baptism, because the "new person" has risen from the waters of baptism, the believer undergoes, once again, severe testing. This attempt by Satan is so that the freshly-baptised believer will focus on who he is not, rather than who he has become. Satan knows that if you really believe all that God has said about you, you will be a major threat to his kingdom, just as Jesus is. In the Garden, Satan suggested the lie that Adam and Eve were missing out on something—that their creation was faulty.

3. Just before the most-impacting step of your life in establishing your identity – just as Christ faced crucifixion by Satanically-inspired men, because He threatened their religious culture and tradition. Matt. 27:22-23, 40. Christ was accused of blasphemy because He claimed to be who He said He was, the Son of God. Finally, evil men put Him to death because of His claim to be Who He was/

Leaders discover their true, God-made identity and live exclusively in whom He has made them.

is. Christ's death, plotted by Satan and evil men, was not a victory for Satan, although it may have looked like it at the time. Christ rose from the dead and thus provided the salvation for all mankind. Leaders often face their greatest Satanic threat at the threshold of major breakthrough.

Satan was not successful with Christ but sometimes he has managed to subvert believers from their greatest mission success and progression as he makes a concentrated attack on the mind, body and life of the believer in various ways. When you are faced with the most impossible task of your life, questions arise that are connected with your identity. You may be tempted to believe that the task apparently set for you is not really for *you*, because it seems beyond all ability you think you possess. However, it is an appointed task given by God to a person that He has made ready and equipped with His ability to accomplish. Judges 6:14-16. It remains for you to reaffirm, "I am the man, this is the hour, I have His ability to accomplish this great task." Ex. 3:11-15 is the example of Moses' identity struggle as he set out to take the people out of Egypt. Was he who he thought he was or who God said he was?

The Bible declares we must have "**a full understanding of every good thing we have in Christ.**" Philemon 6 NASU. God is endeavouring to make "sons" like Jesus. These sons are meant to be powerful, loving and amazingly productive just as their "Dad" is. He has made the "new man" to be indestructible, indefatigable, and unconquerable. When the "new man" lives by faith, in accepting and believing that his or her new identity, is their *real* self, he is released to be who he really is. You can't imagine Jesus making excuse that He was the illegitimate son of a carpenter, from Nazareth (a bad reputation city), with no connections to wealth, government, heritage or social standing.

He grew in understanding and faith in who He was and He progressively displayed who He was. Luke 2:52. When placed "on the spot," He answered unapologetically that He was the Son of God. Do you answer Satan unapologetically that you are a son of God? He is the Accuser and Liar that is always seeking to undermine who you really are from within. Just prior to His death on the Cross, Jesus faced the taunting accusation from demonically-inspired men, "...**if you are** the Son of God...." Matt. 27:40. Demons know who you really are. They suspect *you* don't know who *you really are*. Mark 1:24; Mark 3:11.

Basic Biblical Definitions of Who You are in Christ.
A great pastor many years ago, reflecting on the truth of identity, made this statement: "You are, and you are becoming who you are." The following clear biblical statements of who you are and what you can do (comprising your identity from God's point of view) are what you are and what you are becoming. Just as a child is a person but also is becoming the person they are, as they grow, so also is the believer. The all-wise, loving Heavenly Father chose you to be a unique, one-of-a-kind, special person. Three basic components of identity make up the person God has made you to be:

Leaders discover their true, God-made identity and live exclusively in whom He has made them.

1. Your relationship to God as your Heavenly Father. This relationship is your connection to the Heavenly Family that has provided your family identity and your source of life to live as He intended. One of the essential components of identity is the knowledge of where you came from and where you are going. John 8:13-14. You began, in Him, in Heaven, and you are on a mission that will return you to your home. Phil. 3:20.

2. The character of Christ as your new nature. The spiritual and moral attributes He has ascribed to you as a "new person" or as a son of His. 2 Cor. 5:17 NKJV; 2 Pet. 1:4.

3. The functions or abilities of Christ as your abilities in Him – the gifts and graces He has given you to enable you to minister as He did. There is purpose in design. God made you with a unique set of abilities and inclinations to be used for His glory. 1 Cor. 12:4-11.

God's View of You --- Making it Personal
It is vital to confess aloud and declare aloud who you are "in Christ" even as Christ confessed who He was/is. Luke 22:66-71. From today, you should confess aloud who He has said you are, even as parents call a child's name and then the child calls out their own name when asked.

- I am a child of God – 1 John 3:1-2

- I am Christ's friend – John 15:15

- I am born of God – 1 John 4:7

- I am a son of God – Gal. 3:26

- I am an heir of God – Rom. 8:17

- I am a joint heir with Christ – Rom. 8:17; Gal. 4:7

- I am blessed with every spiritual blessing – Eph. 1:3

- I've been given great promises – 2 Pet. 1:4

- I am more than a conqueror – Rom. 8:37

- I'm redeemed and forgiven – Eph. 1:6-8

- I've been justified, made righteous – Rom. 5:1

- I have eternal life – John 5:24

- I am perfect in His perfection – Heb. 10:14

Leaders discover their true, God-made identity and live exclusively in whom He has made them.

- I am holy in His sight – Heb. 10:10

- I am greatly loved by my Father – John 3:16; John 13:34; Eph. 5:1-2; 2 Thes. 2:16

- I am salt – Matt. 5:13

- I am light – Eph. 5:8; Matt. 5:14

- I am worth more – Luke 12:7-8

- I am bold – Prov. 28:1

- I am very bold – 2 Cor. 3:12

Your Identity and Social Interaction
If the believer does not see Himself in the way God sees him, he tends to relate to others out of the "old self" and perceive others with the same "glasses" or perspective. 2 Cor. 5:16 NKJV says, "Therefore, from now on, we regard no one according to the flesh." If he looks at himself wrongly, he does not tend to look at others from redemption's point of view either. He is, perhaps, aware of the truth of God's ability to love us beyond the necessity of our changing, but does not relate to others as "whole in Christ." He reacts inwardly to their flaws in criticism, anger, resentment, unforgiveness and fear. His carnal and distorted perception of himself automatically distances him from others rather than connecting him with others.

The Father loves us as earthly fathers love their children. Earthly fathers are acutely aware of their children's faults and failures, but never do they withdraw their love from them (that is, godly earthly fathers). Our love for others, given to us from Him, covers others even while they exhibit things that are not lovely. We choose to respond in loving ways. They receive God's unmerited favour through our loving view of them and our loving ways.

Your Identity In Christ and Discipline
God uses the hard things in our lives to move us from what we are **not** into what He has made us to be. The weaknesses we **believe we have**, become where we live. Understanding our true identity, we recognise that our character and relational struggles are simply struggles with who we **were** not who we **are**. Heb. 12:7 says, "Endure hardship as discipline; God is treating you as his children." As our loving Heavenly Father allows hardship in our journey, it is simply to focus our attention on Him and what kind of "son" He has made and is making. Stepping out of weakness, temptation, fear, sin and failure, we step into the favour of His new creation design by the exercise of our faith. We *are not* what the negatives have suggested. We are strong, amazing, beautiful, blessed, powerful, victorious sons and daughters of our Father.

Possession Realities
I am meant to live life in the light of the following "**Possession Realities**…."

Leaders discover their true, God-made identity and live exclusively in whom He has made them.

Possession of the following can only be accomplished by four means: meditating in them and their accompanying Scripture references, declaring them verbally aloud, acting upon them and sitting at Jesus' feet, hearing His voice of affirmation. It is vital to receive a **revelation** of who you are from your spiritual parent, your Heavenly Father. This written and spoken revelation by the Word and the Spirit, combine to establish your soul in who you really are. Mt. 16:15-17 tells us that Peter had a revelation of The Son. Flesh and blood can only inform you of an earthly identity. Hearing God, your Father, who brought you to birth, and gave you a new name, speak *to you* about *who you are*, is very important. Just as an infant looks into the faces of his parents in the beginning of its identity development, so also do we behold Him. 2 Cor. 3:18.

A primary goal of Christian development is the cultivation of the 'new person' that I am in Christ. Without this deliberate cultivation, the leader lives more in the person they used to be, than the one they have been created to be. We are instructed to **'put on'** or clothe ourselves with the "new self." Eph. 4:24; Josh. 1:6-8; Mt. 12:35. The continued internalisation of Divine thoughts is the *internalisation of Divine life*. Taking communion every day and acting out of who you are and denying who you are not, are vital keys to possessing or manifesting the realities of Scriptural identity. John 6:63; John 15:7-8.

- I **have**…Acts 3:6 I actually **possess** what others require to be healed, enabled and delivered…You only have, what you have, if you really believe you have it!

- I have **received**…Mt. 10:8…what I have received I can give away…I must give away…

- I have **access**…Rom.5:2…into the vast "storehouse" of favour, power and resource…Matt. 12:35

- I have **authority**…Mt. 9:8…Jesus accepted the premise that what He did was based on authority—Satan offered authority…Luke 4:6

- I have been **commanded**…Mark. 16:15, 17-18; Mt. 10:8 Inherent in the command is the power to fulfill it (based on faith)

- I have **power**…Luke 24:49; Acts 1:8…I am clothed with power…it is in me, on me and flows from me…John 7:38-39

- I have **blessing**…John 1:16…I have the benefits and enablements of grace in my possession…

- I have **authority to overcome**…Luke 10:19-20…every condition and threat are subject to my authority…

- I can do **greater works**…John 14:12…believing takes me to a higher level…

Leaders discover their true, God-made identity and live exclusively in whom He has made them.

- I am **seated with** Christ…Eph. 2:6…I am superior to…all that is earthly and Satanic

- I am a **king meant to reign** in life…Rom. 5:17…nothing is meant to subjugate me to evil, sickness, disease or disaster…I am meant to rule over all these…

- I have **an example** to follow…1 Pet. 2:21; Acts 10:38; 1 John 4:17…the One within me enables His example to be enacted through me…

- I have **the Satan-work-destroying Christ within** me…1 John 3:8 …I am meant to destroy Satan's works wherever I go…

- I have a **kingdom of power within** me…Luke 17:21; 1 Cor. 4:20

- I have the **mind** of Christ…1 Cor. 2:16

- I am **clothed** with Christ…Gal. 3:27

- I am **hidden** with Christ in God…Col. 3:3

- I have **overcome** the evil one…1 John 2:13

- I have an **anointing** from the Holy One…1 John 2:20

- I have **what I have asked** of Him…1 John 5:15

- I **cannot be harmed** if I believe…Luke 10:19

- I **give orders to evil spirits** with authority and power and they come out… Lk.4:36

- I must **work the works of Him** that sent me…John 9:4

- I am **appointed to go** and bear fruit and receive whatever I ask in His Name… John 15:16 NLT

- I have **keys** to bind and loose…Matt. 16:19…

- I **speak** the words of God…John 3:34

- I **have the Father living in me** doing His work…John 14:10

- I **can ask anything in His name and He will do it**…John 14:14

- I am **in Christ** and Christ is **in me**. 2 Cor. 5:17 NKJV; Col. 1:27.

Leaders discover their true, God-made identity and live exclusively in whom He has made them.

The primary purpose of this lesson is to develop the identity, comprised of relationship, character and function that God has designed for every believer. A leader will develop this by "storing up" these powerful, life-transforming truths in his heart through prayerful meditation upon them. Matt 12:35 says, "The good man brings good things out of **the good stored up in him**, and the evil man brings evil things out of the evil stored up in him."

Leadership is delivering to others what has been "stored up in." No one can do it for the leader. He must be a "self-feeder" all the days of his life. In the secret place, in the place of study, in the place of prayer and in the place of meditation, we "store up" inside ourselves the truth of who we are and what we can do in Christ. The Holy Spirit's agenda is to make us like Jesus in character and function and He works with this powerful process to engrave the Word into our inner man. Leaders minister out of what has been "stored up." What are you "storing up?"

Temptation is an offer to sell your true self for what you are not or what you used to be. Jer. 15:16. Your secret, inner life, determines your depth and your longevity. No person or programme can substitute your own inner personal development. Judg. 16:5-6; Matt. 6:6. You maintain your true identity if you continue to embrace the Word of God and what it says about you, acting as though it is true. John 8:31. The following chart helps define the contexts in which your identity is developed.

Personal Challenges	VS	**Others Challenges**
Appropriating the Word		Ministering
Private		Public
Intimacy		Demonstration
Loving Him		Loving others
How God sees you		How others see you
Family life		The world and the Church
Growing your faith		Demonstrating your faith

Application

- Take time to identify with a small group of others, the particular lies connected with your identity that you have had to deal with. What statements go through your mind i.e. "I can't do that, I am inadequate, I haven't enough training, I am not as talented as others, my faith doesn't really work for me, how others see me is a real problem for me, etc...." Give any insights you have for how the breakthroughs came in stepping into a greater freedom to be who you really are.

- Speak one affirmation over each person in the group, identifying what you believe are strengths, gifts, or abilities that each person has.

Leaders discover their true, God-made identity and live exclusively in whom He has made them.

- On a personal level take the time to read through all the Scriptures and make a regular practice of meditating in the biblical statements of who you are and what you are to do because you are enabled to do so. Do this for the rest of your life.

- Make a list of all the spiritually illegal statements that you have unwittingly accepted about yourself that have run through your head. "I am weak, I am unable, I am not anointed enough, and I am not spiritual enough…." Repent of choosing to believe and accept and use, as excuses, lies that are not how God has defined you and enabled you. Burn the paper you wrote it on as you say, "Yes" to God's statements of who you are and what you can do.

- Set yourself to act out of what He has said. Look for opportunities to heal, prophesy to strangers, do miraculous acts and obey His still small voice, well outside of where you have been living. Decide you are not going to live merely an ordinary Christian life. Blaze a new trail with your inner and outer lifestyle.

- Purchase and read the book, "Living In The Miraculous," by Katharine Ruonala. This book is more a discussion of the foundations of the miraculous than a "how-to" book. It is an excellent treatment of your identity and God's love for you. It is out of this loving and the identity that that loving enables, that miracles flow.

Identity Scriptures

Isa 45:9-10
"Woe to him who quarrels with his Maker, to him who is but a potsherd among the potsherds on the ground. **Does the clay say to the potter, 'What are you making?'** Does your work say, 'He has no hands'? Woe to him who says to his father, 'What have you begotten?' or to his mother, 'What have you brought to birth?'"

Isa. 64:8
"Yet, O Lord, you are our Father. **We are the clay, you are the potter; we are all the work of your hand.**"

Rom. 5:8
"But God demonstrates his own love for us in this: While we were still sinners, Christ died for us."

Rom 5:2
"…through whom we have gained **access by faith into this grace** in which we now stand."

2 Cor. 5:15
"And he died for all, that those who live should **no longer live for themselves** but for him who died for them and was raised again."

Gal 3:26
"**You are all sons of God** through faith in Christ Jesus…."

James 1:23-27
"Anyone who listens to the word but does not do what it says is like a man who **looks at his face in a mirror** and, after **looking at himself**, goes away and immediately forgets what he looks like. But the man who **looks intently into the perfect law that gives freedom, and continues to do this**, not forgetting what he has heard, but doing it — he will be blessed in what he does. If anyone considers himself religious and yet does not keep a tight rein on his tongue, he deceives himself and his religion is worthless. Religion that God our Father accepts as pure and faultless is this: to look after orphans and widows in their distress and to keep oneself from being polluted by the world."

Rom. 14:17
"For the kingdom of God is not a matter of eating and drinking, but of righteousness, peace and joy in the Holy Spirit…."

Gal 4:5-6
"…we might receive the **full rights of sons**…Because **you are sons**…."

Leaders discover their true, God-made identity and live exclusively in whom He has made them.

Ps 139:16

"…**your eyes saw** my unformed body. All the days ordained for me were written in your book before one of them came to be."

Ex 4:10-17

"Moses said to the Lord, "O Lord, I have never been eloquent, neither in the past nor since you have spoken to your servant. I am slow of speech and tongue." The Lord said to him, "Who gave man his mouth? Who makes him deaf or mute? Who gives him sight or makes him blind? Is it not I, the Lord? Now go; I will help you speak and will teach you what to say." But Moses said, "O Lord, please send someone else to do it." Then the Lord's anger burned against Moses and he said, "What about your brother, Aaron the Levite? I know he can speak well. He is already on his way to meet you, and his heart will be glad when he sees you. You shall speak to him and put words in his mouth; I will help both of you speak and will teach you what to do. He will speak to the people for you, and it will be as if he were your mouth and as if you were God to him. But take this staff in your hand so that you can perform miraculous signs with it."

Matt. 2:16

"When Herod realised that he had been outwitted by the Magi, he was furious, and he gave orders to kill all the boys in Bethlehem and its vicinity who were two years old and under, in accordance with the time he had learned from the Magi."

Matt. 3:16-4:11

"**As soon as** Jesus was baptised, he went up out of the water. At that moment heaven was opened, and he saw the Spirit of God descending like a dove and lighting on him. And a voice from heaven said, "This is my Son, whom I love; with him I am well pleased." Then Jesus was led by the Spirit into the desert to be tempted by the devil. After fasting for forty days and forty nights, he was hungry. The tempter came to him and said, "**If you are the Son of God**, tell these stones to become bread." Jesus answered, "It is written: 'Man does not live on bread alone, but on every word that comes from the mouth of God.'" Then the devil took him to the holy city and had him stand on the highest point of the temple. "**If you are the Son of God**," he said, "throw yourself down. For it is written: '"He will command his angels concerning you, and they will lift you up in their hands, so that you will not strike your foot against a stone.'" Jesus answered him, "It is also written: 'Do not put the Lord your God to the test.'" Again, the devil took him to a very high mountain and showed him all the kingdoms of the world and their splendour. "All this I will give you," he said, "if you will bow down and worship me." Jesus said to him, "Away from me, Satan! For it is written: 'Worship the Lord your God, and serve him only.'" Then the devil left him, and angels came and attended him."

Matt 27:22-23, 40

"What shall I do, then, with **Jesus who is called Christ**?" Pilate asked. They all answered, "**Crucify him!**" "Why? What crime has he committed?" asked Pilate. But

Leaders discover their true, God-made identity and live exclusively in whom He has made them.

they shouted all the louder, "Crucify him!" "Come down from the cross, **if you are the Son of God!**"

Judg. 6:14-16
"The Lord turned to him and said, "**Go in the strength you have and save Israel** out of Midian's hand. **Am I not sending you?**" "But Lord," Gideon asked, "how can I save Israel? My clan is the **weakest** in Manasseh, and I am the **least** in my family." The Lord answered, "I will be with you, and you will strike down all the Midianites together."

Ex. 3:11-15
"But Moses said to God, '**Who am I** that I should go to Pharaoh and bring the Israelites out of Egypt?' And God said, 'I will be with you. And this will be the sign to you that it is I who have sent you: when you have brought the people out of Egypt, you will worship God on this mountain.' Moses said to God, '**Suppose I go** to the Israelites and say to them, "The God of your fathers has sent me to you," and they ask me, "What is his name?" Then what shall I tell them?' God said to Moses, 'I AM WHO I AM. This is what you are to say to the Israelites: "I AM has sent me to you."' God also said to Moses, 'Say to the Israelites, "The LORD, the God of your fathers—the God of Abraham, the God of Isaac and the God of Jacob—has sent me to you." 'This is my name for ever, the name you shall call me from generation to generation."

Luke 2:52
"And Jesus **grew in wisdom and stature**, and in favour with God and men."

Mark 1:24
"What do you want with us, Jesus of Nazareth? Have you come to destroy us? **I know who you are** — the Holy One of God!"

Mark 3:11
"Whenever the evil spirits saw him, they fell down before him and cried out, "**You are** the Son of God."

John 8:13-14
"The Pharisees challenged him, "Here you are, appearing as your own witness; your testimony is not valid." Jesus answered, "Even if I testify on my own behalf, my testimony is valid, for I know **where I came from and where I am going**. But you have no idea where I come from or where I am going."

Phil. 3:20
"But our citizenship is in heaven."

2 Cor. 5:17 NKJV
"Therefore, if anyone *is* in Christ, *he is* a new creation; old things have passed away; behold, all things have become new."

Leaders discover their true, God-made identity and live exclusively in whom He has made them.

2 Pet. 1:4
"Through these he has given us his very great and precious promises, so that through them you may participate in the divine nature, having escaped the corruption in the world caused by evil desires."

2 Cor. 12:4-11
"There are different kinds of gifts, but the same Spirit distributes them. There are different kinds of service, but the same Lord. There are different kinds of working, but in all of them and in everyone it is the same God at work. Now to each one the manifestation of the Spirit is given for the common good. To one there is given through the Spirit a message of wisdom, to another a message of knowledge by means of the same Spirit, to another faith by the same Spirit, to another gifts of healing by that one Spirit, to another miraculous powers, to another prophecy, to another distinguishing between spirits, to another speaking in different kinds of tongues, and to still another the interpretation of tongues. All these are the work of one and the same Spirit, and he distributes them to each one, just as he determines."

Luke 22:66-71
"At daybreak the council of the elders of the people, both the chief priests and teachers of the law, met together, and Jesus was led before them. "**If you are the Christ**," they said, "tell us." Jesus answered, "If I tell you, you will not believe me, and if I asked you, you would not answer. But from now on, the Son of Man will be seated at the right hand of the mighty God." They all asked, "Are you then the Son of God?" He replied, "**You are right in saying I am**." Then they said, "Why do we need any more testimony? We have **heard it from his own lips**."

1 John 3:1-2
"How great is the love the Father has lavished on us, that we should be called **children of God! And that is what we are**! The reason the world does not know us is that it did not know him. Dear friends, now **we are children of God**, and what we will be has not yet been made known."

John 15:15
"I no longer call you servants, because a servant does not know his master's business. Instead, **I have called you friends**, for everything that I learned from my Father I have made known to you."

1 John 4:7
"Dear friends, let us love one another, for love comes from God. Everyone who loves has been **born of God** and knows God."

Gal 3:26
"You are all **sons of God** through faith in Christ Jesus...."

Leaders discover their true, God-made identity and live exclusively in whom He has made them.

Rom 8:17
"Now if we are children, **then we are heirs — heirs of God and co-heirs with Christ**, if indeed we share in his sufferings in order that we may also share in his glory."

Gal 4:7
"So you are no longer a slave, but a son; and **since you are a son, God has made you also an heir**."

Eph. 1:3
"Praise be to the God and Father of our Lord Jesus Christ, who has **blessed us in the heavenly realms with every spiritual blessing** in Christ."

2 Peter 1:4
"…He has **given us his very great and precious promises**…."

1 Cor. 12:4-11
"There are different kinds of gifts, but the same Spirit. There are different kinds of service, but the same Lord. There are different kinds of working, but the same God works all of them in all men. Now to each one the manifestation of the Spirit is given for the common good. To one there is given through the Spirit the message of wisdom, to another the message of knowledge by means of the same Spirit, to another faith by the same Spirit, to another gifts of healing by that one Spirit, to another miraculous powers, to another prophecy, to another distinguishing between spirits, to another speaking in different kinds of tongues, and to still another the interpretation of tongues. All these are the work of one and the same Spirit, and **he gives them to each one**, just as he determines."

Rom 8:37
"…in all these things **we are more than conquerors** through him who loved us."

Eph. 1:6-8
"…to the praise of his glorious grace, which he has freely given us in the One he loves. In him **we have redemption** through his blood, **the forgiveness** of sins, in accordance with the riches of God's grace that he lavished on us with all wisdom and understanding."

Rom 5:1
"Therefore, since **we have been justified** through faith, we have peace with God through our Lord Jesus Christ…."

John 5:24
"I tell you the truth, whoever hears my word and believes him who sent me **has eternal life**…."

Heb. 10:14
"…he has **made perfect** forever those who are being made holy."

Leaders discover their true, God-made identity and live exclusively in whom He has made them.

Heb. 10:10
"…we have **been made holy** through the sacrifice of the body of Jesus Christ once for all…"

John 3:16
"For God **so loved the world** that he gave his one and only Son, that whoever believes in him shall not perish but have eternal life."

John 13:34
"A new command I give you: Love one another. **As I have loved you**, so you must love one another."

Eph. 5:1-2
"Be imitators of God, therefore, **as dearly loved children** and live a life of love, just as Christ loved us and gave himself up for us as a fragrant offering and sacrifice to God."

2 Thess. 2:16
"May our Lord Jesus Christ himself and God our Father, **who loved us** and by his grace gave us eternal encouragement and good hope…."

Matt 5:13
"**You are the salt** of the earth. But if the salt loses its saltiness, how can it be made salty again? It is no longer good for anything, except to be thrown out and trampled by men."

Eph. 5:8
"For you were once darkness, but now **you are light** in the Lord. Live as children of light."

Matt 5:14
"**You are the light** of the world. A city on a hill cannot be hidden."

Luke 12:7-8
"Indeed, the very hairs of your head are all numbered. Don't be afraid; **you are worth more** than many sparrows. "I tell you, whoever acknowledges me before men, the Son of Man will also acknowledge him before the angels of God."

Prov. 28:1
"The wicked man flees though no-one pursues, but **the righteous are as bold as a lion**."

2 Cor. 3:12
"Therefore, since we have such a hope, **we are very bold**."

Leaders discover their true, God-made identity and live exclusively in whom He has made them.

Matt. 16:15-17
'But what about you?' he asked. '**Who do you say I am**?' Simon Peter answered, 'You are the Messiah, the Son of the living God.' Jesus replied, 'Blessed are you, Simon son of Jonah, for this was not revealed to you by flesh and blood, but by my Father in heaven."

2 Cor. 3:18
"And we all, who with unveiled faces contemplate the Lord's glory, **are being transformed into his image with ever-increasing glory**, which comes from the Lord, who is the Spirit."

Eph. 4:24
"…to **put on the new self**, created to be like God in true righteousness and holiness."

Josh 1:6-8
"Be strong and courageous, because you will lead these people to inherit the land I swore to their forefathers to give them. Be strong and very courageous. Be careful to obey all the law my servant Moses gave you; do not turn from it to the right or to the left, that you may be successful wherever you go. Do not let this Book of the Law depart from **your mouth; meditate on it day and night**, so that you may be careful to **do everything** written in it. **Then** you will be prosperous and successful."

Matt 12:35
"The good man brings good things out of the **good stored up in him**, and the evil man brings evil things out of the evil stored up in him."

John 6:63
"The Spirit gives life; the flesh counts for nothing. The words I have spoken to you are spirit and they are life."

John 15:7-8
"If you remain in me and my words remain in you, ask whatever you wish, and it will be given you. This is to my Father's glory, that you bear much fruit, showing yourselves to be my disciples."

Acts 3:6
"Then Peter said, "Silver or gold I do not have, but **what I have I give you**. In the name of Jesus Christ of Nazareth, walk."

Matt 10:8
"Heal the sick, raise the dead, cleanse those who have leprosy, drive out demons. Freely **you have received, freely give**."

Rom 5:2
"…we have gained **access by faith into this grace** in which we now stand."

Leaders discover their true, God-made identity and live exclusively in whom He has made them.

Matt 12:35
"The good man brings good things out of **the good stored up in him**, and the evil man brings evil things out of the evil stored up in him."

Matt. 9:8
"When the crowd saw this, they were filled with awe; and they praised God, **who had given such authority to men**."

Luke 4:6
"And he said to him, "I will give you **all their authority and splendour**, for it has been given to me, and I can give it to anyone I want to."

Mark 16:15-18
"He said to them, "**Go** into all the world and **preach** the good news to all creation. And these signs will accompany those who believe: In my name **they will drive out demons**; they will speak in new tongues; they will pick up snakes with their hands; and when they drink deadly poison, it will not hurt them at all; **they will place their hands on** sick people, and they will get well."

Matt. 10:8
"**Heal** the sick, **raise** the dead, **cleanse** those who have leprosy, **drive out** demons. Freely you have received, freely **give**."

Luke 24:49
"I am going to send you what my Father has promised; but stay in the city until you have been **clothed with power** from on high."

Acts 1:8
"But you will **receive power when the Holy Spirit comes on you**; and you will be my witnesses…."

John 7:38-39
"Whoever believes in me, as the Scripture has said, **streams of living water will flow from within him**." By this he meant the Spirit…."

John 1:16
"From the fulness of his grace **we have all received one blessing after another**."

Luke 10:19-20
"I have **given you authority to trample on snakes** and scorpions and to overcome all the power of the enemy; **nothing will harm you**. However, do not rejoice that **the spirits submit to you**…."

John 14:12
"I tell you the truth, anyone who has faith in me will do what I have been doing. **He will do even greater things than these,** because I am going to the Father."

Leaders discover their true, God-made identity and live exclusively in whom He has made them.

Eph. 2:6
"And God raised us up with Christ and **seated us with him** in the heavenly realms in Christ Jesus...."

Rom 5:17
"...how much more will **those who receive God's abundant provision** of grace and of the gift of righteousness **reign in life** through the one man, Jesus Christ."

1 Peter 2:21
"To this you were called, because Christ suffered for you, **leaving you an example, that you should follow in his steps.**"

Acts 10:38
"...how God anointed Jesus of Nazareth with the Holy Spirit and power, and how he went around doing good and healing all who were under the power of the devil, **because God was with Him.**"

1 John 4:17
"In this way, love is made complete among us so that we will have confidence on the day of judgment because **in this world we are like Him.**"

1 John 3:8
"The **reason the Son of God appeared** was **to destroy the devil's work.**"

Luke 17:21
"...the **kingdom of God is within you.**"

1 Cor. 4:20
"For the **kingdom of God is** not a matter of talk but of **power.**"

1 Cor. 2:16
"...we **have the mind of Christ.**"

Gal 3:27
"...for all of you who were baptised into Christ have **clothed yourselves with Christ.**"

Col 3:3
"For you died, and your life is now **hidden with Christ in God.**"

1 John 2:13
"...because **you have overcome the evil one.**"

1 John 2:20
"But you **have an anointing from the Holy One**, and all of you know the truth."

Leaders discover their true, God-made identity and live exclusively in whom He has made them.

1 John 5:15
"And we know that he hears us — whatever we ask — we know that **we have what we asked of him.**"

Luke 10:19
"I have given you authority to trample on snakes and scorpions and to overcome all the power of the enemy; **nothing will harm you.**"

Luke 4:36
"…with authority and power he **gives orders to evil spirits and they come out!**"

John 9:4
"As long as it is day, **we must do the work of him who sent me.**"

John 15:16 NLT
"You didn't choose me. I chose you. **I appointed you to go and produce lasting fruit**, so that the Father will give you whatever you ask for, using my name."

Matt 16:19
"I will give you the keys of the kingdom of heaven; **whatever you bind** on earth will be bound in heaven, and **whatever you loose** on earth will be loosed in heaven."

John 3:34
"For **the one whom God has sent speaks the words of God**, for God gives the Spirit without limit."

John 14:10
"…it is **the Father, living in me,** who is doing his work."

John 14:14

"You may **ask me for anything in my name**, and I will do it."

2 Cor. 5:17 NKJV
"Therefore, if anyone is **in Christ**, he is a new creation; the old things have passed away, behold, all things have become new!"

Col. 1:27
"To them God has chosen to make known among the Gentiles the glorious riches of this mystery, which is **Christ in you**, the hope of glory."

Luke 2:52
"And Jesus **grew** in wisdom and stature, and in favour with God and men.

Leaders discover their true, God-made identity and live exclusively in whom He has made them.

Jer. 15:16
"When your words came, **I ate them**; they were my joy and my heart's delight, for I bear your name, O Lord God Almighty."

Judg. 16:5-6
"The rulers of the Philistines went to her and said, "See if you can lure him into showing you **the secret of his great strength** and how we can overpower him so that we may tie him up and subdue him. Each one of us will give you eleven hundred shekels of silver." So Delilah said to Samson, "Tell me **the secret of your great strength** and how you can be tied up and subdued."

Matt 6:6
"But when you pray, go into your room, close the door and pray to your Father, who is unseen. Then your Father, who sees **what is done in secret**, will reward you."

John 8:31
"To the Jews who had believed him, Jesus said, "If you hold to my teaching, you are really my disciples."

Leaders discover their true, God-made identity and live exclusively in whom He has made them.

The Leader and.....

Exercising Your Spiritual Authority in Ministry

Every leader must learn to use what God has given him, to do the job that God has given him. To fail to use what God has given, is to automatically attempt, to do in human effort, what can only be done by supernatural means. Human effort is attempting to do the miraculous with human resources. If the leader is not invested deeply into the 'power source' of ministry, he will automatically default to human effort. Abiding in the Presence will result in ministry in the power of His Presence, dynamically released to do the job that is necessary. The "Christ in you" longs to do His work through you at a greater level. Col. 1:27.

We are meant to "grow up into Him in all things" which includes the development of greater effectiveness in ministry. Eph. 4:15. However, we must understand that the consciousness of His Presence is to be distinguished from the **way or manner** in which we minister to people. Many sense His Presence but do not minister in the same way as Jesus did in the Gospels. 1 John 2:6 ESV. The traditions of men, even where they have a biblical connection, are often not as effective as God intends because they are not an exact replica of Jesus' ministry.

The Bible makes a clear distinction between Jesus' ministry and the ministry of the Scribes and Pharisees. Jesus exercised authority. The Scribes and Pharisees did not. It became evident. The people sensed and saw the results of ministry with and without **authority**. Mk. 1:22. It became a significant issue for the Scribes and Pharisees as they, too, witnessed the difference between themselves and Jesus' ministry. Mt. 21:23-24. They discerned that Jesus could only do the miraculous, (commanding one condition to supersede another) if he had authority. Mk. 1:27. There is no authority without responsibility and no responsibility without authority. Luke 10:19; John 15:16 NLT. You have received both responsibility and authority to do the miraculous. In Ex. 4:21 God reminds Moses of his responsibility and authority to do the miraculous. You are reminded of the same.

Possession of something as a new covenant believer is often a process. Getting and maintaining a spiritual truth is something to be pursued. Matt. 12:35 says, "The good man brings good things out of the good **stored up in him**...." Phil. 3:16 tells us that we must "live up to what we have already attained."

We must go after our Saviour in faith, in prayer, in study, in meditation, in declaration, and in action. We cannot afford to live where we have lived in the past or be satisfied with the successes we have had or others have had. We must pursue the Lord until

Leaders exercise spiritual authority to change our world.

we are so immersed on the inside, in His Presence, that we operate out of that sphere. The war for your inner man must be won. The distractions must be identified and laid aside. The cares of this life easily take up our days and become the excuse we make to ourselves for powerlessness. We are so busy. We are so tired. Isa. 40:30, 31 NKJV.

Leaders discover a new lifestyle and develop that lifestyle. Otherwise they head "down the road" like all the "lemmings" of this world simply passing through the days. Who will reach our world for and with Christ if we do not? Did God intend you to live internally as you are living now? What are the basic issues to be resolved to live differently so that you live as Jesus did—always having perfect poise, always having perfect peace and always ready to care for others? Do you blame someone else for your weariness, struggle, or difficulty? Rom. 11:36. The source, ability and ultimate destination of all ministry, is Him. Have you discovered a reservoir of strength through waiting on the Lord, through joy and through faith-based obedience? The life of faith demands an authoritative, faith response to every presenting, opposing circumstance. What is there, in your life at the moment that needs to be supernaturally altered in order for you to proceed as Christ lived?

Spiritual authority for doing the works of Jesus comes out of living more and more in His Presence. Mk. 3:14-15. John 15:4, 5, 7 says, "Remain in me, and I will remain in you. No branch can bear fruit by itself; it must remain in the vine. Neither can you bear fruit unless you remain in me…I am the vine; you are the branches. If a man remains in me and I in him, he will bear much fruit; apart from me you can do nothing. **If you remain in me and my words remain in you, ask whatever you wish, and it will be given you.**"

Your Partnership With Christ In Ministry
As long as we make a distinctions between the ministry of Christ and ourselves, we dilute the truth of our union with Him. When we unwittingly undermine the truth of our union with Him, we surrender our greatest effectiveness in ministry. We may have some success but not what we truly desire. How much "union" do we have with Christ? Jesus makes clear that our partnership with Him is the same as His partnership with the Father. To the degree that we grasp our partnership and operate in our union with Him, we have the same results as He did and eventually more….

1. Union with the Father. John 14:9, 11; 1 Cor. 6:17; Col. 1:27; 1 Cor. 1:30; John 14:20.

2. Words of the Father are also the Son's words. John 14:10; His words in us are as powerful as His words spoken from His mouth when He walked in Galilee. John 15:7.

3. Works of the Father also the Son's works. John 14:11 NCV; Our works of the supernatural are the Son's works flowing through us. John 14:12; 1 Cor. 4:17.

Leaders exercise spiritual authority to change our world.

Lifestyle Approach to Greater Authority
Authority is given to those who are meant to be in a position to command. You are meant to be a "king" with authority to command things to be done. Mark 11:23-24 tells us that if you believe *that what **you say** will happen,* it will be done. This is a function of a king, a president, or some other person in a position of authority—it is the natural expression of who they are. Rom. 5:17. The following steps help you to establish the inner mentality and possession of your true identity. You are "in Christ" and He is "in you." He is the King of Kings and you are one of the kings that He is the King over. You exercise His authority in the earth, as you partner with Him, in your union with Him, in His great purpose.

1. Change your lifestyle to accommodate more of Him. Greater exercise of authority begins with consuming more of His Presence. Integrate your daily and family life more with interactions with Him…in singing, praying, and talking the Word. Confess what the Word says about you, who you are, and what you have. Philemon 6 NASU. Union with Christ is a 24/7 intimacy with Him.

2. Discover the legitimate and illegitimate that can/should be eliminated in order to achieve His mission. No one can do this for you. It is a choice you make in consultation with the Holy Spirit who draws you deeper into Him. Don't let anything dilute your **faith** or de-sensitise your spirit. Phil. 3:19; Rom. 12:2.

3. Set in place the decisions you make and follow through with them. John 2:5.

4. Order your life as though Jesus is the Centre. 1 John 4:17 says, "…in this world we are like him." Rom. 11:36.

5. Believe that He is **in** you, **on** you, and **flows from** you. Rom. 8:9 NLT; Acts 1:8; John 7:38-39.

6. Get on with more **doing** of the works of Jesus, as the more you actually do it, the more confident and experienced and bold you become. Acts 10:38 is the "Jesus" lifestyle.

Devotional Approach to Greater Authority.
Your day-by-day focussed and "going on in the background" devotional life, is the foundation and 'well' from which you draw for ministry every day. The Holy Spirit inspires you, directs you, and reveals stuff to you as you take time to wait on Him and for Him.

- Study, meditate, speak, and do…Josh. 1:6-9 is a possession process described. Matt. 7:29; 9:8; 10:1, Luke 10:17-19. Consider the following:

    1. The voice of God through you is designed to produce supernatural impact. *You are commanded to command.* Believing believers are to do what Christ commanded them to do in the way that He did it. John

Leaders exercise spiritual authority to change our world.

20:21. He commanded demons to be quiet and leave. He commanded the storm to be still. He commanded eyes to open. He commanded the fig tree to be withered. Your approach is not tentative or cautious but boldly commanding.

Church traditions often model an approach that not a duplicate of Christ's approach to sickness, disease, demons, situations and need. Your voice, in its tone and words, reveals what you believe about your **position** in relation to the matter you are dealing with and the **authority** you believe you possess in that matter. Stop asking **Him to do** what He has asked **you to do** and given you the power to do through believing, commanding and touching. Jesus had authority to do things. He has given you authority to do things supernaturally. Eph. 2:6; Mark 11:33; Luke 10:19.

2. Your profound faith in your authority is what releases your authority to do its awesome supernatural works. If you are fully persuaded you possess something, you act accordingly. Mark 11:23. You are convinced that what you say will happen, simply because you said it, and it is in alignment with what He says and does. Many things will never happen because no one has used their faith and authority to actually *say them*.

3. Your profound confidence in the Name of Jesus makes wonders take place. One of the awesome names of Jesus is: Wonderful—meaning full of wonders. When you use that name, you are releasing what the Name is full of. John 16:23-24; Acts 3:16.

4. I have an assignment from the Lord…I have an assignment from the pages of the Bible…I must accept the unique assignment I have and complete it with the awesome faith that I have…I carry His powerful Presence wherever I go! Acts 10:38; Col. 4:17 NCV; Col. 1:27.

5. I have a governmental responsibility in the spirit realm…I must operate it! Luke 10:19. Authority is given to be exercised. Rom. 14:12.

Ministry Approach to the Exercise of Greater Authority.
One of the definitions of authority is: to command something with the confidence that it will be obeyed or enacted. Matt. 8:8. What is the point of having a tonne of spiritual authority if you do not use it?

1. Examine **how** you do, what you do. Is it like Jesus' approach? How Jesus used words:

   "Away from me, Satan!" – dealing with Satan in temptation
   "I will go and heal him." -- detailing his response to sickness

Leaders exercise spiritual authority to change our world.

"Go and it will be done just as you believed it would." – responding to a believing man
"Get up, take up your mat and go home." – to a paralytic
"Stretch out your hand." – to a man with a shrivelled hand
"Be quiet, come out of him!" – to a demon who came out
"Follow me." – to a disciple who followed
"Receive your sight...your faith has healed you" – to a blind man
"Lazarus, come out!" – to a dead man
"Be opened!" – to deaf ears
"Be clean!" – to leprous skin
"Peace, be still!" – to a storm
"May no one ever eat fruit from you again!" -- to a fig tree

2. Do you speak with **boldness**? The prayer of the Early Church was to be enabled to speak with *great* boldness. Acts 4:29. That prayer was answered and they did so. Acts 4:31; Acts 9:28; Acts 14:3 says, "So Paul and Barnabas spent considerable time there, **speaking boldly** for the Lord, who confirmed the message of his grace by enabling them to do miraculous signs and wonders." 2 Cor. 3:9-12. What do you give God to confirm? Are you praying for more boldness and then exercising the greater boldness you have received from praying for it? If you believe that you have what you asked, then act as though you now possess what you asked for.

3. Do you have an operational anointing? 1 John 2:20. Do you have more than a knowledge of what the Scripture says regarding your anointing? Is the anointing you have actually operating through you? John 15:4, 7-8. Inwardly abiding in His Presence activates the depth of anointing you possess.

4. Do you do a lot of talking when you are ministering the supernatural to others? "…they think they will be heard because of their many words…" Matt. 6:7. Do you remain focussed on the need and speak **to** it or do you speak **about** it? Are you trying to love, encourage and show compassion more than simply **"do"** the miracle? Show love, encourage, and be compassionate by actually **"doing"** the miracle. Your love, encouragement and compassion are manifested through the power demonstration as they are His love, encouragement and compassion.

Separate the occasion of doing the miraculous, *in terms of words*, from the occasion to encourage, *in terms of words*. Often believers, well-practised in traditions, make ministry or doing of the supernatural, more of a prayer of encouragement than the simple authoritative command of conditions. Unwittingly they can end up asking God to do what He has commanded them to do. He has already shown them how to do the miraculous through Christ's clear example. One of the signs of inwardly expecting God to do this, is how many times they say His Name in their prayer, e.g. "Jesus, "Lord," or "Father" instead of actually

Leaders exercise spiritual authority to change our world.

speaking *to* the condition. Use the Name once in your command but not as a matter of asking God to do what He fully expects you to do.

5. Do you speak with authority? Fundamentally, you obtain operational authority by being with the "Author" of that authority. Matt. 7:29; Matt. 9:6-8; Mk. 11:23. One definition of authority is: the command with the absolute conviction that it will be obeyed. Do you actually believe that because you say it, it will happen immediately? Mark 11:23. Do you actually see yourself commanding one condition to supersede another or are you asking Jesus to come and do it? Do you expect **immediate** results? Is the verbal part of your ministry coming internally more out of **petition** or **declaration**? The carefully chosen words that you speak and the power released in those few words, causes miracles to take place. There is power in your words, *if you believe there is.* Jesus said, "…with man this is impossible." Matt. 19:26. Thus you are classed no longer as a mere man for He also said, "Nothing will be impossible for you!" Matt. 17:20.

Ministering Deliverance to Someone
Leaders sometimes face people who need to be separated from the power and influence of evil spirits. Believers suffer the influence of evil spirits upon their minds and bodies sometimes. This is often defined as oppression. The thoughts they think are not their own but the thoughts injected into their minds by evil spirits. This continual pattern is often referred to as a stronghold. Any believer who recognises this condition can take spiritual authority over what is happening in their own mind, cast it down, and renew their mind with the thoughts of God. 2 Cor. 10:3-5.

However, some believers do not recognise this condition in themselves and struggle on in the pain of failure and loss. Spirit-filled, discerning leaders recognise this condition, inform them of what is happening and then exercise spiritual authority through simple, faith-filled words of authority to dispatch the oppressing evil spirit. The believer is now free of the oppressing work of Satan but still is required to fill the "vacuum" of their thought life with the Word of God lest the old pattern resume. Believers who have never been baptised or filled with the Spirit are most susceptible to this kind of activity but others who have been baptised in the Spirit can also suffer oppression.

Unbelievers can be possessed of evil spirits by having them take up habitation in the part of themselves where spirits live: their spirit. They are simply to be cast out of their illegal home by the "finger of God"—faith-filled words of spiritual authority even as Christ cast them out by saying, "Go!" Luke 11:20.

Deliverance should not ever require wrestling a person to the floor, holding them down for hours, while listening to the demons scream and utter blasphemous and nonsensical things. This is not the New Testament model of Christ in operation. The wrong process wears out the leaders and puts them and others off of ever wanting to undertake the process again. Satan is weak, defeated, and ready to flee whenever

Leaders exercise spiritual authority to change our world.

believers believe and exercise their great covenant authority over him. He would love to get believers to think that it is a "tug of war" with the strongest one winning. Believers **start** from the beginning with the internalised premise that Satan is defeated and must go upon their command. Always command the demon to "be quiet," as Jesus did, if they start to speak. Never get into conversation with a demon or allow them to continue to speak.

Mark 16:17 says, "And these signs will accompany those who believe: In my name they will **drive out** demons…." The original Greek word used here means, "to eject." It does not suggest wrestling, struggling, warring, fighting, pushing, beating with sticks, or anything like that. It is patterned from the work of Christ revealed in the Gospels. It is the very same Christ who is present in the believer to do the very same things in the very same way. Say it now, aloud, "Devil, wherever I find you, you are defeated already in Jesus' Name!" "Look out, here I come with the One who already defeated you!"

Someone may enquire, 'What about the occasion where Jesus said, "…this kind comes out only by prayer and fasting…?" In Matt. 17:19-21 Jesus' first response to the question of why they had failed was that it was due to **unbelief**. Then He goes on to explain the process by which that unbelief is replaced with demon-casting faith—prayer and fasting. Prayer and fasting are designed to enlarge the absorption of His Presence and the growth of discernment (the ability to spiritually read circumstances, people and spiritual activity) and faith. Thus armed, the leader is well able to dispatch the afflicting demon or spirit. The disciples would not have been able to do pre-encounter prayer and fasting for a demonised person they did not know they were going to face. It had to be a part of their lifestyle of growing their faith and their relationship to the Lord.

Sustaining Your Spiritual Authority
Once a leader begins to operate in spiritual authority in supernatural realms he must live safe from downfall. Subtle, Satan-injected thoughts can enter the mind to prepare a path for failure. Keys: humility, honesty, relationship, personal devotional life. So many have "bit the dust" that were once "great" ministries. Acts 13:43; Col. 1:23.

Application
Heal someone in the group. While doing so, have someone not involved, evaluate how authoritatively you seem to be approaching what you are doing. Discuss and repeat. Take less than 40 seconds to do the miracle. Be sure to check for results.

Read Aliss Cresswell's book, "The Normal Supernatural Christian Life."

Leaders exercise spiritual authority to change our world.

Exercising Spiritual Authority Scriptures

Col 1:27
"God has chosen to make known among the Gentiles the glorious riches of this mystery, which is **Christ in you**, the hope of glory."

Eph. 4:15
"Instead, speaking the truth in love, we will **in all things grow up into Him** who is the Head, that is, Christ."

1 John 2:6 ESV
"…whoever says he abides in him ought to walk in the same way in which he walked."

John 14:20
"On that day you will realise that I am in my Father, and **you are in me, and I am in you**."

Mark 1:22
"The people were amazed at his teaching, because he taught them **as one who had authority, not as the teachers of the law**."

Matt 21:23-24
"Jesus entered the temple courts, and, while he was teaching, the chief priests and the elders of the people came to him. **"By what authority are you doing these things?" they asked**. "And who gave you this authority?" Jesus replied, "I will also ask you one question. If you answer me, I will tell you by what authority I am doing these things."

Mark 1:27
"The people were all so amazed that they asked each other, "What is this? A new teaching — and with authority! **He even gives orders to evil spirits and they obey him**."

Luke 10:19
"**I have given you authority** to trample on snakes and scorpions and **to overcome all the power of the enemy**; nothing will harm you."

John 15:16 NLT
"You didn't choose me. I chose you. **I appointed you to go and produce lasting fruit**, so that the Father will give you whatever you ask for, using my name."

Ex. 4:21
"The Lord said to Moses, "When you return to Egypt, **see that you perform before Pharaoh all the wonders I have given you the power to do**. But I will harden his heart so that he will not let the people go."

Leaders exercise spiritual authority to change our world.

Isa. 40:30-31 NKJV
"Even the youths shall faint and be **weary**, and the young men shall utterly fall, but those who wait on the LORD shall **renew *their* strength**; they shall mount up with wings like eagles, they shall run and **not be weary**, they shall walk and not faint."

Rom 11:36
"For **from** him and **through** him and **to** him are all things."

Rom. 8:9 NLT
But you are not controlled by your sinful nature. You are controlled by the Spirit if **you have the Spirit of God living in you**. (And remember that those who do not have the Spirit of Christ living in them do not belong to him at all.)"

Mark 3:14-15
"He appointed twelve — designating them apostles — that they might **be with him** and that he might send them out to preach **and to have authority** to drive out demons."

John 14:9, 11
"Jesus answered: "Don't you know me, Philip, even after I have been among you such a long time? Anyone who has seen me has seen the Father. How can you say, 'Show us the Father'? Believe me when I say that I am in the Father and the Father is in me; or at least believe on the evidence of the miracles themselves."

1 Cor. 6:17
"But he who unites himself with the Lord is one with him in spirit."

Col. 1:27
"To them God has chosen to make known among the Gentiles the glorious riches of this mystery, which is Christ in you, the hope of glory."

1 Cor. 1:30
"It is because of him that you are in Christ Jesus, who has become for us wisdom from God — that is, our righteousness, holiness and redemption."

John 14:20
"On that day you will realise that I am in my Father, and you are in me, and I am in you."

John 14:10

"Don't you believe that I am in the Father, and that the Father is in me? The words I say to you I do not speak on my own authority. Rather, it is the Father, living in me, who is doing his work."

Leaders exercise spiritual authority to change our world.

John 15:7
"If you remain in me and my words remain in you, ask whatever you wish, and it will be done for you."

John 14:11 NCV
"Believe me when I say that I am in the Father and the Father is in me. Or believe because of the miracles I have done."

John 14:12
"Very truly I tell you, whoever believes in me will do the works I have been doing, and they will do even greater things than these, because I am going to the Father."

1 Cor. 4:17
"For this reason I have sent to you Timothy, my son whom I love, who is faithful in the Lord. He will remind you of my way of life in Christ Jesus, which agrees with what I teach everywhere in every church."

Rom. 5:17
"For if, by the trespass of the one man, death reigned through that one man, how much more will those who receive God's abundant provision of grace and of the gift of righteousness reign in life through the one man, Jesus Christ."

Phil. 3:19
"Their destiny is destruction, their god is their stomach, and their glory is in their shame. Their mind is set on earthly things."

Rom. 12:2
"Do not conform to the pattern of this world, but be transformed by the renewing of your mind. Then you will be able to test and approve what God's will is — his good, pleasing and perfect will."

Rom. 8:9
"You, however, are controlled not by the sinful nature but by the Spirit, if **the Spirit of God lives in you**. And if anyone does not have the Spirit of Christ, he does not belong to Christ."

Acts 1:8
"But you will receive power when **the Holy Spirit comes on you**; and you will be my witnesses…."

John 7:38-39
"Whoever believes in me, as the Scripture has said, streams of living water will **flow from within** him." By this he meant **the Spirit**…."

Leaders exercise spiritual authority to change our world.

Acts 10:38
"…how God anointed Jesus of Nazareth with the Holy Spirit and power, and how he went around doing good and healing all who were under the power of the devil, because God was with him."

Josh 1:6-9
"Be strong and courageous, because you will lead these people to inherit the land I swore to their forefathers to give them. Be strong and very courageous. Be careful to obey all the law my servant Moses gave you; do not turn from it to the right or to the left, that you may be successful wherever you go. Do not let this Book of the Law depart from your **mouth; meditate** on it day and night, so that you may be careful **to do everything** written in it. Then you will be prosperous and successful. Have I not commanded you? Be strong and courageous. Do not be terrified; do not be discouraged, for the Lord your God will be with you wherever you go."

Matt 7:29
"…because he taught as **one who had authority**, and not as their teachers of the law."

Matt 9:8
"When the crowd saw this, they were filled with awe; and they praised God, who had **given such authority to men**."

Matt 10:1
"He called his twelve disciples to him and **gave them authority** to drive out evil spirits and to heal every disease and sickness."

Luke 10:17-19
"The seventy-two returned with joy and said, "Lord, even the demons submit to us in your name." He replied, "I saw Satan fall like lightning from heaven. **I have given you authority** to trample on snakes and scorpions and to overcome all the power of the enemy; nothing will harm you."

Matt 8:8
"The centurion replied, "Lord, I do not deserve to have you come under my roof. But **just say the word**, and my servant will be healed."

Acts 4:29
"Now, Lord, consider their threats and enable your servants **to speak your word with great boldness**."

Acts 4:31
"After they prayed, the place where they were meeting was shaken. And they were all filled with the Holy Spirit and spoke the word of God **boldly**."

Leaders exercise spiritual authority to change our world.

Acts 9:28
"So Saul stayed with them and moved about freely in Jerusalem, **speaking boldly** in the name of the Lord."

Acts 14:3
"So Paul and Barnabas spent considerable time there, **speaking boldly for the Lord**, who confirmed the message of his grace by enabling them to perform signs and wonders."

2 Cor. 3:9-12
"If the ministry that condemns men is glorious, how much more glorious is the ministry that brings righteousness! For what was glorious has no glory now in comparison with the surpassing glory. And if what was fading away came with glory, how much greater is the glory of that which lasts! Therefore, since we have such a hope, **we are very bold**."

1 John 2:20
"But **you have an anointing** from the Holy One, and all of you know the truth."

John 15:4, 7-8
"**Remain** in me, and I will **remain** in you. No branch can bear fruit by itself; it must **remain** in the vine. Neither can you bear fruit unless you **remain** in me. If you **remain** in me and my words **remain** in you, ask whatever you wish, and it will be given you. This is to my Father's glory, that you bear much fruit, showing yourselves to be my disciples."

Matt 7:29
"…because he taught as **one who had authority**, and not as their teachers of the law."

Matt 9:6-8
"But so that you may know that the Son of Man has authority on earth to forgive sins…." Then he said to the paralytic, "Get up, take your mat and go home." And the man got up and went home. When the crowd saw this, they were filled with awe; and they praised God, who had **given such authority to men**."

Mark 11:23
"I tell you the truth, if anyone says to this mountain, 'Go, throw yourself into the sea,' and does not doubt in his heart but **believes that what he says will happen**, it will be done for him."

2 Cor. 10:3-5
"For though we live in the world, we do not wage war as the world does. The weapons we fight with are not the weapons of the world. On the contrary, they have divine power to demolish strongholds. We demolish arguments and every pretension that sets itself up against the knowledge of God, and we take captive every thought to make it obedient to Christ."

Leaders exercise spiritual authority to change our world.

Luke 11:20
"But if **I drive out demons by the finger of God**, then the kingdom of God has come to you."

John 16:23-24
"In that day you will no longer ask me anything. I tell you the truth, my Father will give you **whatever you ask in my name**. Until now you have not asked for anything in my name. Ask and you will receive, and your joy will be complete."

Acts 13:43
"When the congregation was dismissed, many of the Jews and devout converts to Judaism followed Paul and Barnabas, who talked with them and **urged them to continue in the grace of God**."

Col. 1:23
"…**if you continue in your faith, established and firm**, not moved from the hope held out in the gospel. This is the gospel that you heard and that has been proclaimed to every creature under heaven, and of which I, Paul, have become a servant."

The Leader and.....

Self-Discipline

Leaders, who intend to remain as leaders for their entire lives, will require a life of self-discipline. Often the very word, "discipline," seems, for some, a loathsome return to some notion of "legalism." Not having thought clearly about either the definition of discipline or how vitally important it is to all of life, they subconsciously resist the idea of some form of discipline being imposed on their lives by themselves or others. They may remember their teen-age years when they struggled greatly with the rules their parents attempted to enforce and thus a negative feeling remains in their minds regarding the whole concept of discipline.

Yet the Bible makes clear that self-discipline is both absolutely necessary and a beautiful life-preserving, fruitfulness-making dimension of a person's life. Leaders will inevitably come to terms with self-discipline or lose their way and ultimately the good life they instinctively desire. 2 Tim 1:7 says, "For God did not give us a spirit of timidity, but a spirit of power, of love and of **self-discipline**." *Without self-discipline a would-be leader will never lead others significantly because their poor life habits will let any team effort down and discourage others from following them.* Poor time management, poor communication, and poor performance in punctuality give the telling message to would-be followers that this endeavour is not that important.

Defining Discipline
Discipline is defined by the dictionary as:

- *Training* or conditions imposed for the improvement of physical powers or self-control

- Systematic *training* in obedience to regulations and authority

- *Instruction* given to a disciple

- The state of improved behaviour as result of *training* or conditions

- Punishment, chastisement or correction

- A system of rules for behaviour or methods of practice

- To improve or attempt to improve the behaviour, orderliness or etc. by *training* conditions or rules

Leaders learn to live self-disciplined lives producing the best for the glory of God.

- *Consistent adherence to boundaries*, responsibilities, and behaviour

All of the concepts mentioned above defining discipline, are mentioned in the Bible. God endeavours by His Spirit and Word to "train us in righteousness" and help us develop the fruit of the Spirit called, "self-control." 2 Tim. 3:16-17; Gal. 5:22-24. Self-control is another word for self-discipline. Paul taught on this dimension of living. Acts 24:25.

The Bible makes plain that discipline is something that is done **to you, for you** and something done **by you**. Deut. 4:36. God, parents, others, and circumstances all endeavour to "discipline" or train us that we might be better people. We enter this world with a nature and tendency to go outside of boundaries. It is God's design that our parents discipline us **to develop the self-discipline within us** to live *inside* the boundaries. Wherever our parents were successful, we live with the blessing of good habits. Wherever they failed to instill in us good habits, by consistent discipline, we suffer the lack of those disciplines or habits in our adult life.

God disciplines us. Ps. 94:12-13. He does so as "**training** in righteousness" or training us to walk in the right ways of God. Heb. 12:11. Hardships, trials, failures, and difficulties all provide us opportunity to develop disciplines (consistent habits) that make our lives better. Heb. 12:7 says, "**Endure hardship** as discipline." God, the Master Trainer, and Master Parent, uses the hard things we go through to train us and develop new realms of fruitfulness in our lives. The boss at work who seems oppressive in his demands may be unjust, but God would use that stressful situation to deepen our prayer life, get us to focus on attitudes we may have toward injustice, and prompt a victorious attitude when we might be tempted to surrender in defeat. Our positive attitude toward hardship and difficulty is vital if we are to be "overcomers, more-than-conquerors, and always in triumph."

1 Cor. 9:25 says, "Everyone who competes in the games **goes into strict training**. They do it to get a crown that will not last; but we do it to get a crown that will last for ever." Our flesh, our carnal nature, or the person that we used to be, does not like the strict training necessary to produce "the crown" we have been promised. Yet it is our wilful, faith-filled embrace of the necessity of such strict training that enables His grace to flood our lives with His ability, when we seem so weak, inadequate, and incapable in ourselves. It is self-delusion to think that I will fully develop my leadership capacity without having to change, develop greater self-discipline and respond correctly to adjustment and correction.

We experience discipline or adjustment by those who are over us in the Lord. They speak and make decisions at times to reinforce the significance of some area of failing that we might find fresh grace to succeed in humility. Heb. 13:17 ESV. How we respond to this discipline determines our forward progress. If we react, rebel, ignore, or decide to quit, we have failed to embrace the discipline that God is using, regardless of how we may perceive the judgment of our leaders.

Leaders learn to live self-disciplined lives producing the best for the glory of God.

Teenagers have this same opportunity presented to them many times. When they refuse to respond positively to the discipline, order, and boundaries set by their parents, they head toward the "cliff of disaster" unknowingly. Thus wise parents begin conditioning their children to respond to rules and instructions long before they become teenagers.

Leviticus 26:23
"'If in spite of these things you do not **accept my correction** but continue to be hostile towards me….'"

Job 36:10
"He makes them **listen to correction and commands them** to repent of their evil."

Proverbs 5:12
"You will say, "How **I hated discipline**! How **my heart spurned correction**!"

Proverbs 10:17
"**He who heeds discipline shows the way** to life, but whoever ignores correction **leads others astray**."

Proverbs 12:1
"Whoever **loves discipline** loves knowledge, but he who **hates correction is stupid**."

Proverbs 13:18
"He who **ignores discipline** comes to poverty and shame, but whoever heeds correction is honoured."

Proverbs 15:5
"A fool **spurns his father's discipline**, but whoever **heeds correction** shows prudence."

Proverbs 15:10
"**Stern discipline** awaits him who leaves the path; he who **hates correction** will die."

Proverbs 15:12
"A mocker **resents correction**; he will not consult the wise."

Proverbs 15:32
"He who **ignores discipline** despises himself, but whoever heeds correction gains understanding."

Proverbs 29:15
"The **rod of correction imparts wisdom**, but a child left to himself disgraces his mother."

Jeremiah 2:30
"In vain I punished your people; they did not **respond to correction**. Your sword has devoured your prophets like a ravening lion."

Leaders learn to live self-disciplined lives producing the best for the glory of God.

Jeremiah 5:3
"O Lord, do not your eyes look for truth? You struck them, but they felt no pain; you crushed them but they **refused correction**. They made their faces harder than stone and refused to repent."

Jeremiah 7:28
"Therefore say to them, 'This is the nation that has not obeyed the Lord its God or **responded to correction**. Truth has perished; it has vanished from their lips."

Zephaniah 3:2
"She obeys no-one, she **accepts no correction**. She does not trust in the Lord, she does not draw near to her God."

Zephaniah 3:7
"I said to the city, 'Surely you will fear me and **accept correction**!' Then her dwelling would not be cut off, nor all **my punishments come upon her**. But they were still eager to act corruptly in all they did."

The Opposite of Discipline
The opposite of discipline is laziness, being "laid-back," irresponsible, undisciplined, self-centred, inconsistent, ambivalent, rebellious and failing. The **attitude** that rejects a more disciplined life is the **attitude** that rejects progress, authority and destiny. In order to be trained as a disciple, a believer must accept the disciplines of that training which produce self-control or self-discipline. The tendencies to live outside prescribed boundaries is a part of the old, carnal nature of who I used to be that must be crucified or put to death.

Many would-be leaders discover that they have arrived at their current age without the level of self-discipline they require. They accurately discern that their attitudes in some areas and their practices, are opposite to a disciplined lifestyle and in some cases a willful defiance of the standards that are required of them. They face a crossroads in their life. Will they embrace greater self-discipline or will they "run" to a less-disciplined church or setting in order to escape the issue? 1 Cor. 11:31-32 says, "…if we judged ourselves, we would not come under judgment. When we are judged by the Lord, we are being **disciplined** (trained) so that we will not be condemned with the world."

Leaders and Self-discipline
Disciples are meant to be a "disciplined" group of people, trained as "soldiers" to accomplish His mission, in His great army. Leaders are even more exercised to be highly trained in self-discipline. They can only lead out of the strength they have embraced through the disciplines of life. Those disciplines come from hardship, God, leaders, parents, trouble, and circumstances. What are you learning from these "teachers"? Prov. 15:31 NKJV says, "The ear that hears the rebukes of life will abide among the wise."

Leaders learn to live self-disciplined lives producing the best for the glory of God.

What actually undergoes the discipline that develops self-discipline?

- My attitude to God, authorities and others
- My attitude toward correction, adjustment and training
- My priorities
- My standards of performance
- My level of consistency in necessary changes
- My level of devotion to Christ in the Word and prayer
- My responses to hardship, injustice, trouble and failure
- My pride and former tendencies to live as I so choose
- My emotions
- My thought life
- My level of diligence and application to rising higher
- My right to myself and self-government

Self-discipline is accepting and imposing a standard of behaviour and living upon *yourself* that enables you to achieve goals and connect with others selflessly. Working within a team, demands self-discipline, lest you let the team down by your own selfish, undisciplined practices. Some would-be leaders, even over time, fail to be consistent in their attendance and attitude, punctual or early, and faithful in communicating with those over them. They live in the fantasy world of believing that they will honour God with their lives and gifts without any greater level of self-discipline. They rationalise the disappointment and frustration they cause others in the team through their undisciplined ways. Meanwhile their progress is stymied and they wonder why. Their unwitting disdain of the responsibility of self-discipline mires them in stagnation and their leaders see them as weak members of the team. Their dream of promotion or greater public ministry is delayed through their own poor choices.

Developing Self-Discipline
You can develop the self-discipline in your life by:

- By responding to the pressures you currently face to meet deadlines, communicate, get tasks finished and order your day in order to allow for a consistent devotional life. 1 Tim 4:7 says, "...**train yourself** to be godly."

Leaders learn to live self-disciplined lives producing the best for the glory of God.

- Sit down and reflect on your areas of weakness in the area of self-discipline. Is it in time-keeping? Is in communication? Is it in finishing jobs assigned to you? Is it in your thought life? Is it in the standard of work you produce? Is it in consistent attendance? Examine what goes on in your mind honestly. What are the specific excuses you are accustomed to making for your lack of self-discipline? Note that these thought patterns and rationalisations keep you from being your best for Him and for others.

- Ask God to help you. **Believe** that He will help you. Make a new plan for your life. God gives abundant grace to those that humble themselves and step out to respond to His voice.

- Learn to make decisions out of **conviction** not *preference or convenience*. Procrastination, unfaithfulness, and failure to complete your assignments, arises out of emotion-based decision-making, not principle-based decision-making. Ps. 119 speaks of "laws, decrees, commands, statutes, and precepts" that bring such amazing blessings to those who live by them.

- Write out the plan you have made in any area of your life that needs self-discipline or self-control. 2 Cor. 8:7 says, "…just as you excel in everything.…" Get started immediately. Meditate in all the verses that speak of self-control and self-discipline.

Application

In small groups discuss the following:

- How I responded to correction as a teenager to my parent(s) attempts to develop self-discipline in me by their application of discipline

- What are ideas or concepts that people hold about training, correction, and discipline today?

- How do I develop more self-discipline today as an adult and a leader?

- How does God use even what I think are wrongly-placed judgments of others to help develop self-discipline in me? (Parents, bosses, government, teachers, church leaders, company rules, protocols or standards of practice, etc.)

- What are the benefits and blessings I have in my life today as a result of the hard things God has used to shape my spirit, attitude, character and behaviour?

Leaders learn to live self-disciplined lives producing the best for the glory of God.

Self-discipline Scriptures

2 Tim 3:16-17
"All Scripture is God-breathed and is useful for teaching, rebuking, correcting and **training** in righteousness, so that the man of God may be **thoroughly equipped** for every good work."

Gal. 5:22-24
"But the fruit of the Spirit is love, joy, peace, patience, kindness, goodness, faithfulness, gentleness and **self-control**. Against such things there is no law. Those who belong to Christ Jesus have crucified the sinful nature with its passions and desires."

Acts 24:25
"As Paul discoursed on righteousness, self-control and the judgment to come, Felix was afraid and said, "That's enough for now! You may leave."

Deut. 4:36
"From heaven he made you hear his **voice to discipline** you. On earth he showed you his great fire, and you heard his words from out of the fire."

Ps 94:12-13
"Blessed is **the man you discipline**, O Lord, the man you teach from your law; you grant him relief from days of trouble…."

Heb. 12:11
"No **discipline seems pleasant** at the time, but painful. Later on, however, it produces a **harvest** of righteousness and peace for those who have been trained by it."

Heb. 13:17 ESV
"Obey your leaders and submit to them, for they are keeping watch over your souls, as those who will have to give an account. Let them do this with joy and not with groaning, for that would be of no **advantage** to you."

Leaders learn to live self-disciplined lives producing the best for the glory of God.

The Leader and.....

Money

Everyone needs money. From the Afghani refugee, living on the border of Pakistan underneath a blanket, with his family and all of his possessions, to the Christian businessman looking to pay his bills and expand his business, we all have a perception of our **need** for money. The leader must exhibit an example of uprightness and transparency where money is concerned. He must be honest, generous, and full of faith where money is concerned and **seen** to be so.

Where does money come from?
Our world system says money comes from the system. The government prints money as a means of exchange. The system is comprised of businesses and industries that employ people. In exchange for working in the business, employees receive money. They use the money they receive, to exchange it for the goods and services they need and desire. As goes the system, so goes the one who subscribes to the philosophy and practices of that system. Many believers unwittingly subscribe to this underlying, subconscious approach to their material lives. Rev. 18:11, 13, 23-24.

Leaders, however, recognise that they connect with an economic system that is not man-made. They can and must work in this world but not be subject to its values, morals, practices, and motivations. They **live** not "for the meat that perishes," but **for** their Father and His great mission and purpose in the earth. John 6:27 NKJV. They recognise:

- Everything belongs to the Creator – Gen. 14:19; 1 Chron. 29:11; Job 41:11. The Creator is the Owner of all things.

- Everything comes from Him who gives us life and breath – James 1:17; 1 Chron. 29:14; Rom. 11:36. Often leaders who are employed by a church, forget that the church is not their source—God is their Source. Luke 22:35. They can and often do forget that their employment may not be for life. They may be released from employment from the church they serve for a host of reasons. If they become bitter about this, no matter how it has come about, they lose their way spiritually and their faith for God's continuing provision. Now they are depending on the world's supply just like everyone else who does not know Christ. Sometimes leaders are released from employment by a church or ministry for the following reasons:

    1. There are not sufficient funds to pay all the outgoings and some cuts must be made.

Leaders set the example in tithes, offerings, generosity and financial transparency.

2. There is a decision to discontinue a particular programme or ministry.

3. There is a change in leadership at a higher level and they want to employ team members of their own choosing.

4. There are relational difficulties that lie unresolved and a staff member(s) must be released from employment in order to go forward.

5. There is no clear or reasonable justification given.

Handling this relational, financial and ultimately, spiritual test, is vital to the spiritual health of the leader and his family and all those he influences. So many leaders, pastors, Senior Pastors, apostles, etc. have been released from employment by a church or group of churches. If they fail to handle this test personally and as a family, they live with anger, bitterness and unforgiveness. Nothing ever catches God by surprise and He always has a way of enabling us to fulfil our life mission apart from what we have already known.

- Everything is to be offered back to Him as we live this life – Rom. 11:35-36; 1 Chron. 29:16; Matt. 6:33. Believers are allowed to enjoy the temporal pleasures of the material world but not be so engrossed in the pursuit of those pleasures as to lose focus on their life mission. 1 Tim. 6:17-19; 1 Cor. 7:29-31.

- The leader, as a believer, has inherited all **things**. Living in your inherited legacy, you need never be in debt or without. Establishing this position inside you is the first step in releasing your faith for it to be manifested. Rom. 8:32; 2 Cor. 9:8 ESV, 11 ESV; Luke 15:31; Ps. 115:16.

The Financial Foundations of A Leader's Life
Leaders are meant to set the example in their financial lives. They are faithful in the basics of tithes and offerings. They are also examples of those who give beyond the Old Testament standard of tithes and offerings in spontaneous, Spirit-directed giving as well. They are ready to pay for a stranger's meal, give a car away, or sow whatever He says, wherever He says. As a result of placing the Kingdom first (Matt. 6:33) motivationally in their giving, they are blessed more and more. God rules their lives financially. He easily puts His hand in their pocket to collect or impart. They live free of greed and live in the unboundaried joy of generosity and have enough to give away all the time. They pay their bills on time, don't live in debt and are a model of selfless giving. They learn to budget, save, pay their taxes and live transparently where finances are concerned. They never use money to manipulate and they don't worship those who have great finances or look down on those who have less.

The Leader and Debt.
This world's economic system is debt-based. As you may be able to discern, our present world economic system is in serious trouble. Its motivations are fundamentally flawed (greed and selfishness) and its structural practices are designed to subjugate people

Leaders set the example in tithes, offerings, generosity and financial transparency.

and maintain poverty. The prince of this world uses the love of money to exalt, and then destroy what has been exalted, to oppress the poor and to enlarge pride and self-sufficiency in the wealthy. The educational system, the media, and the business sector are all geared to promote the inner drive to wealth at any price. The wise leader learns how to disconnect and stay disconnected from this subtle, Satanic motivation and the instincts of the "old man." Satan's promotion of the love of money comes in the following forms:

- I must have it and I must have it now! (a good definition of lust)

- Others have it and thus I am *entitled* as well

- The end justifies the means

- Getting is the goal…giving is foolish

- Live for pleasure and secure what will give you pleasure

- The material world is the world that brings joy and happiness…shout when money comes and weep when it goes, hold tightly to what you gain, secure yourself against any and all loss (not the attitude of Heb. 10:34). Read and meditate in Rev. 13 & 14.

The Leader and Accounting Practice, Taxes, and Loans.
Leaders know the state of their finances. They construct a budget, pay their bills on time, pay cash, balance their accounts each month, and are able to account for how they spend their money. Leaders pay their taxes honestly. Rom. 13:6-8.

Leaders don't make personal loans to members of the congregation. An old adage says, "Give, don't lend, in the long run, it is cheaper." If you can't afford (in your own mind) to give someone some money, don't loan them any. You make a "master-slave" relationship that Satan can exploit, both in you and the person to whom you have made a loan. Prov. 22:7 says, "…the borrower is slave to the lender." Christianity is full of angry, offence-filled people who have made or received loans and when trouble came, they lost their relationship by someone's failure to repay.

Relationships are not to be traded for money. Don't set up this kind of scenario for another or take a loan from some generous, kind-hearted fellow believer or fellow leader. For every successful transaction of loan repayment, there are a thousand failures and the subsequent severing of relationships. Better to look up and focus on the One who owns all and believe His powerful promises for supernatural intervention than subscribe to the logic of this world and suffer twice.

The Leader and Prosperity.
The partnership to prosper is the same as the partnership to do the miraculous as it, too, is a miraculous, favour-operated dimension of our lives.

Leaders set the example in tithes, offerings, generosity and financial transparency.

How prosperity comes – Deut. 28; Mt. 6:33; Ps. 112. Often God's people don't prosper because they don't exercise faith and so their tithes and offerings become simply "dead works." Rom. 14:23 says, "…whatever is not of faith is sin." They also forfeit the prosperity that is theirs because they don't give with the right motivation—the Kingdom motivation. If you put Kingdom first, according to Scripture, God adds the "all things" He has promised. Thus *faith* and *motive* are vital to prosper. 2 Cor. 9:11 says, "You will be made rich in every way so that you can be generous on every occasion."

- How to handle prosperity when it does come – 1 Tim. 6:17-19 tells us that those who have been given significant abundance are to be "rich in good works." They are to recognise that wealth comes with responsibility to bless and enable others, not simply live self-indulgently.

The Leader and Generosity and Great Generosity.
Leaders lead the way in every area of life whether it is the supernatural, loving others, caring and serving, or in generosity. Leaders around the world have discovered that the "generous lifestyle" is a lifestyle that brings the greatest joy and fulfillment to life as well as the greatest security in financial realms. Leaders have become so disconnected from the material world that they have freely given cars, lands, businesses, houses, investments, inheritances, and savings accounts. These are not generally what the world would call "wealthy" individuals although some were. They were generally, ordinary, working class believers with God's heart and faith-filled obedience. They have discovered that if they follow in the steps of their "father" Abraham, in the realm of faith, they can give anything that they are prompted to give and never, never lose.

Leaders, in the last days, will be like the believers in the first century, in being so disconnected from the material world and so deeply connected to generosity and purpose that they will bring houses and lands to offer for His use. They live beyond the material blessing of this life. What could God ask you to give, in developing great generosity, that you might struggle to "let go of?" God will help you "grow" your faith by requiring of you what you may have difficulty in doing. Learn to trust Him at new levels by learning to say "Yes!" with every new instruction regarding giving.

If you would be a money magnet for His purposes, you must be a pipe of generosity *first*. God would prepare you for extravagant receiving by your extravagant giving. Ask Him to take you higher and He will. He will speak to you in your spirit-man and whisper an instruction that may cause you to draw a deep breath. Obey Him! It is with joy and excitement that we walk with an abiding trust in the One who leads us into greater generosity.

We are to be like God who is the Ultimate Giver. His generosity is huge! Luke 6:38 says **how** we are to give, as well as to give…with great measure! God's people are always meant to be generous and leaders even more so, as they are influencing others to be like God, who is amazingly generous.

Leaders set the example in tithes, offerings, generosity and financial transparency.

Giving Spontaneously, Secretly and Publicly and Joyfully.
The Bible tells us the manner in which we are to give so that our giving is acceptable before God. To give in ways different from what He has specified is to cancel our blessings and violate His prescribed methods. Giving starts in the secret place of our hearts. We choose to listen to the Source and obey Him in our giving. It is from that "secret place" that our heart's decisions are instructed to give.

Our general giving in tithes and offerings in our local church is without disclosure to others. Our giving to the needy is also something we do not broadcast to others. Matt. 6:4. The needy themselves may know or may not know who blessed them, depending on the circumstances. Leaders are always ready to respond to need according to the voice of the Holy Spirit. They have a "heart to bless" others and help where need is discovered. If there is a public offering, they can according to their hearing of the Holy Spirit, give as He has directed them. They do not necessarily tell others how much they gave or how they had to exercise faith in their giving or what challenges they faced personally when they were actually giving. They learn to love giving, as loving giving is loving, loving. They have discovered Acts 20:35 which says it is more blessed to give than to receive. Their entire lifestyle is a lifestyle of enabling, blessing and giving to others.

The Supernatural and Money.
Be a believer and not a beggar. Many people are beggars. They do not have a revelation of whom their Father is and how He will provide. Travelling in developing nations I have found pastors, leaders, apostles, and saints consistently asking, texting, emailing and writing asking for money. Often, once they have discovered you are able and generous, they make you their source and you become a regular in their requests for money. They have traded "my God shall supply all my needs" for "my ask" will supply all of my needs.

Debt Cancellation
No leader should be in debt. Make it a goal to eliminate all debt from your life and to remain debt-free for the rest of your life. Rom. 13:8. God's plan is to prosper you so that you will not be in any debt. If you are not good at financial planning, have someone who is good with financial planning sit with you and make a budget that includes paying tithes, paying off all of your debt, making a savings plan (even if only a token amount to begin with) and careful spending of your income. When additional funds come, don't spend them on items not on the budget. Use those additional funds to decrease your debt. Believe God for supernatural debt cancellation. Confess that you are debt-free every day until it manifests. Obey God's voice in your giving. 2 Cor. 9:8-11 ESV; Deut. 15:1-6.

Handling Money
Christians should be scrupulously honest in dealing with money. Paying all the taxes that you owe and paying on time are basic to the honesty of a believer. The leader who is pushing the edges of his tax computation has unwittingly entered into "shortage

Leaders set the example in tithes, offerings, generosity and financial transparency.

thinking." God is not short of money to bless you and pay all the necessary taxes on what He has given you in the first place. Rom. 13:7. Satan will try to get the leader to cut corners and make compromises in paying taxes and bills. This kind of activity does not partner with a generous spirit but hides under the camouflage of "being thrifty." It is really a "shortage mentality."

Listening to a prophetic word given to a woman several years ago that began with, "O how you like nice things!" I thought how common this is to most of humanity. Yet it was a cloud of disappointment and a steely sense of purpose to possess, that swallowed up the life of her inner man and held her back from God's blessing. We can diligently pursue what He is already disposed to favour us with. The world's system is full of people, some who are unwitting believers, who are passionately pursuing wealth—not as a ministry to enable others but to have the joy of possession and the alleged prestige and power that goes with it.

God chooses to bless some men and women extraordinarily with finances for the sake of furthering Kingdom purposes. Such wealthy people will come into the church. They must be treated like everyone else—not worshipped, but loved and accepted as part of the family, having the same needs of affirmation, acceptance and recognition **without reference** to their wealth. They are not to be "hit up" for loans, gifts or favours. Let God direct them. Their ministry will prosper in the same way as others ministries prosper, if we honour the gift that God has given them and bless them as people. Ps. 49:16-18 says, "Do not be overawed when others grow rich, when the splendour of their houses increases; for they will take nothing with them when they die, their splendour will not descend with them. Though while they live they count themselves blessed— and people praise you when you prosper…."

Application
Read "Money Cometh" by Leroy Thompson. Discuss with three others what you benefitted most from this book and how your life and perspective have changed in relation to money.

Read "The Blessed Life" by Robert Morris and make all the adjustments to your heart and your giving that the Holy Spirit speaks to you about.

Ask God for the name of someone in your leadership team that you should bless financially and how much you should give **anonymously**. Then obey God. Get started on hearing and obeying God in relation to giving. Adopt a lifestyle of generous giving. Expect that God will at some time ask you to give away something greatly significant. Don't hesitate…just do it…just as Abraham gave Isaac.

If you are married, discuss with your spouse how you should "upgrade" your financial giving life. Take the steps you agree on.

Leaders set the example in tithes, offerings, generosity and financial transparency.

Money Scriptures

Rev 18:11-13
"The merchants of the earth will weep and mourn over her because no-one buys their cargoes any more — cargoes of gold, silver, precious stones and pearls…**and bodies and souls of men.**"

Rev 18:23-24
"Your **merchants were the world's great men. By your magic spell all the nations were led astray.** In her was found the blood of prophets and of the saints, and of all who have been killed on the earth."

John 6:27 NKJV
"Do not labor for the **food which perishes**, but for the food which endures to everlasting life…."

Gen 14:19
"…he blessed Abram, saying, "Blessed be Abram by God Most High, **Creator of heaven and earth.**"

1 Chron. 29:11
"Yours, O Lord, is the greatness and the power and the glory and the majesty and the splendour, for **everything in heaven and earth is yours.**"

Job 41:11
"Who has a claim against me that I must pay? **Everything under heaven belongs to me.**"

James 1:17
"Every good and perfect gift is **from above**, coming down from the Father of the heavenly lights, who does not change like shifting shadows."

1 Chron. 29:14
"But who am I, and who are my people, that we should be able to give as generously as this? **Everything comes from you, and we have given you only what comes from your hand.**"

Luke 22:35
"Then Jesus asked them, "When I sent you without purse, bag or sandals, did you lack anything?" "Nothing," they answered."

Rom. 11:35-36
"Who has ever given to God, that God should repay him?" For **from him** and **through him** and **to him** are all things."

Leaders set the example in tithes, offerings, generosity and financial transparency.

1 Chron. 29:16
"O Lord our God, as **for all this** abundance that **we have provided for building you a temple** for your Holy Name, it **comes from your hand**, and **all of it belongs to you**."

Matt 6:33
"But seek first his kingdom and his righteousness, and all these things will be given to you as well."

1 Tim. 6:17-19
"Command those who are rich in this present world not to be arrogant nor to put their hope in wealth, which is so uncertain, but to put their hope in God, who richly provides us with everything for our enjoyment. Command them to do good, to be rich in good deeds, and to be generous and willing to share. In this way they will lay up treasure for themselves as a firm foundation for the coming age, so that they may take hold of the life that is truly life."

1 Cor. 7:29-31
"What I mean, brothers, is that the time is short. From now on those who have wives should live as if they had none; those who mourn, as if they did not; those who are happy, as if they were not; those who buy something, as if it were not theirs to keep; those who use the things of the world, as if not engrossed in them. For this world in its present form is passing away."

Rom 8:32
"He who did not spare his own Son, but gave him up for us all — how will he not also, along with him, graciously **give us all things**?"

2 Cor. 9:8, 11 ESV
And God is able to make all grace abound to you, so that having all sufficiency **in all things at all times, you will abound in every good work. You will be enriched in every way** to be generous in every way, which through us will produce thanksgiving to God."

Luke 15:31
"'My son,' the father said, 'you are always with me, and everything I have is yours."

Ps. 115:16
"The highest heavens belong to the Lord, but the earth he has given to man."

Rom. 13:6-8
"This is also why you pay taxes, for the authorities are God's servants, who give their full time to governing. Give everyone what you owe him: If you owe taxes, pay taxes; if revenue, then revenue; if respect, then respect; if honour, then honour. Let no debt remain outstanding, except the continuing debt to love one another, for he who loves his fellow-man has fulfilled the law."

Leaders set the example in tithes, offerings, generosity and financial transparency.

Matt. 6:4
"…so that **your giving may be in secret**. Then your Father, who sees what is done in secret, will reward you."

2 Cor. 9:8-11 ESV
"And God is able to make all grace **abound** to you, so that **having all sufficiency in all things at all times, you may abound in every good work**. As it is written, "He has distributed freely, he has given to the poor; his righteousness endures forever." He who supplies **seed to the sower and bread for food** will supply and multiply your seed for sowing and increase the harvest of your righteousness. **You will be enriched in every way for all your generosity**, which through us will produce thanksgiving to God."

Deut. 15:1-6
"At the end of every seven years you must cancel debts. This is how it is to be done: Every creditor shall cancel the loan he has made to his fellow Israelite. He shall not require payment from his fellow Israelite or brother, because the Lord's time for cancelling debts has been proclaimed. You may require payment from a foreigner, but you must cancel any debt your brother owes you. However, there should be no poor among you, for in the land the Lord your God is giving you to possess as your inheritance, he will richly bless you, if only you fully obey the Lord your God and are careful to follow all these commands I am giving you today. For the Lord your God will bless you as he has promised, and you will lend to many nations but will borrow from none. You will rule over many nations but none will rule over you."

Rom. 13:7
"**Give everyone what you owe him**: If you **owe taxes, pay taxes**; if revenue, then revenue; if respect, then respect; if honour, then honour."

Leaders set the example in tithes, offerings, generosity and financial transparency.

The Leader and.....

Attitude

There is an old saying, "Nothing ever goes wrong for a Christian but his attitude." Attitude is the disposition, opinion, outlook, belief, perspective, and what comes out of your spirit and mouth as a result of that view. (The words that are translated, "attitude" in the New International Version mean "the spirit of your mind" and "what you think.") Your attitude is also what informs your judgment and it is what reveals, partly, your **character**. It is a leader's responsibility to help others when their attitude suffers from decline. He recognises the downcast look, the angry face, the resistant spirit, the hopeless demeanour, the broken heart, the grieving eyes, and all the other outward expressions of struggle in attitude. He must also discern his own attitude and make certain that it is always what it should be to preserve himself and to benefit others. Eph. 4:22-24. Having a right attitude, all the time, is one of the great tests of life and leadership.

To fail to acknowledge a negative attitude that you have and to change it, is to set in motion your own spiritual decline. Often leaders may be sophisticated enough to hide fairly discreetly their own wrong attitude. However, whether some other person discerns this wrong attitude or not, God knows that it exists and that it is eating away at your success from the inside. Often those in senior leadership discern a change in attitude, as God gives them the ability to detect this, just as parents detect it in their children. Sometimes leaders struggle with their attitudes in the following ways:

Resentment of:

- Work load
- Standards necessary to be a leader
- Other leaders
- Pastor
- Believers who criticise
- Difficult people or people who seem to waste the leader's time
- Tasks or assignment they have received
- Others who hold a different view from what they do
- Others who they believe do not hold them in respect and esteem

Sometimes the attitude shift represents a "disconnect" from the vision of the House. This attitude must be examined and dealt with, in order for it to keep from being a source of discouragement and division. When a leader discovers he or she has a

Leaders guard their attitude with their lives for it is their life.

disconnect from the Church, its vision or its leadership, he or she must first pray, then if no change has taken place, go and see the Senior Pastor.

Attitude in Scripture
We can see how significant our attitude or disposition is important in our continual progress in the Lord as it is discussed in Scripture.

- In the story of Jacob and Laban we see the revelation of having a good attitude *when you are being mistreated*. Gen. 31:2-7.

- In the story of Joseph we see how Joseph had a right attitude *when it appeared he had been forgotten*—he was forgotten by man but not by God. Gen. 40:23; 41:16.

- In the story of Solomon we see that having the wrong attitude caused Solomon to *lose the kingdom*. 1 Kings 11:10-11.

- In the story of the king of Assyria we can see how powerful a right attitude is in enabling the *work of God to go forward*. Ezra 6:20-22.

- In the story of Nebuchadnezzar we can see how an evil attitude infected by satanic notions *sought the extinction of believers*. Dan. 3:19-20.

Phil. 2:5-9 exhorts us to have the same attitude in all situations as Christ has…He did not grasp for position, recognition, or acclaim but was a servant who lived in humility and obedience. He never resented His fellow workers, His circumstances, His enemies, or His calling. Leaders have that same spirit or attitude that we see Christ as having.

Attitudes Can Be Changed by Your Decision to Do So
Sometimes a leader may be tempted to stay rooted in a wrong attitude. After a while, it seems in the view of such a leader, that the state of their own attitude is hopeless. Yet the liberating truth is that we have the power to change our attitude, disposition and perspective. We can choose by our own act of volition to frame, consider or take a perspective on life, people, issues, and circumstances, differently than we have been doing.

To change an attitude, you must first *yield* to God. Unwittingly, we can decide to maintain a disposition that God cannot work with and our choice to do so is subtly mired in stubbornness. It is this *yielding to God* that enables us to open up and hear Him and in our repentance adopt a new attitude.

I once felt myself resisting a colleague over a period of time and I felt and believed my stance was the "right one." However, the situation did not improve and the tension and difficulty only escalated. The pressure became unbearable. One day, while praying, I *yielded* to God. I told Him, "Lord, I am willing to do whatever you want. I will find your grace to work with the situation as I am clearly not walking in it." In my brokenness, peace came. I was in a different place in my relation to God in the

Leaders guard their attitude with their lives for it is their life.

matter. Whatever happened, I was now free and not imprisoned within myself but free to operate in His grace toward this colleague. It was such a blessed release. Not long after that, the colleague moved away. God knew they would leave but they were not to leave until my attitude had risen to the right place in God.

Changing your attitude does not require a miracle or even an understanding of how you can see something is going to work better. Often we cannot figure out with human resources how a matter will be resolved but God holds victory in store for us and releases it *when* our attitude (far more important than circumstantial change) changes. Prov. 2:7.

Continuity and Attitude
An attitude that is contrary to the Word of God and our relationship to the Lord will inevitably lead us into demise. Our leadership opportunity will eventually cease if we fail to address what stifles our progress and offends the spirit of holiness. The subtle rationalisations that hold in place our justification for a wrong attitude, are an evidence of pride. Pride, as a sinful attitude, is a deception. It is a deception, held in place by the originator of pride, the Devil. As long as we believe we are "Ok" when we are in fact not "Ok," we are living in the fog of prideful deception.

Leaders walk in humility continuously. This means they are humble and honest before God first, then humble and honest before others. Marriages break simply over pride. No one wants to go first and take responsibility for failure in attitude and action. Minimising something that is wrong, by comparing it with the alleged maximum wrong of others, makes it no less wrong—wrong is wrong and it is an unenviable pit of failure regardless of its "size." Humility acknowledges what is nakedly wrong. It is an inward, Holy Spirit-enabled honesty before God that labels wrong, as wrong, in one's own disposition and seeks to address it with repentance and grace.

Humility and faith sustain longevity. We often can perceive the wrongful attitude in another and sometimes fail to see our own wrong attitudes. This is why the Scripture tells us that while we seek to preserve and better the spiritual life of another, we must do it in humility. Gal. 6:1 ESV; Matt. 7:3-5. Always check to see if there is some level or form of the same thing in yourself that you see in another that is not good.

Conflict and Attitude
Often in conflict or disagreement situations, leaders can lose the "high ground" of having a right attitude. In their passionate discussion of what they so strongly believe and feel, they can unwittingly display an attitude that reveals some level of uncrucified ego connected to their expression of their view. A view is either right or wrong. If our attitude "assaults" others who do not hold the same view, we most often lose the opportunity to influence their position. It is not fundamentally wrong to hold a strong view but it **is** wrong to use sarcasm, denigration, or rejection of others in the expression of our strongly-held view. Christ, the meekest of all who ever lived, is The Truth. He persuaded by love and clear communication of the truth. When condemned,

Leaders guard their attitude with their lives for it is their life.

abused, maligned, and rejected, He answered meekly or not at all. Sometimes in the "heat of discussion" a leader can fail to remember that it is the Holy Spirit that brings revelation to others, as well as to ourselves. We can get in His way if we are not careful about our attitude.

Attitude and Repentance
When a leader loses a right attitude and reflects a wrong or sinful attitude, he or she should repent (turn and go the opposite direction) of manifesting a wrong attitude. This does not necessarily mean that his viewpoint is wrong, simply his attitude. He then is obligated to apologise unequivocally (without qualification or justification) for having a wrong attitude in expressing his opinion. To say, "I am sorry, I was wrong in the way that spoke about (insert the issue) and though I believe in the things I was saying, I was wrong in the way I spoke…would you forgive me?" is a valuable way to affirm the higher value of relationship over viewpoint. It also helps reset the standard for discussion.

Application

- In small groups, discuss occasions when you had a wrong attitude (leaving out of your telling, the names and places) and how it affected you and others and what you did about it.

- If someone is struggling with a wrong attitude about some thing, person or condition, pray for them and give them any encouragement from the Scriptures the Holy Spirit provides.

- Give testimonies of how breakthrough in attitude changed circumstances.

Leaders guard their attitude with their lives for it is their life.

Attitude Scriptures

Eph. 4:22-24
"You were taught, with regard to your former way of life, to put off your old self, which is being corrupted by its deceitful desires; to be made new in **the attitude of your minds**; and to put on the new self, created to be like God in true righteousness and holiness."

Gen 31:2-7
"And Jacob noticed that Laban's **attitude towards him** was not what it had been. Then the Lord said to Jacob, "Go back to the land of your fathers and to your relatives, and I will be with you." So Jacob sent word to Rachel and Leah to come out to the fields where his flocks were. He said to them, "I see that your father's **attitude towards me** is not what it was before, but the God of my father has been with me. You know that I've worked for your father with all my strength, yet your father has cheated me by changing my wages ten times. However, God has not allowed him to harm me."

Gen. 40:23
"The chief cupbearer, however, did not remember Joseph; **he forgot him**."

Gen. 41:16
"I cannot do it," Joseph replied to Pharaoh, "but **God will give Pharaoh the answer** he desires."

1 Kings 11:10-11
"Although he had forbidden Solomon to follow other gods, Solomon did not keep the Lord's command. So the Lord said to Solomon, "Since **this is your attitude** and you have not kept my covenant and my decrees, which I commanded you, I will most certainly tear the kingdom away from you and give it to one of your subordinates."

Ezra 6:20-22
"The priests and Levites had purified themselves and were all ceremonially clean. The Levites slaughtered the Passover lamb for all the exiles, for their brothers the priests and for themselves. So the Israelites who had returned from the exile ate it, together with all who had separated themselves from the unclean practices of their Gentile neighbours in order to seek the Lord, the God of Israel. For seven days they celebrated with joy the Feast of Unleavened Bread, because the Lord had filled them with joy by **changing the attitude** of the king of Assyria, so that he assisted them in the work on the house of God, the God of Israel."

Dan 3:19-20
"Then Nebuchadnezzar was furious with Shadrach, Meshach and Abednego, and his **attitude** towards them changed. He ordered the furnace to be heated seven times hotter than usual and commanded some of the strongest soldiers in his army to tie up Shadrach, Meshach and Abednego and throw them into the blazing furnace."

Leaders guard their attitude with their lives for it is their life.

Phil 2:5-9

"Your **attitude** should be the same as that of Christ Jesus: Who, being in very nature God, did not consider equality with God something to be grasped, but made himself nothing, taking the very nature of a servant, being made in human likeness. And being found in appearance as a man, he humbled himself and became obedient to death — even death on a cross! Therefore God exalted him to the highest place and gave him the name that is above every name…."

Prov. 2:7

"He holds victory in store for the upright, he is a shield to those whose walk is blameless…."

Gal 6:1

"Brothers, if someone is caught in a sin, you who are spiritual should restore him gently. But watch yourself, or you also may be tempted."

Matt. 7:3-5

"Why do you look at the speck of sawdust in your brother's eye and pay no attention to the plank in your own eye? How can you say to your brother, 'Let me take the speck out of your eye,' when all the time there is a plank in your own eye? You hypocrite, first take the plank out of your own eye, and then you will see clearly to remove the speck from your brother's eye."

Leaders guard their attitude with their lives for it is their life.

The Leader and.....

Destiny

Where Do We Go From Here….?

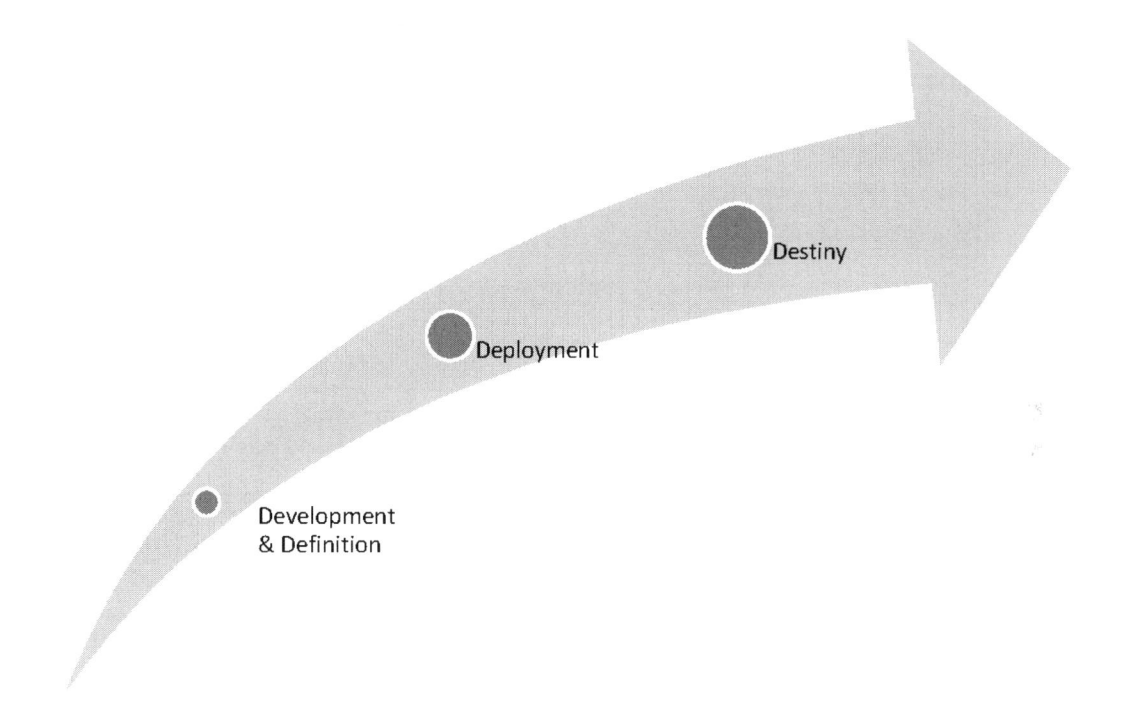

Discipleship

Introduction
When I was seven years of age, I attended church services every Sunday with my family. On one Sunday we had a visiting speaker, an evangelist. In the middle of his message he stepped off the platform and came to where I was sitting. He placed his hand on my head and prophesied, "This boy will preach the gospel in a foreign land someday." Many years later, as I stood on a platform in Pakistan preaching to approximately forty thousand Muslims, I was reminded of that prophetic word. God had that day of preaching, placed in "my folder," from before time and announced it, when I was but seven years old. He has such a huge plan for your life. Will you discover it? Will you enter into its unfolding? Will your faith sustain you all your days, so you can say you finished the course that He had designed?

Life is a Journey
Mk 6:8. Our lives are spiritually defined as a journey from Heaven to earth (we are born from above), and then back to heaven. Rom. 11:36 says, "For from Him, through Him and to Him are all things." Saving grace flowed from the Father (John 3:16),

Leaders step into their intended destiny with their faith and obedience.

through the Son and then back to the Father from your life. You started spiritually in Heaven, (as your earthly life was sentenced to death), and then you were awakened to take up your mission on earth via the Son's indwelling and enablement, which ultimately you present back to Him. There are three primary dimensions of this Heaven-sent mission you have received:

1. Revelation from Him – Your spiritual eyes are opened to your calling. Acts 9:8, 17-18; Acts 26:19. Like Saul/Paul, your life radically changed when you saw and accepted your mission.

2. Resource from Him – 2 Pet. 1:3 ESV. Everything you need to complete the mission you have been given. 1 Cor. 4:7; 2 Cor. 4:7.

3. Equipping – 1 Thes. 2:13; 2 Tim. 2:2. There is the "word" that you have received that is working within you, enabling you and releasing ability through you, as you step out in faith.

If you see yourself as simply earth-based, earth-defined, and thus earth-limited, you will find yourself often lost on the journey…circumstances, contradictions, conflicts, betrayals, disappointments. All of these will tend to tie you to this earthly life and its limitations, restrictions, disappointments, frustrations, and failures. You will live like a man or woman full of lead weights, rather than the soaring eagle who sees earth from Heaven. Isa. 51:6 says, "Lift up your eyes to the Heavens, look at the earth beneath…." When you look up, you change the position from which you look at the earth and all that is going on there. Eph. 2:6 says you are now "seated in heavenly places."

Discipleship – every believer is to become a disciple (one who follows another to learn their life and their ways). Many believers want to be a Christian (someone going to Heaven) but not subscribe to discipleship—a life disciplined and conformed to the amazing ways of the Lord. Mt. 28:19. Just as children are born into a family, fragile, ignorant and incapable of much, so also are believers that are "new-born," when they enter into the Christian life. They receive spiritual parents to train them and develop them into full-grown disciples of Jesus. Prov. 29:15 says, "…a child left to himself, disgraces his mother." The disciples were called disciples because they left their own ways and followed Christ. Some believers live in the vain hope that simply by attending services they will become what they should become and actually possess what the Bible says they have.

Development – there is a sense in which you are always undergoing development, as your life is from beginning to end, an unfolding of your partnership with Him. Yet there is a distinct season of development that has to do with your earth-mission that is time-based. God reveals, in general terms, His development plan. His plan prepares men and women for expression of their life purpose--the reason they were born in time and the time expression of that specific purpose that they were intended to have.

Leaders step into their intended destiny with their faith and obedience.

- Moses – hiding, palace, desert -----all to prepare for deployment

- Joseph – home, fields, cistern, slavery, Potiphar's house, prison ---- all to prepare for deployment

- Saul – Damascus, Jerusalem, Caesarea, Tarsus – all to prepare for deployment to Corinth and then the world…

- Christ – Bethlehem to Nazareth to Capernaum…

Development is the season of training, in any kind of context, where there is a gathering of the "seed" that someday you will dispense. Matt. 12:35. That seed can take the form of:

1. The Word -- Luke 8:11; Mt. 13:23. There is a season of "gathering the seed" of the Word. Studying, being taught, attending conferences, and meditating in the Word during this time of "storing" is vital to day of "sowing" that is coming when you will be so busy you won't have as much time to store up the seed. Mt. 12:35.

2. Experience that gives wisdom (Gen. 30:27 NKJV), establishes a lifestyle of fruitfulness (Acts 10:38) and releases power and authority. Success in influencing others and releasing supernatural grace into people and situations is an important foundation for even greater fruitfulness. Maturity requires valuable experience.

3. Relational growth…today's intimacy prepares you for tomorrow's demonstrations – there is great danger in ministry deployment while living in relational poverty— there must be a learning of relationship skills, and how to become a problem-solver. Eph. 5:1-2; 1 Pet. 1:22; Rom. 14:7. Leaders that are insecure, feel threatened, jealous of others' opportunities, lacking in close friendships and suffering from "father" issues, ultimately derail themselves and damage others regardless of how gifted they are. Intimacy with God first, then relational development with colleagues. You will always be on a team. Learning team dynamics is essential to future success. There is always a "pull" or tension to move you away from others and "go it alone." Relational instability is a sign of major issues unaddressed.

4. Specified training contexts…school of the prophets, Bible colleges, understudy, on-line courses, mentoring, discipleship, mission work, street work, outdoor crusades in other lands, serving others in the local church, and becoming an intern where an intern programme exists are all potential-focussed training contexts.

Leaders step into their intended destiny with their faith and obedience.

Development is Also the Season of *Definition*
It is this "defining season" where you begin to develop your true identity—the person He has made you to be and the person you are becoming. It is in this season that you begin to discard the definitions of yourself that are illegally held. He has not made you to be weak, inadequate, spiritually dull, unhearing, and incapable. He has poured the fullness of Himself uniquely into you. Col. 2:9-10. It is in this season of development that you discover what and Whom is inside you and how to live acceptably in that consciousness. It is meant to be a development of your partnership with Him—a strong sense of knowing that you "carry Him" all the time and His immediate availability. John 14:20.

The "season of definition," as a part of your overall development as a leader, is a period of time, training, and experience, that helps to define the gifts you possess. Many "would-be" leaders aspire to something at the beginning that may not be a part of their ultimate role. Some want to "preach." Some want to "prophesy." Some want to "teach." Some want to be "a worship leader." All of these desires are good desires but they may not be the gifting or calling of the person who holds them.

Distinction has to be made between *activities* and *callings*. There is no calling to simply be a "preacher." Preaching is an activity done as part of a wider and deeper calling—that of being an elder or one of the five-fold ministry in a narrow sense. In a wider sense, everyone is a preacher or proclaimer of truth. Some may aspire to be "in the pulpit," "on stage," or "preaching to the masses," without reference to any other responsibility. These imaginations or desires are not callings but in a positive sense, perhaps, a prophetic picture of where a life is headed in terms of expression of gifts. In a negative sense, they may be simply a desire for public affirmation or profile.

Someone may desire to be a worship leader. However, examination of their God-given ability reveals He has not gifted them with the ability to sing well. If they can sing well, they may not be gifted with the grace of leading worship. This period of definition is sometimes a difficult period as expectations are re-aligned to spiritual realities. I must lay down any expectation I have of my future responsibility that is not consistent with my ability. What He has designed for me is the best and only place of fruitfulness, blessing and fulfillment. What He has called me to do, He has gifted me to do. The gifts that He has really given me will show verifiable evidence—they may not be what I hoped I had been given. In the secular world, not everyone who enters a singing talent contest possesses what they dream and believe they possess. Some have no singing talent at all but they are firmly self-persuaded that they are a "star-in-the-making."

A person who prophesies is not necessarily a prophet. A person who teaches children is not necessarily a five-fold teacher. Both activities are vital and important to the life of the Body, but are not, in themselves, an indication of the distinctive abilities and graces of a five-fold ministry. One man said his calling was to be a "preacher." He wanted to do nothing except "preach." There is no such calling. A preacher is one who must live

Leaders step into their intended destiny with their faith and obedience.

and declare the Word of God **and** take responsibility for caring for God's flock. This means he or she is ultimately more than a "preacher." He or she is a pastor, an elder, or another one of the five-fold ministries described in Ephesians 4:11.

One man who endeavoured to pastor churches, finally laid down that desire in discouragement, after he nearly emptied four churches. He left that role and entered a very large congregation. He shared his desire to lead. The elders agreed to give him a small group of believers in their house group configuration. It was one of the larger groups with mature believers attending. Soon the complaints came that he simply used these informal meetings to be his "pulpit" and most began to cease to attend. He was "asked to step aside" from leading a small group which was a hard "blow." His stepping aside from that responsibility was not a correction of some moral fault, but a recognition of what his gifting was **not**. Later on, he was given the opportunity to teach in the Christian school connected with the church and he found his "niche" or rightful placement in the Body and functioned very well with great fruitfulness for many, many years.

1 Cor. 12:15 says, "If the foot should say, "Because I am not a hand, I do not belong to the body," it would not for that reason cease to be part of the body." This verse tells us that some believers actually err in determining their role and function in the Body. Many have said in discouragement, and sometimes even resentment, as they left a church, "they just don't recognise the gifts that I have." Their criticism of their previous church is often an expression of their unwillingness to undergo a season of definition that proves their particular grace or gifting or to develop in other areas of character and relationship that are necessary. In their disappointment, they "trample" on their own progress because they fail to submit and to communicate and **to learn about themselves realistically**. They have, in effect, become "do-it-yourself" developers of their own ministry. *God most often uses the hands of men to "shape the clay" that He ultimately shapes.* 2 Tim. 2:2.

How long is the developmental season? As long as God so chooses…Ps. 105:18, 19 NKJV. God prepares every person differently, as each person is unique and thus the mission they carry is unique--there is, however, an acceleration of the process in our day. Amos 9:13. As you study the people of the Bible, some rose to prominence and great expression very quickly. Others, God processed them for a longer period according to His wisdom and His knowledge of what He knew they were to eventually do.

Dangers
Many believers enter some formal ministry training. When they finish that season of training, they enter another season of training. It is the season of being led by God apart from the previously assumed structure they had. Now, where I live, where I function in a local church, what job I take, and what friends I make, are questions that are to be answered by listening and hearing and obeying the voice of the Lord. Many ex-students flounder because they have not been this way before and must solely lean

Leaders step into their intended destiny with their faith and obedience.

on their devotional hearing from the Lord for themselves. They have "saved" others, now, they must "save" themselves. Acts 2:40. Some of the dangers they encounter are:

- Isolation -- separated from the positive influence of intimate and loving relationships, we become the more vulnerable target of spiritual attack – Eccl. 4:8-12

- Discouragement – losing our faith perspective, we slip to the default position of governing our lives through logic and feeling-based decisions – Heb. 10:35

- Drifting – moving away from stability and Word and Spirit-directed living, we meander and drift into carelessness, then compromise, then denial…Heb. 2:1

- Temptation – the opportunity to accept a definition of myself that is not true to who I really am in Christ – James 1:23-24 (adrift from purpose, I can subtly be drawn into wrong relationships and activities that appear to ease the pain)

- No father connection -- 1 Cor. 4:15 – never making an earthly spiritual "Father," we live in insecurity, lack of accountability, poor relation to authority, and ultimately, internally, self-government -- 2 Cor. 10:8. Wrongful independence is destructive ("no one is going to tell me what to do"). Our lives and ministry also do not model the need for a loving relationship with a spiritual father if we do not have one.

Deployment

Having stored the seed (Matt. 12:35), where do you now go to dispense what you have stored? How does God deploy the ministries He has created?

Two fundamental things God is passionate about:

1. His House, His Bride, His Church, His Home, His Family – Eph. 5:25. Often in our time, God's people devalue, neglect or ignore the Church because their experience and their perception of the Church is negative. It remains for them to study His Word on the subject and receive His heart that they might cherish what He cherishes and build with Him, in loving partnership, alongside their Kingdom expansion efforts. Regardless of how it appears, Christ loves the Church and died for the Church. Eph. 3:10, 11.

2. The Kingdom – John 3:16; Luke 17:21; 1 Cor. 4:20; Matt. 10:8 NASU. The Kingdom within, is demonstrated in power, and the result is expansion. When it expands, (others receiving the Kingdom within by salvation through faith), every new Kingdom-person enters into the discipleship phase commanded by God through agency of the local church. Without the discipling, fathering, shepherding, training, and the loving of a local church family, the Kingdom-person fails to learn how to work in partnership with the Church and embrace vital maturity-making truths.

Leaders step into their intended destiny with their faith and obedience.

When you have had Kingdom training, you now have to live in the House. So what house you choose becomes all important, as well as how you adapt to living in the House. Some Houses have House rules that preclude or prohibit some of the things you have learned to do. You will not feel at home there. Yet your life process is not to be governed by logic. Moses would never have voted for the desert, Joseph for the prison, or Saul for hiding out. So God rules. Let Him direct your steps. Expect to have to exercise your faith at a personal level, not just to minister to others by the exercise of faith. 1 Kings 17:9. The "widow" never looks like the place of supply.

Practical Considerations: Ps. 68:6 NKJ; Prov. 15:19 KJV; 1 Cor. 12:18. The One who called you is the One who plants, sets and settles you in the House and provides the Kingdom "launching pad" that He has in mind.

1. Selecting the local church, the family home, where you will belong and make a "body-life" contribution. Eph. 4:16. Responsibility, accountability, serving, joining in loving relationships and developing a lifestyle of loving are all a part of living in "family." Receiving adjustment and commissioning are also a vital part of your local church life.

   - A worshipping church
   - A Word-preaching, faith-building church
   - A visionary church
   - A church that values the supernatural
   - A church that values the prophetic
   - A loving spiritual family

   Pray, enquire, visit churches expecting God to lead you. Speak with the Pastor. Disclose your heart, your training, and your desire. Don't make the mistake of looking to start in some position. Come to serve and let the Master promote you by causing those over you to see the grace that He has placed on your life. Matt. 20:28.

   Don't expect it to be like any other place you have been. It is not likely it will. Decide to make others successful and bring success to the vision of the House. Ruth 1:16-17. One of the basic revelations of early discipleship is: "Us" is more important than "me" in terms of ministry. Yes, you do need of a revelation of who you are and what you have been given, but you need to know that you are **always a part of** the Body of Christ, not the whole, in the way you live out the ministry He has given you. Jesus sent out His disciples in twos. They had to learn how to live, walk, and work as a team.

2. Getting a job, finding an earthly place to live, and making friends, are also basic components of your life foundation. Building your Heavenly home life on earth is vital because you go out of your Heavenly home, spiritually, when you go out of your earthly home to reach the world. Eph. 2:6; 2 Thes. 3:10-12; Rom.

Leaders step into their intended destiny with their faith and obedience.

12:13. Make certain that you are transparent with your oversight regarding any immigration issues that you have. Don't expect God to bless you in taking your life and ministry forward, if you are living a lie in relation to your immigration status. If you need to return to another country, do it in faith and let God exalt you from a platform of honesty and legality. He is big enough to do that. Don't live in the denial of the truth, simply because you want to remain in the country where you are illegal. Rom. 12:17 KJV says, "Provide things honest in the sight of all men." You cannot ultimately succeed building on a wrong foundation.

3. Deployment is also about accepting a significant level of responsibility, having proved yourself faithful in little things. Matt. 25:21. It is the immaturity of a self-focussed adolescent (in spiritual terms) that seeks major responsibility, without having been proved faithful in little things. 2 Cor. 4:2. Some that are trained, step into a new place and see all the things that are "wrong," "not as they should be," needing to be fixed, or not like I think we should do it." They make the mistake of **assuming** a position of authority they do not have, upset people and then unjustifiably decide that this "is not where God is planting me."

Change operates primarily by influence. If others don't see you as an example or as a more mature, wise person, they don't readily accept your ideas as "gospel." It takes time to love, serve and show humility before God exalts you in others' eyes. Take it easy. Don't be in a hurry to fix everything or anything. Become known as a loving, generous, gracious, encouraging servant to all. You are not called to a place to fix what is wrong.

Destiny – is about carrying out the assignment you have been called, prepared, equipped, and given to do. John 9:4. In your Divine placement, you are now "doing the stuff" that you were purposed to do from before time. Having built a network of loving relationships, established your deep connection to His House, you are now focussed on the expanding parameters of His work through you, *along with others.*

Application
In small groups have each person share with the group where they believe God is taking them with their lives and ministry. Be careful that no one person monopolises the available time so that each person can have opportunity to share. Pray and prophesy over each other as time permits.

Leaders step into their intended destiny with their faith and obedience.

Destiny Scriptures

Mark 6:8
"These were his instructions: "Take nothing for the journey except a staff — no bread, no bag, **no money in your belts.**"

John 3:16
"For God so loved the world that he gave his one and only Son, that whoever believes in him shall not perish but have eternal life."

Acts 9:8
"Saul got up from the ground, but when he opened his eyes he could see nothing. So they led him by the hand into Damascus."

Acts 9:17-18
Then Ananias went to the house and entered it. Placing his hands on Saul, he said, "Brother Saul, the Lord — Jesus, who appeared to you on the road as you were coming here — has sent me so that you may see again and be filled with the Holy Spirit." Immediately, something like scales fell from Saul's eyes, and he could see again. He got up and was baptised…."

Acts 26:19
"So then, King Agrippa, I was **not disobedient to the vision from heaven**."

2 Peter 1:3
"His divine power **has given us everything we need for life and godliness** through our knowledge of him who called us by his own glory and goodness."

1 Cor. 4:7
"For who makes you different from anyone else? **What do you have that you did not receive?** And if you did receive it, why do you boast as though you did not?"

2 Cor. 4:7
"But **we have this treasure in jars of clay to show** that this all-surpassing power is from God and not from us."

1 Thess. 2:13
"And we also thank God continually because, when you received the word of God, which you heard from us, you accepted it not as the word of men, but as it actually is, the word of God, which is at work in you who believe."

2 Tim. 2:2
"And the things you have heard me say in the presence of many witnesses entrust to reliable people who will also be qualified to teach others."

Leaders step into their intended destiny with their faith and obedience.

Isa. 51:6
"Lift up your eyes to the heavens, **look at the earth beneath**...."

Matt. 28:19
"Therefore go and **make disciples** of all nations, baptising them in the name of the Father and of the Son and of the Holy Spirit...."

Matt 12:35
"The good man brings good things out of **the good stored up in him**, and the evil man brings evil things out of the evil stored up in him."

Luke 8:11
"This is the meaning of the parable: **The seed is the word of God**."

Matt 13:23
"But the one who received the seed that fell on good soil is the man who hears the word and understands it. He produces a crop, yielding a hundred, sixty or thirty times what was sown."

Gen 30:27-28 NKJV
"And Laban said to him, "Please *stay*, if I have found favor in your eyes, *for* **I have learned by experience** that the LORD has blessed me for your sake."

Acts 10:38
"...how God anointed Jesus of Nazareth with the Holy Spirit and power, and how he went around doing good and healing all who were under the power of the devil, because God was with him."

Eph. 5:1-2
"Be imitators of God, therefore, as dearly loved children and **live a life of love**, just as Christ loved us and gave himself up for us as a fragrant offering and sacrifice to God."

1 Peter 1:22
"Now that you have purified yourselves by obeying the truth so that you have sincere love for your brothers, **love one another deeply**, from the heart."

2 Tim. 2:2
"And the things you have heard me say in the presence of many witnesses **entrust to reliable men** who will also be qualified to teach others."

Rom. 14:7
"For **none of us lives to himself alone** and none of us dies to himself alone."

Ps 105:18-19 NKJV
"They hurt his feet with fetters, he was laid in irons. **Until the time that his word came to pass,** the word of the LORD tested him."

Leaders step into their intended destiny with their faith and obedience.

Amos 9:13
"The days are coming," declares the Lord, "when the reaper will be overtaken by the ploughman and the planter by the one treading grapes. New wine will drip from the mountains and flow from all the hills."

Acts 2:40
"With many other words he warned them; and he pleaded with them, "**Save yourselves** from this corrupt generation."

Eccl. 4:8-12
"There was a man all alone; he had neither son nor brother. There was no end to his toil, yet his eyes were not content with his wealth. "For whom am I toiling," he asked, "and why am I depriving myself of enjoyment?" This too is meaningless — a miserable business! Two are better than one, because they have a good return for their work: If one falls down, his friend can help him up. But pity the man who falls and has no-one to help him up! Also, if two lie down together, they will keep warm. But how can one keep warm alone? Though one may be overpowered, two can defend themselves. A cord of three strands is not quickly broken."

James 1:23-24
"Anyone who listens to the word but does not do what it says is like a man who looks at his face in a mirror and, after looking at himself, goes away and immediately **forgets what he looks like**."

1 Cor. 4:15
"Even though you have ten thousand guardians in Christ, you do not have many fathers, for in Christ Jesus I became your father through the gospel."

2 Cor. 10:8
"For even if I boast somewhat freely about the **authority the Lord gave us for building you up** rather than pulling you down, I will not be ashamed of it."

Matt. 12:35
"The good man brings good things out of **the good stored up in him**, and the evil man brings evil things out of the evil stored up in him."

Eph. 5:25
"Husbands, love your wives, just as Christ loved the church and gave himself up for her...."

Eph. 3:10
"His intent was that now, **through the church**, the manifold wisdom of God should be made known to the rulers and authorities in the heavenly realms...."

Leaders step into their intended destiny with their faith and obedience.

John 3:16
"For God so loved the world that he gave his one and only Son, that whoever believes in him shall not perish but have eternal life."

Luke 17:21
"…nor will people say, 'Here it is,' or 'There it is,' because the kingdom of God is within you."

1 Cor. 4:20
"For the kingdom of God is not a matter of talk but of power"

Matt 10:8
"Heal the sick, raise the dead, cleanse those who have leprosy, drive out demons. Freely you have received, freely give."

1 Kings 17:9
"Go at once to Zarephath of Sidon and stay there. **I have commanded a widow** in that place to supply you with food."

Ps 68:6 NKJV
"**God sets the solitary in families**; He brings out those who are bound into prosperity…."

Prov. 15:19 KJV
"…the way of the righteous is **made plain**."

1 Cor. 12:18
"But in fact God has arranged the parts in the body, every one of them, just as he wanted them to be."

Eph. 4:16
"From him the whole body, joined and held together by every supporting ligament, grows and builds itself up in love, as each part does its work."

Matt 20:28
"…just as the Son of Man did not come to be served, but **to serve**, and **to give his life** as a ransom for many."

Ruth 1:16-17
"But Ruth replied, "Don't urge me to leave you or to turn back from you. Where you go I will go, and where you stay I will stay. **Your people will be my people** and your God my God. Where you die I will die, and there I will be buried. May the Lord deal with me, be it ever so severely, if anything but death separates you and me."

Leaders step into their intended destiny with their faith and obedience.

Eph. 2:6
"And God raised us up with Christ and seated us with him in the heavenly realms in Christ Jesus…."

2 Thess. 3:10-12
"For even when we were with you, we gave you this rule: "**If a man will not work, he shall not eat**. "We hear that some among you are idle. They are not busy; they are busybodies. Such people we command and urge in the Lord Jesus Christ to settle down and **earn the bread they eat**."

Rom. 12:13
"**Share with God's people** who are in need. **Practise hospitality**."

Matt 25:21
"His master replied, 'Well done, good and faithful servant! **You have been faithful with a few things**; I will put you in charge of many things. Come and share your master's happiness!'

2 Cor. 4:2
"Rather, we have renounced secret and shameful ways; we do not use deception, nor do we distort the word of God. On the contrary, by setting forth the truth plainly we commend ourselves to every man's conscience in the sight of God."

John 9:4
"As long as it is day, we must do the work of him who sent me. Night is coming, when no-one can work."

Leaders step into their intended destiny with their faith and obedience.

The Leader and.....

Team Dynamics

Introduction
One of the features greatly needed in our time is the understanding and practice of how to work within a team. Working well *within a team* demands a knowledge of how a team works. It also demands a knowledge of the particular role of every person on the team and how they connect in relationship, authority, accountability, and function with one another. Many leaders unwittingly sabotage what they are charged with building, by not functioning well as a team member. Jesus sent His disciples out in "twos." They had to learn teamwork.

There are several other specific teams mentioned in the Bible. Moses and the elders, James and the elders, Jesus and the Disciples, and the team at the Antioch church. Acts 13:1-3. The Bible records that some of these teams had their issues and struggles to resolve in order to accomplish the great Commission. Paul revealed, partially, the sense of teamwork in which he operated, in his opening remarks to the church at Thessalonica, when he began with, "Paul, Silas, and Timothy." 1 Thes. 1:1. He refers to his partner in ministry, Silas, and his own spiritual son, Timothy, who by now had become an established and mature ministry.

The First Team You Are In
You will always be in a team and you will always be developing a team. The family is the first team placement for every person. There are generally some other people in the family and they function as a team, well or poorly. Authority, accountability, responsibility, communication, problem-solving, roles, work distribution, training, relationship, support, affirmation, loving, deadlines, faithfulness, morale, change, loyalty, confidentiality, initiative, creativity and compensation are a few of the issues that arise in the "family team" effort. The family is also the first "team-training" centre that you live in. It becomes the subconscious default model you live by, until you learn differently.

The Character of Team
A leadership team is made up of godly men and women who love each other and the team as a whole. They also love the Church that Christ loves and gave Himself for and they love the lost, even as God loves the lost. They, as lovers, lay down or sacrifice themselves for what they love, even as Christ did. John 3:16; Eph. 5:25-27; Eph. 5:1-2. They exhibit the fruit of the Spirit in their families and in their team relationships, at all times. When the *work* of team members takes supremacy over their *relationships*, the team becomes vulnerable to tensions, frictions, and misunderstandings that lead

Leaders always love, value and support all the other members of the team as Christ did.

to further decline. Work must be done. However, *relationship* is greater than *work* and must be what enables the work to be done at the highest level and the greatest continuity. Matt. 10:40-42. Anyone, in the heat of disagreement, who loses sight of the significance of relationship, in attempting to accomplish the mission, is temporarily blind to the greater value.

Team Defined
Definition – co-operative or coordinated effort on the part of a group of persons acting together as a team or in the interests of a common cause. Teams are potentially powerful because they can accomplish so much more than a single individual.

In terms of the concept of "team," the part is not the whole and the whole is not the part. Any part, no matter how talented or valuable, can be sacrificed for the health and life of the whole. There is an "affordable but regrettable" loss of any individual team player who jeopardises, by behaviour or attitude that is uncorrectable, the unity and effort of the entire team.

The Character of Each Team Member
The foundation of every business, school, organisation, or church is built on *character*. It is the character of those in leadership that sustains the momentum of that endeavour in accomplishing objectives. Where any endeavour fails, it most often fails due to character issues. Leaders in a local church are always in a character development mode. When they choose not to be, they set themselves on the road to ruin and damage.

Good leaders are always learning how to relate to various kinds of people. They learn what to say and what not to say and how to say it. They also learn about changing their own specific attitudes and practices to be the best team player they can be. To have continual upsets with people and then claim, "this is who I am…others just need to recognise and adjust to it," is not a legitimate excuse. We learn to love others in wisdom, caring, and all the fruit of the Spirit in manifestation.

Character determines the quality of team life and its effectiveness more than any other factor. Paul and Barnabas took a young team member with them, John Mark. However, in the midst of severe trial, John Mark, bailed out or left the team. Acts 15:38. Later when they were to go out again, Paul was adamant that he did not want to take John Mark. Thus the team was split and two teams went out. Later Paul saw that John Mark had matured and asked for him to come to him as he said he had become "profitable." 2 Tim. 4:11.

Many teams are occupied with greatly talented or gifted people. However, their ability to work together in the long term is dependent on their character or the degree in which the fruit of the Spirit is continually manifested through their lives. Egotism, selfishness, insecurity, comparison, politics, manipulation, fear, gossip, pride, critical

Leaders always love, value and support all the other members of the team as Christ did.

spirit, unforgiveness and poor relational skills all destroy the team and the potential of a team to be powerfully effective and fruitful.

The greatest team ever, also, suffered betrayal and was almost lost entirely. Jesus' team of twelve faced character tests. They failed but recovered themselves to do an awesome job in taking the gospel over the globe. It is an amazing fact that God uses flawed vessels to perfect His Body. There is a lot at stake in being part of a team. Let us all grow in grace that we might not unwittingly destroy what we are trying to build with our loving and with our gifts.

Responsibility, Accountability and Authority
At some point, every would-be leader will volunteer to take some responsibility for something or will be asked by those over him to do something. This is an indication and an expectation that the "ability to respond" to a task is within the leader. This is *response-ability*.

No one is given responsibility without *accountability*. Accountability is the expectation and ability to "give an account" of the responsibility or task you have been given. You are, as a team member, to give an *account* to someone over you. Someone will ask you to give an on-going account of what is being done, how it is progressing, what challenges or difficulties you have encountered and any other issues related to your assignment. This means that you, as a team member, learn to be a communicator regarding your assignment. Even if those over you aren't "in your face" all the time, you should give those over you a regular report of your area. If there is little to report, make your report accordingly brief.

When you are given responsibility, you are also given *authority* in the area where you have responsibility. If there is anyone working with you in the designated assignment that you have, they respond to your authority in decision-making. It is an authority that is responsibility-specific. It is not an authority that "authorises" you to speak into anything and everything that is going on **outside** your assigned task. If you have tasks that interface with others and that affect their operation, then you will want to work cooperatively with them through positive communication. You will not want to make assumptions regarding someone else's response to decisions that you take that affect them. You will want to act unselfishly and communicate with them "before the fact."

Input and Humility. Some team members may bring their long-practised ways of giving input to people and situations that is unwittingly damaging to both. They do not realise that they come across pushy, proud, and even bullying. This kind of input is characterised by often injecting their ideas of how something should be done when they are not the leader of an endeavour. It seemingly does not occur to them, that if they are not leading a matter, they should take instruction and follow the path laid out for them by the one who is leading. They do have the option of making a suggestion, as a suggestion, humbly and occasionally, in the right way and right time. They are not to make the leader look stupid or incapable as they would not want to be made

Leaders always love, value and support all the other members of the team as Christ did.

to look stupid or incapable. Private suggestions are best but the occasional "on the spot" suggestion can be made in a humble manner. It can be worded in the following manner: "I would **suggest**...." After having given the suggestion, leave the matter with the Lord and get on with making the operation a success whether it was taken up or not **with a good and right attitude**. This makes for good teamwork. If you are a person that is always making suggestions, you will appear to be attempting to lead the group without having been given the leadership of the group. If you get upset because your ideas are not taken up you are immature. There will be other opportunities for your wisdom to be recognised for its value in God's timing. Relax and "chill out."

Honouring Others
Respecting the value and legitimate contribution of every team member is vital. Encouraging and inviting the input of others, rather than "taking control" or "taking over" a team meeting is vital. Many years ago I worked in a large team. One of the team members didn't say a lot and often when he did his ideas seemed out of touch with the situation or wisdom. He made his comment and stopped. His idea was not taken up. However, once in a while, he had an extremely worthwhile and valuable input that enabled the process and solution to go forward. Had he been marginalised, we would have suffered without his valuable contribution.

When leaders gather together there is leadership among the leaders. However, it is not a domineering type of leadership but an inviting, affirming, welcoming style that succeeds in bringing out the best from everyone. Those that tend to be quiet or less apt to speak up have to have their opinion solicited in a positive way so they can make their valuable contribution. Otherwise the consensus is made up of the vocal ones instead of everyone. 1 Cor. 12:22-25.

Communication in a Team
In a marriage there are four kinds of communication that are necessary for the "team" to work well. These same types of communication are necessary for any church team to function well with stability and longevity. They are:

1. Operational Communication. Operational communication is the verbalised response to all lines of authority and accountability, the information that enables everyone to work well together. Any plans that involve others, meetings, changes, major difficulties, and new opportunities all require regular and consistent communication. Speaking to others in advance as much as possible is important as it gives some time and opportunity to plan and prepare.

2. Bonding Communication. Bonding communication is the verbalised or spoken affirmation and affection that Christians share with each other. It is the thankfulness that recognises the value and contribution of others on the team. It is communicated by words *and* acts of kindness. Practising consistently the affirmation of others on the team develops a culture of identity-releasing security. When each person believes that the others on the team believe that

Leaders always love, value and support all the other members of the team as Christ did.

they make a unique and valuable contribution, the team is a good "place" to live.

3. Remedial Communication. Remedial communication is the verbal effort to resolve any and all problems with solutions. Satan often causes misunderstandings and amplifies the alleged impact of mistakes and thus this type of communication is absolutely imperative in order to keep "the ship" moving and on course. Humility, carefulness and wisdom, mean you measure your words carefully, having the right attitude and approach, choosing the right time and place and bathing the whole process in prayer. Where offences have been caused, (whether carelessly or unintentionally), the biblical process is followed, so there can be forgiveness requested and granted, and the wounds healed. Whatever issues remain to be resolved, can now be resolved, without the paralysing element of offence.

4. Reflective Communication. Reflective communication is what takes place where leaders sit to discuss objectives, progress, dreams, plans and goals. It is often in this atmosphere that new ministries are recognised or birthed. As each person shares his or her heart on the matters being discussed, the team is broadened and deepened, becoming more inwardly linked with each other and the team as a whole. Recognising the unique differences in each team member and embracing each other in this process makes a stronger and more effective team.

Loving the Team
We are commanded to love one another and thus we develop Christ-like relationships in a team by loving the team members. That loving process takes specific steps that reveal our investment of value and love. As every member of the team contributes the following elements, a strong, enduring, powerful and loving team develops.

- Building through encouragement

- Self-sacrifice

- Communication

- Covering weakness

- Upholding standards.

Team Core Values
Vital to the success of a team are the underlying values or core beliefs held and practised by every member of the team. The following team values, lived out within the life of a team, make the team a wonderful "place" to live that is also safe and secure, growing and powerfully effective. It is a microcosm of the Church as a whole where He has said He is happy to live.

Leaders always love, value and support all the other members of the team as Christ did.

1. "Us" is more important than "me." Selflessness is a basic of Christian living. 2 Cor. 5:15. A team is full of selfless people looking to make others successful in their mission. Everything that divides begins with the sin of selfishness.

2. Love -- "Team," for believers, is different from the world's concept of team. It is to be, in relational terms, like a loving family. It still is to be efficient, effective, organised, disciplined and well-administrated. However, these things do not prevent the deep and powerful bonds of loving that sustain longevity and release creativity and gifting to the highest levels. *Relationships are always greater in importance than issues.*

3. Humility. When team members walk in humility, they are careful to entreat those that are older or more experienced. 1 Tim. 5:1 KJV; Phil. 4:3 KJV. They also evidence their humility by their willingness to submit to anyone who is leading some operation and give them their full support. Eph. 5:21. Their humility and respect for other members of the team is also evidenced in their tone of voice that is full of kindness, joy and excitement, not a parental, judgmental or "I know better" tone. Sometimes team members get upset if others don't take their suggestions. Suggestions are **not** commands to be obeyed.

4. Honesty and transparency. No team can be powerfully effective if leaders are not open and transparent with their lives. A leader that "hides out" giving the faulted and feeble excuse, "I am a very private person," can never remain part of team as each member belongs to the other members. If we are to be self-giving (for that is what love is) we have no right to live so privately that others we labour with have great difficulty getting to know us. Such a tendency is fear-based and engenders suspicion and distrust. Honesty means also that you don't hide your true feelings or opinions when it is vital to share them for the sake of relationship growth and mutual input. There is a principle found in the verse of Jer. 48:11 which says, "…like wine left on its dregs, not poured from one jar to another…so she tastes as she did, and her aroma is unchanged." There is the *principle of exchange* in transparent, self-disclosure. Your ideas, concepts, practices and feelings are exposed to the views of others and the process makes for mutual understanding, change, growth, and encouragement. The person who remains "private" can never make a good team member. They must open themselves up and reveal their hearts and lives in order to grow and help others to grow. Rom. 12:17 TLB says, "Do things in such a way that everyone can see you are honest clear through."

5. Encouragement. Team members are always building up the other members of the team from a pure motivation, releasing grace for each one to fully express the grace that is on their lives, to the benefit of the team and others. Eph. 4:29. If you know that a member of the team is about to lead something, send them an encouraging text or Scripture.

Leaders always love, value and support all the other members of the team as Christ did.

6. Servant spirit. The willingness to make others a success and the collective efforts of the team a success, requires everyone on the team to have a "servant spirit," or the disposition to serve. Being a helpful person, even when there is sacrifice is involved, is vital to a great team. Who gets the glory for accomplishment and success is something that comes ultimately from the One who sees and knows all. Gal. 5:13 says, "…by love serve one another." The mature team member is not a "glory-seeker" but a loving servant.

7. Faith. Faith is the underpinning attitude and conviction that makes a team powerful and effective. We believe God. We believe in the mission. We believe each other. We believe every obstacle is overcome. We believe there is great fruitfulness coming from our God-inspired, God-honouring efforts! Heb. 11:6; 2 Cor. 5:7; Num. 13:30.

8. Recognition not competition. 1 Cor. 12:26 says, "If one part suffers, every part suffers with it; if one part is honoured, every part rejoices with it." Team members recognise the particular and unique grace that is on every other team member and celebrate that grace and their success. They always have encouraging words before an event and after. Rom. 12:6 says, "We have *different* gifts according to the grace given us." Different is not wrong. Because there is such deep caring for each other, (something that is developed), when a team member experiences great news or sorrow, the whole team "feels" it and acts accordingly. When there is a great spiritual threat to one, the whole team gets behind that person and adds their faith to the cause for the sake of success.

Decision-making.

Although this topic is too great to cover comprehensively here, some general principles of decision-making will be addressed, so there will be a common understanding within a team. Decisions are taken within circles of reference or counsel, depending on the structure of a team. The structure of family is a good illustration. Husband and wife take decisions for the sake of their family together. They share their opinions. They pray for God's wisdom and input. If there is unanimity, the consensus decision of husband and wife is taken and the children follow along with that decision. If there is no consensus between husband and wife, the husband makes the final decision based on all the input he has received. His wife supports his decision even if she disagreed at the input stage. The children are taught to support it as well. The children weren't (in most instances until older) allowed even to give their input. The circle of reference or counsel was simply husband and wife.

In a leadership team, there are decisions taken within different circles of reference. Where a decision has to do with a particular department, the department head takes decisions with his fellow team members if he invites them into the discussion. Sometimes he may invite them to give input, sometimes he may not, depending on the type of decision that is to be made. In the end, however, he/she has the final say within that department and will give account for the decision and its outcome.

Leaders always love, value and support all the other members of the team as Christ did.

If the elder, pastor or Senior Pastor over the department head believes the decision requires consideration or review, they may choose rightly to meet with the department head and go over it. They may see the need for the sake of all concerned to alter the decision the department head has made or was about to make.

The authority above you (and there is always an authority above you) has the right to intervene and make a change if they believe it is best. This is **not** a support for "micro-managing" someone's department. That is foolish and detrimental. If they were considered capable of doing the job, the leader over them should let them get on with it, staying in communication, of course.

- A leader should be allowed to make some mistakes as well (as long as they are not colossal).

- A leader should never make a major decision regarding his/her responsibility without conferring with the authority over him/her. A major decision is the type of decision that can impact the overall effort of others who are not under his/her authority or the wider operation. It can also be any decision that affects the entire department in a major way or a decision to shut it down. Sometimes leaders of departments have been known to take on themselves, exclusively, decisions that they would never have taken in the secular world. This is not functioning in the proper way inside authority structures and counsel of reference. Communication is absolutely a vital key to keep any department running smoothly within itself and in concert with all other departments.

- In eldership teams, where numerous major decisions are made, consensus (everyone agreeing) is the goal. Some decisions are taken however, when there is no consensus, by the Senior Pastor, as he is responsible to take the work forward. He will always be listening to the Holy Spirit and in some matters can choose to delay a decision until there is unanimity or consensus. The Church is governed ultimately by the Head of the Church, Christ, by the Holy Spirit speaking to those who are working with Him.

- Wise, loving, leaders in close relationships, talk together. However, a leader should not propose to adjust another leader or criticise another's decision unless invited to do so. He then should only do so humbly and wisely. He can preface his idea in attempting to help by a comment such as, "Just a suggestion…but perhaps, you might consider _____." Or he might simply ask a question i.e. "…I am curious…what is the reasoning or goal behind _____?" This type of approach is less threatening and can have the positive effect of bringing about consideration from another view and even change. The goal is not to offend the person while attempting to help bring about change.

Leaders always love, value and support all the other members of the team as Christ did.

We all need each other and it is a wise and secure leader who invites his fellow leader's to share, **on selected occasions**, their view of something that is not their responsibility. This occasional invitation to reflect an opinion is not, a carte blanche (an unrestricted free hand) to continually say, "You should…." 1 Thes. 4:11 says, "…mind your own business."

Exiting the Team

How do you leave a team? Leave it well…regardless of your views of what has happened. You have a future as a leader, still, if you leave well. If you fail to leave well, you can carry the resentment, anger, and resistance that keeps you from ever being a good leader elsewhere, especially where you might take up senior leadership. Do your very best to leave no "friendly-fire casualties" if you believe you are to leave a church or a team of leadership. Make certain you have contacted anyone who you may have a hurt or wounded and assure them of your love for them and ask for forgiveness for anything that may have wounded them. Give thanks for the opportunities, blessings, and input you have received from being on the team. Celebrate the people and the team and the church where you have been planted. Determine to speak well of them and not leave a trail of negative gossip regarding the place where you served. No place is perfect, with you or without you and your faithfulness to speak well is a mark of your spiritual maturity. No grudges, no offences, and no wounds will be allowed to live in your spirit. That would handicap your future. Prov. 18:14 NCV. You want to be released or sent with blessing.

Sometimes a leader is prepared by God to leave a team for ministry in another context. It may be to lead a ministry elsewhere or some mission effort. If he or she does not recognise what God is doing, he or she may react unwisely. When God is preparing a person to leave the "nest" where they have been settled for a season, the nest becomes uncomfortable. Just as a mother eagle begins to take away some of the items that make the nest comfortable and expose the thorns to give the little eaglets a message, so also does the Lord allow tensions, pressures, and troubles to arise to loosen the heart-strings from the current place. He is preparing the heart to be devoted to a major new focus and release. The "labour-pains" of change come.

The wise leader does not get angry at others, resent his oversight or become distant but waits on the Lord for clear direction allowing nothing to "cloud" his spirit. When some clarity has come, the wise leader goes to his oversight and shares humbly his heart and what he has heard the Lord say. In so doing, he is placing his life in the Lord's hands as he places it in the hands of his leaders. Patiently trusting and waiting before the Lord, the Lord causes all the blocks to fall into place. Lam. 3:24-26.

When my wife and I presented our call to go to the United Kingdom the first time, all 24 elders said, "No." They did not believe this was the will of God. I believed it was the will of God. We waited on the Lord. In the following year of waiting, allowing the Holy Spirit to work, the Lord refined the vision in **our** heart. When we presented our hearts to the eldership the second time, there was unanimous conviction that what

Leaders always love, value and support all the other members of the team as Christ did.

we had now arrived at was of the Lord. We were commissioned, blessed, celebrated, and sent. We were launched with a rocket blast of grace and faith instead of a great tearing. Prov. 16:1-3 NLT.

Application

1. As a project have each member of the team take one of the issues just mentioned and show how that issue is evidence in the "family team" and how it parallels all other team efforts i.e. education, business, church.

2. Read the book, "The Blessed Church" by Robert Morris. Carefully reflect on the values and processes He encourages churches to subscribe to so that the church might be greatly enabled through great teamwork.

Leaders always love, value and support all the other members of the team as Christ did.

Team Dynamics Scriptures

Acts 13:1-3
"In the church at Antioch there were **prophets and teachers**: Barnabas, Simeon called Niger, Lucius of Cyrene, Manaen (who had been brought up with Herod the tetrarch) and Saul. While they were worshipping the Lord and fasting, the Holy Spirit said, "Set apart for me Barnabas and Saul for the work to which I have called them." So after they had fasted and prayed, they placed their hands on them and sent them off."

John 3:16
"For God so loved the world that he gave his one and only Son, that whoever believes in him shall not perish but have eternal life."

Eph. 5:25-27
"Husbands, love your wives, just as Christ loved the church and gave himself up for her to make her holy, cleansing her by the washing with water through the word and to present her to himself as a radiant church, without stain or wrinkle or any other blemish, but holy and blameless."

Eph. 5:1-2
"Be imitators of God, therefore, as dearly loved children and live a life of love, just as Christ loved us and gave himself up for us as a fragrant offering and sacrifice to God."

Matt 10:40-42
"He who receives you receives me, and he who receives me receives the one who sent me. Anyone who receives a prophet because he is a prophet will receive a prophet's reward, and anyone who receives a righteous man because he is a righteous man will receive a righteous man's reward. And if anyone gives even a cup of cold water to one of these little ones because he is my disciple, I tell you the truth, he will certainly not lose his reward."

Acts 15:38
"...but Paul did not think it wise to take him, because **he had deserted them in Pamphylia and had not continued with them in the work.**"

2 Tim. 4:11
"Only Luke is with me. Get Mark and bring him with you, because **he is helpful to me in my ministry.**"

1 Cor. 12:22-25
"On the contrary, those parts of the body that seem to be weaker are indispensable, and the parts that we think are less honourable we treat with special honour. And the parts that are unpresentable are treated with special modesty, while our presentable parts need no special treatment. But God has combined the members of the body and has given greater honour to the parts that lacked it, so that there should be no division in the body, but that its parts should have equal concern for each other."

Leaders always love, value and support all the other members of the team as Christ did.

2 Cor. 5:15
"And he died for all, that those who live should no longer live for themselves but for him who died for them and was raised again."

1 Tim. 5:1
"Do not rebuke an older man harshly, but exhort him as if he were your father. Treat younger men as brothers…."

Phil. 4:3 KJV
"And I intreat thee also, true yokefellow, help those women which laboured with me in the gospel, with Clement also, and with other my fellow labourers, whose names are in the book of life."

Eph. 5:21
"Submit to one another out of reverence for Christ."

Eph. 4:29
"Do not let any unwholesome talk come out of your mouths, but only what is helpful for building others up according to their needs, that it may benefit those who listen."

Heb. 11:6
And without faith it is impossible to please God, because anyone who comes to him must believe that he exists and that he rewards those who earnestly seek him."

2 Cor. 5:7
"For we live by faith, not by sight."

Num. 13:30
"Then Caleb silenced the people before Moses and said, "We should go up and take possession of the land, for we can certainly do it."

Prov. 18:14 NCV
"The will to live will get you through sickness, but **no one can live with a broken spirit**."

Lam 3:24-26
"I say to myself, "The Lord is my portion; therefore **I will wait for Him**." The Lord is good to those whose hope is in him, to the one who seeks him; it is good to wait **quietly** for the salvation of the Lord."

Prov. 16:1-3 NLT
"We can make our own plans, but **the Lord gives the right answer**. People may be pure in their own eyes, but the Lord examines their motives. Commit your actions **to the Lord**, and your plans will succeed."

Leaders always love, value and support all the other members of the team as Christ did.

The Leader and...

The Supernatural

Introduction
Many believers live in a "room" that is almost exclusively natural, human, and limited. Apart from the supernatural dimension of their salvation and the occasional Divine intervention, there is no continuing expression of the power of God, in and through their lives. They learn to live at the lower level of limitation, restriction and suffering. Their circumstances rule their lives. It is as though they have no power in their lives to make a difference to what happens. They may be beautiful in character and kindness but deficit in the manifestation of power that gives the awe, wonder, and exuberant celebration to their lives. They live far beneath the privilege that Christ's death and resurrection have provided.

Often they *develop* a theology to accommodate their powerless lifestyle, all the while living in the secret hope that things would be different. This *experience-developed* theology becomes the wall that prevents their progress. Only until they get a revelation outside their thinking and exercise their faith for what lies "beyond" what they have known, will they advance into the unboundaried joy that God intended.

Unwittingly, they have hung a sign over themselves visible to the Devil and all of his spirit-help, "vacancy here." The first line of Satan's attacks is met with their *experience-developed* theology. Their inner responses often are:

- "I must deserve this for sins or flaws in my character…"

- "This is my 'thorn' in the flesh, like Paul…"

- "God is sovereign and so He must have willed this, so I must accept it…"

- "I will reveal God's glory through this ordeal by simply gritting my teeth and enduring it…"

They have not sown any of the verses of their strength, power, authority, faith and victory, deeply into their spirit, so that they live out of the life and power of those verses. Matt. 12:35. They have not seen, that even in the Old Testament, that God led His people to impassable places that He might reveal His power and glory--not for their "death by a thousand cuts." Eph. 6:10 commands us, "Finally, be strong in the Lord and in His mighty power."

Leaders learn to live in the supernatural realm.

God will lead every leader into impossible and impassable places so that the leader can become familiar with how to handle the impossible. Don't be surprised when it is your turn to face a new set of impossible circumstances. The Christian life is a cycle of impossibilities leading into another set of impossibilities. This is clearly illustrated by God's leading of Israel out of Egypt (a great miracle) into numerous other impossible situations.

Your steps are ordered of the Lord and no matter whether the circumstances are engineered by Satan or the result of following the leading of the Holy Spirit, you are well able to meet those circumstances with the power of Him who is in you. God never intended our Christian lives be simply a matter of logic, human effort and earth-based wisdom in decision-making. The Almighty lives inside the believer that He might display His ways, His truth, His life and His power through him. There is little point in having the All Powerful One living inside you, if it makes no difference in the circumstances of life when He is most needed. It makes no sense at all to have Bill Gates (one of the richest men in the world) as your intimate friend, if he is glad for you to walk around in rags.

Jer. 17:12 says, "A glorious throne, exalted from the beginning, is the place of our sanctuary." The sanctuary of all believers is a throne where rule, government, victory, and dispatch take place. It is from this "sanctuary" that grace flows to supernaturally bring about God's great purposes in the earth. Every leader and every congregation is meant to inhabit this sanctuary of power. We learn to live from Heaven to earth, as that is our spiritual origin. John 8:23; 1 Cor. 15:48; Rom. 11:36. Your life is supernatural because God is supernatural and He is your life. Col. 3:4.

Your Supernatural Life and Lifestyle
Christianity is fundamentally supernatural because it is a faith and a life, created and operated by God. From recorded beginning to end (of the Bible), the supernatural realm is the realm that controls all human existence. You were either under the control of God or the Devil. Eph. 2:1-9. Everything about your existence in Christ and your walk in Christ every day, is supernatural, in God's mind. He upholds you and everything else by the word of His power. Heb. 1:3 NKJV. You couldn't tie your shoe laces if He didn't provide the strength of your hands to do so. He miraculously saved you. He has you sitting with Him in heavenly places. He gives you commands to live a lifestyle that is humanly impossible. He holds you accountable for things that are only accomplished by His supernatural power. When you die, you leave this life supernaturally and enter the next one. Only the release of His wisdom and power can enable you to live with Him, for Him, and by Him. Settle it in your heart. You cannot live like most humans do with human efforts, human wisdom, human resources and human endurance. You were made new to live in a totally new way—the supernatural way.

The old covenant law was a powerful school teacher to tell us that human efforts to live acceptably are doomed to failure. Gal. 3:5 AMP. With the best of intentions,

Leaders learn to live in the supernatural realm.

"Ishmaels" abound. Western education teaches you to consciously and subconsciously rely on your own best efforts. This fatal mentality compromises your Christian walk. You are in Him and He is in you. You have His fullness (character and power and mind), not so you can live as though you didn't. You carry with you a supernatural atmosphere. Luke 24:49; John 7:37-39. Jesus said, "...with man this is impossible." Mk. 10:27; Luke 18:27. However, He also said, "Nothing will be impossible for you." Matt. 17:20. It is clear He does not see the believer as a mere man and thus you should not see yourself as a weak and powerless "earthling," but as Moses, powerful in speech and action." Acts 7:22.

How often believers are prone to say, "Well, I did my best." What are they really saying? They are saying in effect, "I accessed the inventory of my ability, intelligence, skill, strength, experience, intuition, know-how and knowledge and gave hundred per cent application. That should suffice...or at least be acceptable." Not. Ps. 20:7-8; Ps. 147:10-11. How often there are tears of disappointment when our best fails dismally. We perhaps, have failed many times, because we failed to access His power to succeed supernaturally. We were trying to "do something," rather than operating out of "who we really are." Ask yourself, "What is missing from my life when I don't have the supernatural being manifested regularly?" Also, ask yourself, "What is *invading* my life that is not God's best because I don't have the supernatural manifested in my life?" These two questions help us to re-focus on the most basic nature of our Christian life. The first question focusses on a potential deficit; the second question focusses on a potential negative intrusion.

Your Road Into The Impossible
Throughout the Bible we can see that God led His people into places that required His supernatural help to survive, as well as to progress. God, the Master Teacher, always takes us where we must partner with Him in supernatural ways. Your *life* journey will not escape the necessity of supernatural power displays. Your *ministry* journey also will not escape the necessity of supernatural power displays and the Divine energy to persevere.

Israel's journeys were directed by God. It was the Cloud of His Presence that took them out of Egypt and across the desert wilderness into the Promised Land. In that journey, God deliberately led them to places where human ability and human effort would fail. He said in 1 Cor. 10:9-10 that all of these experiences were recorded for our example and learning. He intended that we learn how to negotiate the impossible, with the amazing power we possess, through our own exercise of faith—the awesome resource He provided for doing just that. We can, like many believers, allow ourselves self-pity, fear, and despair or we can speak the words that "calm the storm" on the horizon of life as He fully expects us to do.

Jesus' command to go to other side of lake as recorded in Matt. 8:18; 23-27, is a valuable insight that God has commanded us to go to places where our lives are threatened or something quite significant is imperilled. His intent is that we "deal with it." Mark

Leaders learn to live in the supernatural realm.

4:40. You are meant to move from living a lifestyle of petitioning God, to a lifestyle of dealing with circumstances, in spiritual authority and power, as a mature son or daughter of God. Children are always expecting and asking for help. Mature adults get up and do. If He has called you to this kind of lifestyle, He has constructed you as a new creation with the capability of doing the job. Accept the job and the equipping that has come with it! (No, I am not saying that there never is an occasion for petition – see Heb. 5:7 but also see Mark 11:24).

Not long ago I heard firsthand the story of a small missionary woman confronted by a number of terrorists that poked their machine guns into the windows of her car. She started laughing. Immediately, the "intimidators" were intimidated by this "little woman" because she knew who she was, what she carried and Who was with her. In the end, she told them what they were to do for her and they did.

Responding To the Impossible With Supernatural Power
It is very clear from the Bible accounts of God's people, that often when God led them into some great difficulty, they responded with faith or fear. God will take the leader through circumstances that He permits, in a journey of inner development, so that their faith will always be their response to the challenge. When inadequacy, insecurity, fear, weakness, and resignation rise up within you, you learn to recognise the source of those thoughts and emotions. God has led you to this moment that He might work through you for His glory. When contrary emotions and thoughts rise within you (because emotions follow thoughts or are the result of thoughts), you know that those thoughts are not from God. They are not the thoughts of the "new you" that God has made you to be.

They can come from only one other source: Satan. Satan will send you his ideas or attempt to resurrect your old nature so that you will not rise to the challenge and see supernatural things transpire.

Faith is **first** a decision based on information received from Heaven. We must make a decision to go with what we have received from God (via the Spirit-quickened Word or the voice of the Holy Spirit). We choose to act in accordance with who we are in Christ and with what He is saying. To fail to pursue the lifestyle of supernatural demonstration by the exercise of faith is to automatically fall back into the "default" position of human effort based on human logic. You are a "faith" person, who lives by faith, in every area of your life and you regularly see the demonstration of God's power in and through your life.

Faith is **not** a feeling or emotion. It most often operates when feelings are absent or even contrary.

You begin to see yourself as a powerful, capable, strong, miracle-producing believer exercising your inherited authority and power as a son. The old excuses are no longer relevant. You think and act from a newly informed position. You have shed the old

Leaders learn to live in the supernatural realm.

carcass of inadequacy, weakness, fear, self-denigration, false humility and have *put on* the new clothes of power and wisdom. Nothing scares you any longer. No sickness, no aging, no financial difficulty, no past weaknesses, no failures, no disappointments, and no trouble threaten your success. You have become "more than a conqueror" in all areas of life.

Using your faith, you bring God's power to bear on everything in your life. You get the Word into your heart and mind and so meditate on it, that it works for you. You speak differently. You speak boldness and faith. 2 Cor. 4:13; Acts 4:29; 2 Cor. 3:12. You do not consider any other alternatives than the biblical outcome. You have become "strong in the power of His might."

Establish Your Superiority Over the Devil
God expects you to deal with every work of Satan just as Jesus did. 1 John 3:8; John 20:21. In order to approach those works of the Devil you must have an established attitude of superiority over the Devil and all of his works. You have been transferred to another Kingdom and are no longer **under** Satan's domain, rule or influence. Col. 1:13, 14 NASU. You now live **above** all of Satan's domain, rule and influence. John 8:23; Eph. 2:6; Rev. 12:12. Woe is pronounced to the inhabitants of the earth as Satan is loosed to continue his work until the appointed time. You are **not** an earth-dweller because your address is Heaven, your citizenship is Heaven and you are, as a result of new birth: *from there*. Phil. 3:20.

You are now to approach everything in life from your established position—from Heaven to earth. You now "come down on stuff" that needs to be conformed to Heaven's standard of life even as the Father directs your steps.

Application

1. Make a list of things that are currently in your life that require the impact of your faith, authority and power. Get the Scriptures that relate to those issues to hand. Meditate in them. Begin to speak to them with the awesome power that you possess and do whatever He tells you to do. Isa. 51:16 says, "I have put my words in your mouth…."

2. In a small group share the testimony of a victory you have had in exercising your supernatural identity and authority.

3. Pray and prophesy over each person in your group.

4. Read the book, "Your Words Hold a Miracle," by John Osteen.

Leaders learn to live in the supernatural realm.

Supernatural Scriptures

Matt. 12:35
"The good man brings good things out of the good **stored up in him**, and the evil man brings evil things out of the evil stored up in him."

John 8:23
"But he continued, "You are from below; I am from above. You are of this world; I am not of this world."

1 Cor. 15:48
"As was the earthly man, so are those who are of the earth; and as is the man from heaven, so also are those who are of heaven."

Rom 11:36
"For from him and through him and to him are all things."

Col. 3:4
"When Christ, **who is your life**, appears, then you also will appear with him in glory."

Eph. 2:1-9
"As for you, you were dead in your transgressions and sins, in which you used to live when you followed the ways of this world and of the ruler of the kingdom of the air, the spirit who is now at work in those who are disobedient. All of us also lived among them at one time, gratifying the cravings of our sinful nature and following its desires and thoughts. Like the rest, we were by nature objects of wrath. But because of his great love for us, God, who is rich in mercy, made us alive with Christ even when we were dead in transgressions — it is by grace you have been saved. And **God raised us up with Christ and seated us with him in the heavenly realms** in Christ Jesus, in order that in the coming ages he might show the incomparable riches of his grace, expressed in his kindness to us in Christ Jesus. For it is by grace you have been saved, through faith — and this not from yourselves, it is the gift of God — not by works, so that no-one can boast."

Heb. 1:3 NKJV
"…who being the brightness of **His** glory and the express image of His person, and upholding all things by the word of His power…."

Gal 3:5
"Does God give you his Spirit and work miracles among you because you observe the law, or because you believe what you heard?"

Luke 24:49
"I am going to send you what my Father has promised; but stay in the city until you have been **clothed with power from on high**."

Leaders learn to live in the supernatural realm.

John 7:37-39
"On the last and greatest day of the Feast, Jesus stood and said in a loud voice, "If anyone is thirsty, let him come to me and drink. Whoever believes in me, as the Scripture has said, **streams of living water will flow from within him." By this he meant the Spirit**…"

Ps 20:7-8
"Some trust in chariots and some in horses, but we trust in the name of the Lord our God. They are brought to their knees and fall, but we rise up and stand firm."

Ps 147:10-11
"His pleasure is not in the strength of the horse, nor his delight in the legs of a man; the Lord delights in those who fear him, who put their hope in his unfailing love."

Matt. 8:18, 23-24
"When Jesus saw the crowd around him, he gave **orders to cross** to the other side of the lake…Then he got into the boat and his disciples followed him. **Without warning, a furious storm came up** on the lake, so that the waves swept over the boat. But Jesus was sleeping."

John 8:23-24
"But he continued, "You are from below; I am from above. You are of this world; I am not of this world. I told you that you would die in your sins; if you do not believe that I am [the one I claim to be], you will indeed die in your sins."

Acts 9:15-16
"But the Lord said to Ananias, "Go! This man is my chosen instrument to carry my name before the Gentiles and their kings and before the people of Israel. I will show him how much he must suffer for my name."

2 Cor. 4:13
It is written: "**I believed; therefore I have spoken**." With that same **spirit of faith** we also believe and therefore speak…."

Acts 4:29
"Now, Lord, consider their threats and enable your servants to **speak your word with great boldness**."

2 Cor. 3:12
"Therefore, since we have such a hope, **we are very bold**."

1 John 3:8
"He who does what is sinful is of the devil, because the devil has been sinning from the beginning. The **reason the Son of God appeared was to destroy the devil's work**."

Leaders learn to live in the supernatural realm.

John 20:21
"Again Jesus said, "Peace be with you! As the Father has sent me, **I am sending you**."

Col. 1:13-14 NASU
"For He rescued us from the domain of darkness, and **transferred us** to the kingdom of His beloved Son…."

John 8:23
"But he continued, "You are from below; I am from above. You are of this world; I am not of this world."

Eph. 2:6
"And God raised us up with Christ and **seated us with him** in the heavenly realms in Christ Jesus…."

Rev. 12:12
"Therefore rejoice, you heavens and you who dwell in them! But woe to the earth and the sea, because the devil has gone down to you! He is filled with fury, because he knows that his time is short.

Phil. 3:20
"But our citizenship is in heaven."

Leaders learn to live in the supernatural realm.

The Leader and.....

Criticism

Every person alive faces criticism. Leaders face criticism more than those who are not functioning as leaders because what they do has wider exposure and greater consequence. Mark 14:27. Vital to the longevity and fruitfulness of a leader is their response to criticism. There is no avoiding of criticism but the necessity of a wise response to it. A wise response guarantees the leader will be enhanced through what seems to be a negative, discouraging, circumstance.

Misplaced Criticism

- Sarah's criticism of Abram for Hagar's son. Gen. 16:5. In this story, Sarah gave her maidservant, Hagar, to Abram to have children by her. When it turned out badly, she blamed Abram. Abram was not responsible for Hagar's attitude toward Sarah.

- Israel's criticism of Moses for difficulties in the journey. Num. 21:4, 5. The Israelites criticised Moses for the hard things they had to endure. They had no faith in the God who brought them out and so they turned their deep disappointment and unbelief into criticism of Moses. Often people going through difficult things blame others in an effort to lessen the pain and pressure of their discouragement.

- Men of Ephraim's criticism of Gideon – Judges 8:1. The men of Ephraim were upset that they were not allowed to be a part of Gideon's victory over the Midianites. Gideon appeased them by saying, that what he had accomplished, was nothing compared to their past victories.

- Circumcised believers criticised Peter – Acts 11:2-3, 18. When Peter went into the house of an uncircumcised person, he received criticism from circumcised believers. Their criticism was based on wrong beliefs as the New Covenant was extended to all men, not just the 'circumcised' Jewish believers.

Criticism can threaten spiritual longevity. Leaders have given up their churches, their marriages, their faith and their calling through criticism. Criticism can come at varying levels…even to the level of betrayal, where a very close friend 'stabs' you with words and deeds. The pain, the shock, the confusion and contradictory nature plunge the knife of such criticism deep into the soul of the leader. Only those who are close and trusted can inflict such deep wounds. Those closest to Jesus betrayed Him. Ps. 55:12-14.

Leaders learn to respond wisely to all criticism.

Attempts to Understand the "Why?" of Criticism
Sometimes through investigation, a clear understanding as to why the criticism has come, is evident. On other occasions there is no obvious condition that points to why the criticism has come. Where reasons for the criticism are not evident **after investigation**, it will be most likely due to issues of the heart on the part of the one criticising.

- They may be discouraged generally. Under a load of unresolved problems and weak in their Word and Spirit-life, they are critical of others. Often possessing an overall negative outlook on life, it has become a subconscious or instinctive practice to criticise others. Their futile attempts to "feel better" by criticising others is fruitless and destructive. They require loving correction.

- They may have other painful issues they seem powerless to resolve unconnected to whom they are criticising. In this instance they may be under great financial pressure, marriage pressure, or secret habits they feel powerless to overcome. In their "pain," they lash out in criticism of others, hoping to take the focus off of their own struggle.

- They may be jealous, envious, or have anger or unforgiveness issues unconnected to whom or what they are criticising.

- They may simply be selfish, frustrated individuals lashing out for more attention. Sometimes weak and immature believers attack the Church verbally, claiming there is "no love" in the Church and that they have been deeply disappointed in the alleged hypocrisy of the Church. However, close examination reveals they have had an extensive amount of care and love and been the recipients of great generosity. Their criticism is simply the selfish attempt to manipulate to gain even more "benefits" and attention. In many cases they have gone from church to church with this lifestyle, sucking all they can get from kind-hearted, generous, and loving believers until the "well" seems to run dry. Then off they go to another place.

- They may be leaders wanting position, status or profile that they believe they are not rightly getting. Their criticisms are a form of complaining, which hide the hidden agenda of attention-seeking.

- They may be leaders simply resentful of standards that are expected of them that they are not prepared to embrace.

- They may be the unregenerated "fool" as described in numerous terms, in the book of Proverbs, bent on attacking others.

- They may be a person undergoing some discipline and are angry, upset and bitter about it and thus lashing out at others and especially a leader(s).

Leaders learn to respond wisely to all criticism.

Where women criticise, it actually may be, (to a man), regarding an issue, seemingly unconnected to what they are talking about, simply because women often communicate laterally. In this instance, great care and investigation can reveal what is the exact nature of the criticism, so it can be properly addressed.

Regardless of whether significant reasons for criticism can be determined or not, the most important issue is the leader's response to the criticism that has come. Even if the "Why?" cannot be satisfactorily determined, it is vital to have a wise response to the criticism. Men are often tempted to not lay down what they cannot determine the cause of and thus continue to frustrate themselves and others by their fixation with the question of "Why?" something has occurred. If you ask God and He tells you that is insight. If He does not tell you or you do not hear why the criticism has come, arise from the "autopsy" and get on with a wise and godly response to the criticism.

Well-placed Criticism
Well-placed criticism is a constructive criticism or recognition of a condition or problem that needs solving. It is **not** an attack *on a person*, especially the person deemed responsible for the condition or issue involved. It is a means of bringing something to a person's attention that they may know or not know about, in order to secure a change or improvement. It should always be done with the sincere desire to obtain a solution, not merely to "vent a frustration."

It is also wisdom to have in mind some possible suggestions or solutions for the issue involved, as that is what leaders are meant to be: solution-providers. The words or terminology used to bring an issue that needs addressing, should be carefully and wisely chosen, in order to get the most objective hearing. Often immature leaders don't present their view of some condition, need or practice, in a positive way. Wise leaders maintain their respect of those over them, as they seek to better some situation through discussion. It is always a good idea to preface the subject with a simple statement i.e. "I want to bring something to you for your advice and opinion as I think it may require some changes."

In the Acts 6:1 some of the widows who received sustenance from the church were being left out. It was a situation that needed to be addressed lest they suffer. Leaders took on board the criticism and met to discuss what should be done. A solution (the appointing of deacons) was found and the issue resolved.

Responding to Criticism
Sometimes believers take all criticism as a "Satanic attack" on themselves and reject the criticism completely as a "work of the Devil." They may be correct in some instances but not in all instances. In completely casting aside all criticism, they lose the benefit of hearing what they do not want to hear that can improve their lives and the lives of others. It is very important to pause and listen to the Holy Spirit for any message He wants to speak regarding the criticism in order to know how to respond.

Leaders learn to respond wisely to all criticism.

- Judges 8:1-3 -- sometimes an explanation of the reasoning behind some actions or policies can cause resentment to subside. Prov. 24:3-4; Acts 11:2-4.

Listening **very carefully**.
Asking for greater explanation and clarification before responding. "What are you actually saying? What exactly is the issue you are concerned about?"

- Respond – in words, in changes, in affirmation, or in explanation (Acts 11:2-4). Sometimes it is valuable to invite one or two others who are not directly connected to the criticism to evaluate the criticism you have received in confidence, honesty and humility. David invited Jonathan to judge his behaviour when Saul came against him. 1 Sam. 20:8.

  If the fact that criticism is to be revealed, it is best to keep the source of that criticism anonymous for evaluation purposes. You are attempting to gain another's honest evaluation of the criticism itself, its merits and demerits--not allow another to take up an offence on your behalf. If you have upset the person who criticised you, you can apologise humbly, without making the assumption that you agree with their point of view. Whether someone else (not a party to the situation) thinks you spoke well or poorly is irrelevant. The person who is upset and thus criticising you or criticising something you are responsible for, is the one with whom you must resolve the relational aspect.

- Ignore – Matt. 26:59, 63; Matt. 27:12-14; Mk. 15:3-5; 1 Pet. 2:23. On several occasions Jesus did not answer his accusers. Leaders must know when to keep silent and let the Father handle the accusers. This type of approach is **not**, however, a warrant for refusing to discuss honestly with other leaders, matters that are needing to be resolved.

- Warn – Titus 3:10. People who persist in criticising others without reference to a godly approach to their concerns are to be warned and if they fail to respond, disassociated. They have become a railer and divisive.

- Remove – 1 Cor. 5:11, 13 tells us that a railer or a slanderer who is simply indiscriminately criticising and tearing down others must be removed from the fellowship of believers if they refuse to repent.

The Huge Danger of Wrongly Responding to Criticism
Satan is called the Accuser in the Bible. He wants to destroy the Church whether it is through legitimate criticism or unfounded criticism. It is extremely important to have a wise response to criticism, lest a serious wound take place that is wholly unneccesary. Where churches or leaders have failed to respond wisely to criticism, churches and leaders have imploded. Leaders have resigned and become ill. Bitter people die prematurely and numerous believers are spiritually assaulted with life-destroying discouragement when criticism is not handled with wisdom. Prov. 24:3-4.

Leaders learn to respond wisely to all criticism.

Sometimes someone comes with the statement attached to their criticism saying, "Others are saying this as well...." – just exactly whom? Are their criticisms exactly the same or different? If they will not reveal the names, they have taken up an evil report and are not really interested in solutions but are simply ventilating frustration. This kind of criticism or accusation is not to be received but prayed about that God might reveal what is truly going on. When He reveals what is really happening, leaders lovingly, wisely and methodically pursue the process of "putting the fire out" if there is really a "fire." If it is discovered that there are a few that have discussed their disagreement, the wise leader confronts them **individually**, not as a group. He does not go in the assumption of anything, but he goes asking questions. To start with hearsay is to open the door to a multitude of complications. Each person has their own story to tell in a unique way. It has been well documented that "groups" who band together always have differing agendas and complaints among themselves than what is presented to the one who is the "accused."

When To "Chase Down" Criticism

Every criticism need not be pursued and attempts made to "satisfy" the accuser. Prov. 12:16 says a prudent man overlooks an insult. Some people choose to attack another person verbally with insults. These are a form of criticism but should be ignored. Other substantial issues or critical reports may need to be investigated even if only to put a stop to destructive and divisive speech. One woman continuously told others in public contexts, "There is no love in this church." She had, in fact, received much loving expressed in financial gifts, help finding employment, numerous prayers and encouragements and a multitude of other ways. On one occasion, as people were moving out of a service she raised her voice and said it again. I happened to be nearby and so I spoke up in front of all that could hear and said, "What you have just said is a lie. If you really believe that, leave." I had already confronted this woman several times, but this rebuke, was the impetus she took for leaving the fellowship. I was sad to see her go because we had great hopes for her life but she refused to be adjusted and corrected. Today she has a positive relationship to the church family although she attends elsewhere.

Any criticism from within the congregation that goes viral, through any media means, must be addressed. It must be addressed with Holy Spirit generated wisdom.

The Carefulness that Minimises Criticism

There is an attitude and practice of openness in which the culture of transparency is balanced wisely with a confidentiality that protects others and minimises criticism. 2 Cor. 8:20-21. There is no absolute deterrent to, or prevention of, destructive criticism, as men and women can step out of carefulness and loving into carnal ways. However, when leaders refuse to entertain an "evil report" about others they are developing a biblical culture of honour. When leaders readily and immediately seek reconciliation when necessary and they are seen to be doing things openly without suspicion-arousing secrecy, such a culture of honour is again being developed.

Leaders learn to respond wisely to all criticism.

Is There a Difference Between Criticism and Complaint?
It is vital to distinguish between issues and people. Some accuse or criticise people in terms of their motives and judgments and some complain about practices or conditions. A complaint is: verbally raising a perceived, negative, condition without reference to a solution. Constructive criticism by a leader is: referencing a perceived negative condition with a positive attitude and an attempt at a solution. This is maturity. The two spies, distinct from the other ten spies, acknowledged the giants but came with a faith-founded response to the condition of giants. Wise leaders are always looking for "faith's response" to any negative condition. Destructive criticism often focuses on individuals and comes with no positive solution to an issue. It can often simply "venting" carnal emotions toward another person. Whether criticism or complaint, whether destructive or constructive, the leader must have a wise response.

Maintaining A Right Spirit While Being Criticised
The tendency of the "old person" I used to be, is to be defensive or to instinctively respond to criticism with anger, defence and resistance, before actually really hearing and evaluating the criticism. If I get angry with the one who is criticising, I can easily lose my objectivity in evaluating the actual criticism they are bringing. Leaders are always meant to be calm and in control of their spirit and mouth. Prov. 29:11 says, "A fool gives full vent to his anger, but a wise man keeps himself under control."

Holding yourself steady and quiet while the criticism is taking place is vital, so you can listen to the Holy Spirit while the accusation is taking place. Prov. 16:32. You will want to know how to respond when the criticism has ended. This also allows the "accuser" to 'spend the emotion' connected with their accusation or complaint. After they have gotten it "off their chest," they are in a better position to hear objectively, a response from you.

Anger, frustration, disappointment, hurt and offence, cloud their ability to *hear* a solution and you want them to be at their best when you open your mouth. Resist the temptation to interrupt them and correct some misplaced notion or non-factual assumption. Wait till the end of their speech. Before responding directly to some issues, ask any questions you may need answers to in order to give a wise and well-founded response. Prov. 18:13 NLT says, "Spouting off before listening to the facts is both shameful and foolish." Prov. 18:19, 20 NLT.

A woman not connected to our congregation rang very angrily to accuse me of failing one of our congregational family members. I listened while she made her tirade of indignation and sarcastic attack. She had a lot of misinformation and ignorance of facts connected with the incident she was addressing. I let her talk without interruption until she came to the end even though she asked several rhetorical questions in the middle of her speech. I resisted the temptation to try and answer those questions. When she had finished, I then began to softly (a soft answer turns away wrath—Prov. 15:1) give information she did not have and explain the matter carefully and graciously. She calmed down and admitted she had not known the facts I had presented and that

Leaders learn to respond wisely to all criticism.

with that information I was not to be faulted. She ended the conversation no longer at odds with me and more focussed on a solution.

Wrong responses to criticism and accusation can serve to inflame the emotions and distort the issues. Mired in anger and misunderstanding, two parties often remain at odds with each other, rather than reconciled. Leaders are wise and avoid this reactive tendency through the fruit of the Spirit called self-control. When a leader "loses it," he must go and "clean it up." Asking forgiveness for a wrong attitude then opens the door to address issues that may need to be cleared up.

Practical Application
In small groups discuss the following:

1. How you have failed to handle criticism in the past and the consequences of mishandling criticism.

2. What you have personally discovered what works for you when you are being criticised—both warranted and unwarranted criticism.

3. On a scale of 1-10 with ten being the highest level, tell how you would rate yourself on being a defensive person and why you gave yourself that rating.

4. How does a wise leader handle the most hurtful criticisms and accusations?

5. Read the book, "Criticism Bites," by Brian Berry.

Leaders learn to respond wisely to all criticism.

Criticism Scriptures

Mark 14:27
"You will all fall away," Jesus told them, "for it is written: "'I will strike the shepherd, and the sheep will be scattered.'"

Gen 16:5
"Then Sarai said to Abram, "You are responsible for the wrong I am suffering. I put my servant in your arms, and now that she knows she is pregnant, she despises me. May the Lord judge between you and me."

Num. 21:4-5
"They travelled from Mount Hor along the route to the Red Sea, to go round Edom. But the people grew impatient on the way; they spoke against God and against Moses, and said, "Why have you brought us up out of Egypt to die in the desert? There is no bread! There is no water! And we detest this miserable food!"

Judg. 8:1
"Now the Ephraimites asked Gideon, "Why have you treated us like this? Why didn't you call us when you went to fight Midian?" And they **criticised him sharply**."

Acts 11:2-3, 18
"So when Peter went up to Jerusalem, the circumcised **believers criticised him** and said, "You went into the house of uncircumcised men and ate with them." When they heard this, they had no further objections and praised God, saying, "So then, God has granted even the Gentiles repentance unto life."

Ps. 55:12-14
"If an enemy were insulting me, I could endure it; if a foe were raising himself against me, I could hide from him. But it is you, a man like myself, my companion, my close friend, with whom I once enjoyed sweet fellowship as we walked with the throng at the house of God."

Judg. 8:1-3
"Now the Ephraimites asked Gideon, "Why have you treated us like this? Why didn't you call us when you went to fight Midian?" And **they criticised him sharply**. But he answered them, "What have I accomplished compared to you? Aren't the gleanings of Ephraim's grapes better than the full grape harvest of Abiezer? God gave Oreb and Zeeb, the Midianite leaders, into your hands. What was I able to do compared to you?" **At this, their resentment against him subsided**."

Prov. 24:3-4
"By wisdom a house is built, and through understanding it is established; through knowledge its rooms are filled with rare and beautiful treasures."

Leaders learn to respond wisely to all criticism.

Acts 11:2-4
"So when Peter went up to Jerusalem, the circumcised **believers criticised him** and said, "You went into the house of uncircumcised men and ate with them." Peter began and explained everything to them precisely as it had happened…."

1 Sam. 20:8
"As for you, show kindness to your servant, for you have brought him into a covenant with you before the Lord. If I am guilty, then kill me yourself! Why hand me over to your father?"

Matt. 26:59, 63
"The chief priests and the whole Sanhedrin were looking for false evidence against Jesus so that they could put him to death. But **Jesus remained silent**. The high priest said to him, "I charge you under oath by the living God: Tell us if you are the Christ, the Son of God.""

Matt. 27:12-14
"When he was accused by the chief priests and the elders, he gave no answer. Then Pilate asked him, "Don't you hear the testimony they are bringing against you?" **But Jesus made no reply, not even to a single charge** — to the great amazement of the governor."

Mark 15:3-5
"The chief priests accused him of many things. So again Pilate asked him, "Aren't you going to answer? See how many things they are accusing you of." **But Jesus still made no reply**, and Pilate was amazed."

1 Peter 2:23
"When they hurled their insults at him, **he did not retaliate**; when he suffered, he made no threats. Instead, he entrusted himself to him who judges justly."

Titus 3:10
"Warn a divisive person once, and then warn him a second time. After that, have nothing to do with him."

Prov. 12:16
"A fool shows his annoyance at once, but **a prudent man overlooks an insult**."

1 Cor. 5:11-13
"But now I am writing to you that you must **not associate with** anyone who calls himself a brother but is sexually immoral or greedy, an idolater or **a slanderer**, a drunkard or a swindler. With such a man do not even eat. What business is it of mine to judge those outside the church? Are you not to judge those inside? God will judge those outside. "Expel the wicked man from among you.""

Leaders learn to respond wisely to all criticism.

2 Cor. 8:20-21
"We want to **avoid any criticism** of the way we administer this liberal gift. For we are taking pains to do what is right, not only in the eyes of the Lord but also in the eyes of men."

Prov. 29:11
"A fool gives full vent to his anger, but **a wise man keeps himself under control**."

Prov. 16:32
"Better a patient man than a warrior, a man who controls his temper than one who takes a city."

Prov. 18:13 NLT
"Spouting off before listening to the facts is both shameful and foolish."

Prov. 18:19-20 NLT
"An offended friend is harder to win back than a fortified city. Arguments separate friends like a gate locked with bars. Wise words satisfy like a good meal the right words bring satisfaction."

Leaders learn to respond wisely to all criticism.

The Leader and.....

Judgment

The doctrine of judgment begins in the Garden, where God, the Judge of all, pronounced the judgment against sin before sin was committed. Throughout all of redemptive history, from that early beginning, God has lovingly acted in His role of the Ultimate Judge of all people and matters. He offered His Son to receive the judgment upon sin as the sacrifice that would enable mankind a way to escape eternal judgment in Hell. The end of the Bible wraps up redemptive history with God judging all of mankind, the Devil and all evil angels. Heb. 6:2 tells us that the doctrine of eternal judgment was one of the foundational doctrines of the Early Church. It is vital for us to understand this complex and wide-ranging truth as it has major implications for how we live.

In a world of blurred lines, indistinct values, and moral haze, leaders must be increasingly clear about the issue of judgment. Every person is involved in judging and judgment. From what we will wear and won't wear, to who we will relate to and at what level we will relate, we all are "judges." But to avoid being judgmental (having a harsh assessment and a disposition not tempered with mercy) or being indifferent to evil and sin, we must have a clear grasp of the doctrine of judgment.

Judgment is first an internal activity that must be exercised correctly so that the external forms of judgment are biblically valid and right as well. Often leaders, individual believers, and congregations, disagree over matters of judgment and division takes place unnecessarily. Paul and Barnabas, great friends, disagreed over the spiritual maturity of John Mark, and so parted company. Acts 15:37-41. Later on, Paul sent for John Mark, recognising that regardless of whom was correct in their earlier judgments, John Mark, was now mature and capable. 2 Tim. 4:11.

Because of the wide scope of treatment that the Bible gives to the subject of judgment it is vital to understand *all* that the Bibles says about the subject. To form any opinion, about any Bible issue, without reference to all that the Bible says about the subject, is to form an incomplete and sometimes inaccurate conclusion. Because the Bible *appears* to be in conflict with itself at times, it does not mean that it *is* in conflict with itself. It simply means, we need further insight into how it actually fits together and does not contradict.

For example, John 7:24 says, "**Stop judging** by mere appearances, and **make a right judgment**." Yet the Scripture also says in Matt. 7:1, "**Judge not**, or you too will be judged" and yet further, in 1 Cor. 11:31 which says, "But if **we judged ourselves**, we would not come under judgment."

Leaders exercise judgment with great care, the Holy Spirit and biblical insight.

Defining "Judgment."
The word, "judgment is defined in the following ways:

- an *act or instance* of judging or drawing a conclusion between things being considered

- the *ability* to judge, make a decision, or form an opinion objectively, authoritatively, and wisely, especially in matters affecting action; good sense; discretion: i.e. "…a man of sound judgment."

- the *demonstration or exercise of such ability* or capacity: i.e. "The Major was decorated for the judgment he showed under fire."

- the *forming of an opinion, estimate, notion, or conclusion*, as from circumstances presented to the mind: i.e. "Our judgment as to the cause of his failure must rest on the evidence."

- the *opinion formed*: i.e. "He regretted his hasty judgment."

Conscience – An Inner Judge
Every person is born with an "inner judge" which weighs and decides on the right or wrong of behaviour or some considered action. Rom. 2:14-15 says, "Indeed, when Gentiles, who do not have the law, do by nature things required by the law, they are a law for themselves, even though they do not have the law since they show that the requirements of the **law are written on their hearts**, their **consciences** also bearing witness, and their thoughts now *accusing*, now even *defending* them."

This God-created facility of conscience is part of what leads a person to Christ. This inner "gavel," slams down the pronouncement that some behaviour is wrong. The guilt that a person feels, as a result of this inner judging activity, is something that God designed would lead a person to Him. The guilty person would want to escape these feelings of guilt and look for some way to live apart from them. (Yes, a conscience can be misinformed on some matters but that is not the matter under consideration here).

Judging Yourself
Along with the conscience, every person makes or draws conclusions about themselves. Where they draw Biblically-based conclusions about themselves, they are able to prosper as their conclusions are aligned with those of their Creator, Redeemer and Perfecter. Where they draw wrong conclusions or judgments about themselves, they live in condemnation, fear, limitation, and failure. Thus how we judge ourselves is vital. One distinction made in Scripture is revealed in the difference between the words, "guilt" and "condemnation." Guilt is what I feel as a result of violating some standard of truth or morality. It is the conscience and sometimes the Holy Spirit speaking a "judging" word about my behaviour, attitude, words or motives. Condemnation, is defined as: what I feel as a result of "passing a sentence on myself that God does not pass." Rom. 8:1; 1 John 3:19-21. I "feel" guilty but in actuality, before God, I am not

Leaders exercise judgment with great care, the Holy Spirit and biblical insight.

guilty. These "feelings of condemnation" (misplaced or wrongful self-judging) come from having wrongly judged myself. It is a judgment, albeit an illegitimate one. I think and believe I have done wrong, therefore I have "feelings" of self-condemnation that go with such a self-judgment. This is most often a work of Satan, the Accuser.

There is a right and a wrong self-judgment. The right self-judgment referred to in 1 Cor. 11:28-32 ESV tells us that we should examine ourselves and judge (come to a correct conclusion) regarding how we stand in relation to the Lord and His Body. If we have forsaken the foundation of walking in forgiveness with all others, we come into God's judgment and redemptive discipline that we might return to the Lord by reconciling with others. If we judge ourselves and do what needs to be done to recognise Him by recognising His Body in love and forgiveness, we live in blessing and communion takes its powerful effect. The word translated "recognising" in this passage has the same root as the word translated "judge" in the New Testament.

Wisdom in Judgment or Decision-making
Gen. 31:36-53 (It is necessary to hear the whole story and then render a wise and just decision). Judgment, in decision-making, is the process by which we 'separate' what is in view, into categories. Some elements are placed on "one side" and some placed on the "other side," facing each other in distinction or opposition. Attempting to weigh the matters, we conclude or decide. The wisdom, insight, facts, and truth we use to conclude a matter and render a decision is referred to as our "judgment." People are often said to have good judgment or poor judgment. It is a reference to their ability to come to a wise conclusion of a matter based on their accurate discernment or analysis of the matter **and** their use of wisdom (God's intelligence). Ps. 119:66.

A leader with good judgment must both "read" situations correctly as well as *conclude* wisely. Prov. 24:3-4. If you do not read a map or a satellite navigation device correctly, you make poor, wrong, and costly judgments. 1 Cor. 6:5 says, "Is it possible that there is nobody among you **wise enough to judge** a dispute between believers?" Deut. 1:17 says, "Do not show partiality in judging; hear both small and great alike. Do not be afraid of any man, for judgment belongs to God." Seeing both "the part" and "the whole" in a matter is necessary in order to make wise judgments or decisions. Some leaders "see" only the "part" and not the whole matter. Some leaders "see" or focus on the whole and appear to neglect the "part." Often in church life, a group of leaders discussing a matter bring together both the "part" and the "whole" through their collective input. Having heard the issues and the facts connected with them, it is vital to then hear the Holy Spirit. The Spirit of wisdom enables us to make judgments as He did. Isa. 11:3.

There are sometimes issues that can "cloud" or sway our judgment or potentially "cloud" our judgment that can prevent us from making wise decisions. We can be:

1. Deeply emotionally aligned to a *person* that the decision will affect.

Leaders exercise judgment with great care, the Holy Spirit and biblical insight.

2. Deeply emotionally aligned to an *outcome* of a decision and how it will affect us or others.

3. Thinking of the possibility of being *personally* advantaged or disadvantaged by a decision.

4. Weighing the decision's impact on how *others may perceive* us or others. Others may or may not be aware that we are part of a decision-making process.

    - Correct balance of mercy and truth in judging – 1 Kings 3:6 NKJV; Ps. 25:10 NKJV; Ps. 85:10 NKJV; Prov. 16:6 NKJV Paul's letters to the Corinthians are a great study of the balancing of mercy and truth in judging. In the first letter to the Corinthians he comes straight out with some information for the entire church that is vital to the church's longevity. It is negative information about a condition, that unaddressed, will "leaven" the whole loaf of the body of believers. His Spirit-led writing reveals to us some vital understanding of the issue of judgment.

Leaders must learn to wisely and rightly hold the tension between mercy and truth. The truth in relation to salvation is: if you do not repent, you suffer the continuing judgment upon sin (i.e. that it is wrong and carries a sentence) and ultimately die and go to Hell. If you repent, you receive God's mercy, the pronounced judgment is removed and you live in cleansing and redemption. The Word of God provides for us and all generations, how mercy and truth are handled in judging sinful activity. Let us examine some of the principles revealed in this instructive narrative of 1 Cor. 5:1-5 ESV.

1. A decision or judgment is given about an *unrepentant* sinner in the congregation. Believers learn to walk in repentance, but if they refuse to repent, they threaten their own life of blessing and the spiritual purity of others. 1 Cor. 5:1-5 ESV; 1 Pet. 4:17. (It is **not any particular sin** that warrants being excluded spiritually from the family of believers **but the refusal to repent** of such sin.) This is made clear in the second epistle to the Corinthians, where believers were charged with forgiving and taking the man back into fellowship because he had truly repented. 2 Cor. 2:6-8.

2. An instruction of how discipline is to be exercised, based on biblical judgment, is given. The man is to be spiritually removed or disfellowshipped or excommunicated as a result of his contumacy (unwillingness to repent). 1 Cor. 5:1-5 ESV. It is a judgment with a *redemptive* view. The man is to be spiritually removed from the covering of God's Presence and returned to the attacks of Satan at a greater level, so he can come to his senses spiritually and return to a loving relationship with Christ. It is not harsh, but redemptive, and is actually the most loving thing that can happen to anyone who has been trapped in deception, as it is the "medicine" for releasing them. It is the pain, spiritual

Leaders exercise judgment with great care, the Holy Spirit and biblical insight.

separation and trouble that is connected with sin and Satan's attacks that helps to smash the deception and bring the revelation of truth. The personal brokenness that the disciplined person undergoes, through Satan's attacks on their life, opens them to the revelation that their sin is:

- exposed
- has painful consequences
- not God's plan for them

Deception is believing a lie. Discipline, biblically and lovingly, exercised, exposes the lie for what it is and provides opportunity to embrace truth, mercy, forgiveness, and reconciliation. What a marvellous and loving plan God has for bringing us out of what could keep us in a lifestyle of pain and death!

God, The Judge -- Gen. 18:25
Out of Whom God *is*, He makes right decisions. He is holy, so His holiness governs His judgment. He is merciful, so mercy governs His judgment. He is omniscient, (knows and sees all), so His total knowledge of all circumstances and the hearts of men governs His judgment. God is love, so love governs His judgment.

Some may think that under the New Covenant that God is no longer acting as a judge. Under such a view, God is now fundamentally different from what He was under the Old Covenant. Wrong, in their view, is never to be punished. Discipline is spiritually illegal and forgiveness and mercy must reign in every circumstance regardless of any repentance. Grace must mean that favour is granted in every case of wrong-doing, whether there is repentance or not. These premises, however, are not consistent with the entire Bible. Hell is a reality. As such, it is a statement that judgment, instituted by the Great Judge, remains. He has determined that those who reject Him are cast into Hell by virtue of their choice. It is not His desire they suffer eternal punishment, but He has set the consequence of their final decision. 2 Pet. 3:9, 10. To forsake mercy is to invite the consequence that mercy would have prevented.

God still hates sin and His wrath (a holy and righteous response) against sin still remains. John 3:36; Rom. 1:18; Rom. 2:4-8. However, His love and His mercy restrain the expression of His wrath against sin, in judging the sinner, when His love and mercy are embraced. Because His wrath was demonstrated and exercised on sin in Christ's substitutionary death, it does not mean that He has somehow put away His holiness where sin is concerned. Although He acts in His omniscient mercy, He will, in some way, at some time, act in judgment against sin. Heb. 10:29-31. If believers act with blatant disregard to a moral law, He will, as a loving father, exercise judgment **unto redemption** or **reconciliation** in their behalf and "chastise" them that they might return to Him in contrition and humility. James 4:6 ESV; Heb. 12:4-11. His loving discipline is a pain that leads to a corrected heart and life.

Leaders exercise judgment with great care, the Holy Spirit and biblical insight.

Understanding how the great truth of judgment is meant to function in our lives is vital, if we are to represent the Great Judge, accurately, in our judging activity. Leaders can sometimes shrink from the heavy responsibility of exercising judgment in order to avoid being called, "judgmental or harsh." However, when they do so, they dilute the standard of righteous living that God requires, release the "leavening" effect of sin to do its work and expose themselves to God's discipline for failing to do so. Vital to the weighty responsibility of exercising judgment, while holding the balance of mercy and truth, the leader depends entirely on the Holy Spirit to give supernatural wisdom for the process. Isa. 11:2-3 reveals that leaders operate with the same spirit that was on Christ. They do not judge simply by "hearing of the ears and seeing of the eyes," but by the Spirit-given wisdom and counsel of God.

God Judges
Nineteen times, the Scriptures, both in the Old Testament and in the New Testament, refer to God the Father, in judging. He is not disconnected from all that He has created and He ultimately decides how His redemptive plan for man is to be exercised. From the Garden of Eden in the book of Genesis to the Garden of Paradise in the book of Revelation, the Father exercises judgment. He is, as it says in Gen. 18:25, the Judge of all the Earth. Gen.31:53; Ex. 6:6; 1 Cor. 5:13; 2 Tim. 4:1; Heb. 12:23; Heb. 13:4; Rom. 2:16; Rev. 11:18; Rev. 20:7-15.

Jesus Judges
John 9:39-41 says, "Jesus said, "For **judgment I have come into this world**, so that the blind will see and those who see will become blind." Some Pharisees who were with him heard him say this and asked, "What? Are we blind too?" Jesus said, "If you were blind, you would not be guilty of sin; but now that you claim you can see, your guilt remains." John 5:27-30; Acts 17:31.

John 8:26 says, "I have much to say **in judgment** of you. But he who sent me is reliable, and what I have heard from him I tell the world." Acts 10:42; Isa. 11:3.

The Holy Spirit Judges. John 16:8-11 says, "When he comes, he will convict the world of guilt in regard to sin and righteousness and **judgment**: in regard to sin, because men do not believe in me; in regard to righteousness, because I am going to the Father, where you can see me no longer; and in regard to **judgment**, because the prince of this world now stands condemned." When a believer sins, it is the **Holy** Spirit that comes to speak that such behaviour, motive, or attitude is wrong or sinful. The Spirit of Holiness faithfully guards our lives with His voice that we might always walk in repentance and love.

The Word Judges
Heb. 4:11-12 says, "Let us, therefore, make every effort to enter that rest, so that no-one will fall by following their example of disobedience. For the word of God is living and active. Sharper than any double-edged sword, it penetrates even to dividing soul and spirit, joints and marrow; it **judges the thoughts and attitudes** of the heart."

Leaders exercise judgment with great care, the Holy Spirit and biblical insight.

Virtually every page of Scripture is setting right on one side and wrong on another. It is defining the moral content of everything God has made. The Word is an expression of His thought, so it thus is an expression of God Himself. Such expression cannot be amoral (without moral judgments) for He is, in Himself, the Ultimate Standard by which all things are morally measured as right or wrong, acceptable or unacceptable.

Parents Judge

God associates pain with sin, through the response to sin, in judgment. Heb. 12:11. The Cross, God's ultimate statement and judgment on sin, was extremely painful. God also associates or connects the punishment of sin with pain in a redemptive manner, so that man will have one of two motivations at least, for refraining from sin. Rom. 2:9 says trouble, distress, anguish and tribulation comes on every person who does evil. God made it so. This connection is potentially redemptive. If there was no pain associated with sin, we would continue in sin.

In our world today, parents are taught by social scientists (those charged with constructing society) that it is not morally right to associate pain with disobedience. Some other method of persuasion must be sought in order to train a child to do right. However, unrestrained children develop no curbs to their inner tendencies that are selfish and wrong, and thus go on to destroy their lives and the lives of others. 1 Sam. 3:13. Our prisons are full of rebellious, unrestrained, undisciplined people. They had to be secured inside lockable boundaries because they couldn't live inside moral or behavioural boundaries set by the laws of the land. The law-keeping tendency was never placed inside them. Divorce courts are busy granting divorces to believers who never learned to live selflessly inside biblical boundaries. Their divorce from selfless intimate relationships often began when they were three years old when self-will was never judged effectively.

A few years ago the U.K. had a wide outbreak of rioting and violence in the streets all across the country. Politicians, teachers, and the public all watched what seemed to be a shocking, inexplicable, phenomena. In the aftermath, there was a considerable "autopsy" on the issue to discover its cause. One man interviewed on the street on national television, observed, when asked why he thought the riots had taken place said, "The government took away my right to discipline my children, so guess who gets to do it now."

Years ago, I injured my eye by accidentally poking a broom (the bristles end) into my eye while using the handle to break up some loft insulation. I went to the doctor. He put one drop of substance into my eyes. In an instant the considerable pain was gone. I asked him if I could have the bottle. He said, "No, because people would abuse medication like this. If you have pain, it is for a reason and the reason needs to be investigated and dealt with, not merely have the symptoms removed." No one likes pain but it becomes our servant, if, because of it, we examine our lives and turn from sin to the Saviour.

Leaders exercise judgment with great care, the Holy Spirit and biblical insight.

Parents understand that willfulness and rebellion are innate or born in every child. Every child comes out of the womb, not a saint, but a sinner. Every child is born with the nature to disobey, rebel, and be selfish. It is the privilege and assignment of parenting, to judge their wrong behaviour as wrong, and bring correction, just as it is their privilege and assignment to encourage and bless right behaviour. Eph. 6:1. If a parent does not achieve brokenness in the will of the child (not broken in spirit), the child will grow up to struggle with rebellion against all standards and authorities. Prov. 22:15 TLB.

To fail in either discipline or encouragement, is to create great difficulty for the person the child is becoming. Prov. 20:11 NCV. Col. 3:20-21. 1 Tim. 3:4, 12 NLT. Discipline, a form of judgment, is both corrective and redemptive. A small sapling in a fruit orchard is often tied to a stake to insure that it grows up straight. If there is not something straight that the child is constantly connected to (a standard of behaviour), he or she will grow up crooked. That behavioural constant is both affirming and judging—both of which, are parental responsibilities.

The Church Leadership Judges.
Just as parents are required by God to assess and judge their children's behaviour, so also the spiritual parents in the church family have to make some judgments at times regarding their "spiritual children's" behaviour for biblically-based reasons. I Cor. 5:12, 13. To fail to exercise discipline (a judging process) is to allow the leavening power of sin to spread throughout the entire church family. It is not an easy process or a pain-free process but a vital one. Church history is full of terrible stories of churches that have dissolved because there was no biblical approach to unrepentant sin amongst its members.

The world system, governed by Satan, wants to be all-inclusive with no one excluded from any context of association, yet somehow maintain some fabric of society that is peaceful and does not violate anyone else's boundaries. This is a foolish and unrealistic notion that is unachievable. Believers can and do get sucked unwittingly into such notions thinking they are kind, broadminded, and rightly tolerant. They can hold such a notion until the impact of such thinking radically impacts their own life or family in a negative and destructive way. When the serial rapist rapes their 14 year-old daughter and gets a three month sentence, they tend to re-examine their view of how judgment is to be rendered.

Religion is progressively moving away from any clear definition of sin lest lines have to be drawn and judgment have to be exercised. It is a trend to have a totally non-judgmental world. If there is no sin, there is no need for any judgment. Evil becomes good and good becomes evil. The "evil" people in this world's view, are more and more, the devout Christians who actually believe there is such a thing as evil, wrong, and sinful behaviour. One of the definitions of sin in the New Testament is lawlessness. If there is no law, then there is no consequence for breaking a law. This

Leaders exercise judgment with great care, the Holy Spirit and biblical insight.

is a great deception and not consistent with Scripture or even God Himself, who is defined by Himself, as holy.

As difficult as judgment is, the leader must always speak and act on the truth. He must also carry out the responsibility of speaking the truth about everything. Eph. 4:15. It is this weighty responsibility that the leader carries, that causes him to act and speak in judgment in relation to others carefully and wisely. He knows that he himself is measured by the very same "measuring rod" of truth with which he is required to measure all other things.

Believers Judge.
1 Cor. 6:3-4; Gal. 6:1 ESV (to see a brother overtaken in a fault requires the discernment of right and wrong and the observation of another involved in it.) To set out to restore someone who is "overtaken in a fault," requires an assessment or judgment that such an activity or attitude that is wrong and self-destructive, has taken place. We cannot restore others lovingly if we step back from doing so because we don't want "to judge." Our judgment is not based on personal opinion or the accusations of others but personal, first hand observation of our sinning brother or sister measured only by the Word of God. Only a clear violation of the Word of God can form the basis of such an approach.

Because this type of loving confrontation is so rare in Christian circles, it does not mean it should not be done. You may approach a sinning brother or sister lovingly by saying, "I may be wrong, but it seems that you may be struggling in your attitude toward your boss. If so, I would love to pray with you about it." (This may have been observed first hand in hearing the erring brother speak angrily and most disparagingly against his boss). In this way you have highlighted a failure in a way that the offender can affirm or deny. You have come across not in a condemning way. You have framed your approach lovingly and redemptively by offering to pray with them. If the person rejects such an offer, you lay aside that topic in your conversation and go on loving them and praying for them. If they do not judge themselves according to the Word of God, any perception and offer you make will not go forward positively. *It does not mean that simply because you say it that it makes it so.* Relax and let the Holy Spirit find another way to help your brother or sister while you go on loving and praying for them. You would want the same treatment yourself.

Many years ago I met for coffee with a dear Christian friend of mine. He had decided to divorce his wife, not because of any infidelity, financial issues, or apparent conflict—simply because as he insisted, he did not love her anymore and wondered if he had ever loved her. I knew his wife and children and loved them as dear friends. With tears, I asked him if he believed he was doing right according to the Scripture. He sidestepped the question. I pleaded with him to reconsider this step and get some help. He was not for seeking help. I left off the subject and we spoke of other things and after a few minutes, finished and left the restaurant. We remained friends. The attempt to restore someone who is "overtaken in a fault" is not always immediately

Leaders exercise judgment with great care, the Holy Spirit and biblical insight.

successful or ultimately successful. It is, however, a biblical step. This does not mean that the believer sets himself up as the Holy Spirit going around looking for whom he can correct or adjust. Such an attitude and practice would unwittingly be based in pride.

Governments Judge.
The Bible makes clear that governments are involved in judgment. The believer relates to the judgments that governments make, according to the Word of God, not their own feelings of what is just and right.

Rom 13:1-5 says, "Everyone must submit himself to the governing authorities, for there is no authority except that which God has established. The authorities that exist have been established by God. Consequently, he who rebels against the authority is rebelling against what God has instituted, and those who do so **will bring judgment on themselves**. For rulers hold no terror for those who do right, but for those who do wrong. Do you want to be free from fear of the one in authority? Then do what is right and he will commend you. For he is God's servant to do you good. But if you do wrong, be afraid, for he does not bear the sword for nothing. He is God's servant, an agent of wrath to bring punishment on the wrongdoer. Therefore, it is necessary to submit to the authorities, not only because of possible punishment but also because of conscience."

Judgment and Grace
Sin exists. The one who sins, (before salvation or after), must have a remedy. In order to have a remedy, the "sinner" must first acknowledge the presence of sin. He must "judge himself" according to the Word that judges him, given by the great Judge. The sinner cannot save himself, cleanse his own record or place himself in the position he was before sin. He must have a redeemer who does what the sinner cannot do—cleanse, reset the record, and put the sinner into justification (as though he had never sinned). Rom. 3:24. When the "sinner" confesses his sin (the word, 'confess' means, "… to say the same thing about something that God says"), he receives God's unmerited, unearned, unwarranted favour or grace. He does not *experience* favour or grace **until** he judges himself according to the judgment that God judges. 1 John 2:1; 1:9; Matt. 6:12 NLT. If he fails to judge himself, in the same way that God judges him, he does not confess, and thus he does not repent, and there is no redemptive grace applied to his life or lifestyle at that time. James 4:6 ESV.

In God's great redemption there are two major dimensions that the leader must always be aware of: provision and application. God has provided for all of man's needs in redemption. However, the provisions of redemption (Christ's finished work) are only applied when man cooperates with God's means of application—faith, confession, and repentance. Scripture says that God is not willing that any should perish but that all should come to repentance. 2 Pet. 3:9. He has made provision. It remains for man to acknowledge that provision has been made. To fail to take up provision is to reject the need for provision. Provision is necessary because sin was judged and is judged by

Leaders exercise judgment with great care, the Holy Spirit and biblical insight.

God as wrong and unacceptable and it carries punishment or painful consequence. Rom. 2:8-9.

God desires to take and keep man out of the prison of sin's consequences and the death inherent in sin itself. To restore man to an intimate and holy relationship with Himself, He provided the means of restoring that relationship. The man or woman who rejects the means of that restoration is rejecting the self-judgment that agrees with God's judgment of their behaviour and attitudes. Provision still exists—there is simply no application of that provision and the "sinner" continues in the deception of sin and its subsequent, no-matter-how-delayed consequences. God lovingly placed painful consequences in connection with sin so that man might consider God's assessment of evil (His judgment "of" and His judgment "on") and His gracious provision to remove sin and its consequences. God's attitude, His provision, and His faithfulness to act in redemption, is the essence of grace. God has provided the "living water" for the sinner "dying of thirst." If the sinner rejects the "water of salvation" because he wrongly judges that his condition is not due to lack of "water," he dies. God's redemptive compassion is an expression of His gracious favour that He would love to see us experience. Rom. 5:8 says, "…while we were yet sinners, Christ died for us."

This expression of **provision** is a dimension of God's disposition toward man—He loves all and does not desire that any should perish. However, unless the sinner accepts this offer of grace provided through a faith confession of sin, he lives outside the benefits of the grace provided. Ps. 66:18 NLT.

What is Being Judged by God? When a holy God judges us, He judges motive, attitude, and behaviour. He has already judged or pronounced sin as sin in the Garden of Eden. Now, His judging activities are intended to be redemptive. Pain focusses. Hardship inclines the heart to look up. Rom. 2:4-6, 9; When the pain of a guilty conscience, circumstantial hardship and Holy Spirit rebuke come to us, we examine ourselves that we might realign ourselves with a Holy God our Redeemer and Friend. This self-judgment is a judgment unto righteousness or reconciliation with God. 1 Cor. 11:31-32.

What is not to be Judged by Believers?
The believer is also not to go around judging others in the Body of Christ and condemning them for their alleged "wrong doctrine" or wrong practices. If you met up with a person the following day after you had condemned them, would they want to listen to you carefully so as to learn of the great revelation and wisdom that you have?

The web is such a judgmental, gossiping, slandering tool for division through wrongful judging of anyone and everyone. It is used by Satan to tarnish, discredit and destroy God's influence in the earth through criticising other parts of the Body of Christ. However, the Bible forbids us to judge other believers in the following ways:

Leaders exercise judgment with great care, the Holy Spirit and biblical insight.

- The **motives** of others. No one is allowed to judge the motives of another person as motives arise from the hidden place of the heart. Only God can see the heart of another and it is His job to deal with the heart. 1 Sam 16:7 ESV says, "Man looks at the outward appearance, but the Lord looks at the heart." Prov. 21:2; 1 Chron. 28:9. Believers are required to make judgments about sinful behaviour that is "in their face." They do not become a judgmental person by their lifestyle and thus separate themselves spiritually from others who may or may not be doing wrong. We can righteously condemn (recognise a sin is sin) what He condemns, in terms of sinful behaviour, but *still love those who commit sinful acts.*

Often believers wrongfully judge or make a determination that someone else's motives were wrong, evil, or selfish. This is spiritually illegal to do. Satan would always attack another person, in a believer's mind, by claiming the other had a wrong motive, in order to separate and cause hurt and division. Wise believers live a life of love which always trusts or believes the best about others. 1 Cor. 13:7 NASU. When circumstances reveal the wrong ways of a person you have loved, you can still act lovingly, wisely and humbly toward them. Gal. 6:1 ESV.

- Other believers who have committed past mistakes. Satan always wants to make the mistakes of others larger than life that we might weigh their "huge mistakes" so great that we carry "a distancing attitude" toward them rather than a loving one. Saul was a murderer and one of the challenges of the Early Church believers was to believe that he was no longer such a person. They did, however, succeed in doing so and God used him greatly in their lives and in ours. Can you so totally bury the past mistakes of others that they actually get a "new beginning" like you have received many times? Continuing to judge them as the person they used to be is wrong and invites the same wrong judgment upon yourself.

You are not the person you used to be and not the person yet that you are becoming. Let not the "gavel of judgment" continue to slam down on another that says, "You are still as you were." 2 Cor. 5:16 NLT says, "So we have stopped evaluating others from a human point of view." Everyone has flaws but no one is a flaw. Our perspective of all others is both loving and redemptive even as His perspective is loving and redemptive. A well-known ministry went to prison in a highly-publicised case. His first visitor was Billy Graham who went there to pray with him and give him hope.

- Other parts of the Body of Christ, the Bride of Christ. Leaders become aware of other churches, movements or Christian organisations that are believing and practising what they believe is error or unwise. However, it is not the leader's responsibility to allow their "judgment" of the other group to distance themselves from them. Loving others we can find opportunity to serve and help them. In the grace of God, they sometimes can learn, grow and receive. No group or church or movement has "all truth" or walks perfectly even in all

Leaders exercise judgment with great care, the Holy Spirit and biblical insight.

that they believe. All of us are "learners on the journey" acknowledging that we are all **part** of the Body of Christ, not the whole, needing the input of others.

Bless, build, and encourage all others and be open to learning new ways founded in Scripture and the wisdom of God. Does Jesus love all those that you think are wrong? Does He grant them some measure of success and blessing in spite of their alleged faulty ways and teaching? If so, then He is doing nothing different from what He does with you, as you are not probably 100% totally perfect, accurate and all-wise. Never let some words condemning other movements, believers, leaders, or groups come out of your mouth. Be ready to humbly bless and care for all others.

- People and situations that are nothing to do with you. In matters that are not your responsibility, you often don't have all the facts in your possession to even make a judgment. Often believers get caught up with great passion and displays of anger and strong emotion in matters that are not their responsibility. They are offended at the injustice, folly, consequences, or apparent madness of some other person or situation. Their conversation reveals they are not bearing this person or situation in intercessory prayer but "venting" their own disdain and emotional steam. This kind of behaviour is negative and potentially divisive. Satan loves for you to be greatly upset or "steamed up" about matters that are not your responsibility. Prov. 26:17 ESV.

- Judging with a view to condemn, rather than discerning wrong with a view to redeem. Rom. 2:1-5 makes clear that judging others to condemn them while doing the same things or worse yourself puts you in a serious position of an appointment with God's wrath. Leaders always take a redemptive view of others in spite of their obvious faults, as they fully expect God to take a merciful and redemptive view of them in view of their obvious faults. The disposition to be negative, critical and to condemn is fully wrong from this passage. We don't relate to the person they "used to be" but who they are in Christ as a new creation. Sometimes, as leaders, we have to make decisions regarding the unrepentant in order to preserve the wholeness of the spiritual family. However, it is still with a view that such persons will return to becoming who they really are in Christ.

Biblical Balance in Exercising Judgment
Ps. 2:12 says, "Kiss the Son, lest he be angry and you be destroyed in your way, for his wrath can flare up in a moment." If you embrace the Son, who is **Truth**, you receive **mercy** from Him. Prov. 16:6 KJV says, "By mercy and truth iniquity is purged: and by the fear of the Lord men depart from evil."

One of the most challenging parts of judgment is **the balancing of mercy and truth**. It is for this reason that leaders must depend on the Holy Spirit in carrying out matters of judgment that are biblically legitimate. The foundational principle is this: embrace

Leaders exercise judgment with great care, the Holy Spirit and biblical insight.

the truth and mercy is granted. This principle is throughout the Scripture and even in the broader context of life. Where people refuse to embrace the truth (a moral standard of righteousness determined by God), there is the consequence of that refusal. Those consequences may be delayed in mercy (in theology this is called a "space to repent"), but consequences will come. Even where a person refuses to repent there is, in God's mercy, often an apparent delay, in the painful consequences of discipline that God uses to restore us to Himself. Mercy, in such a manner, is a restraint of bringing the pain of consequence, giving further time for the errant one to consider and turn in repentance.

There does come a point, however, when the judgment is made, and activated in consequences. Men and women who walk in flagrant sin cannot remain in leadership or in some public role representing the church. 1 Tim. 5:19, 20. Their opportunity to "leaven" the wider body of believers or misrepresent Christ must be removed as much as possible. Asking them to "step down" is an act that should take place in order for them to consider the seriousness of what has taken place, as well as provide opportunity to work more intensively on their own issues. This focus is healthy and redemptive. When their repentance has been fully worked out, in the assessment of those over them, they return to "active service" at one level or another.

Some who have been given a place of leadership and then enter of time of great marital discord and conflict must step aside until they recover the first "flock" of their responsibility, their own home. 1 Tim. 3:5. This is not referring to the occasional argument a married couple may have from time to time but a serious state of unforgiveness, communication breakdown, unresolved conflict and serious relationship deterioration. To make the judgment that they must step aside is not a maligning of them as people but a loving of them enough, to make the hard steps in judgment, that are necessary for them pause, reflect and work on what is most important.

Where a person is truly contrite and embraces truth, mercy is granted. Our granting of mercy (not bringing any consequence to the guilty) is merely the mercy that God grants. This is why there must be such carefulness in the discipline of the local church as we represent Him in both the granting of mercy or the bringing of some level of discipline.

Discernment is an insight informed by the Holy Spirit and the Word. It gives perspective and wisdom to decision-making. Vital to the process and the decisions that are taken in judgment in the local church, is the insight and wisdom of the Holy Spirit. Isa. 11:3. Good judgment is **not** founded in the mere collection of facts as can be collected and the logical processing of such information, although that is necessary. It is, like everything in leadership life, a combination of hearing the Holy Spirit and applying the test of the Word to what is heard. A swift or rush to judgment, does not give pause to the process of weighing the matter before the Lord. On the other hand,

Leaders exercise judgment with great care, the Holy Spirit and biblical insight.

unnecessary delay can cause the widening of gossip and a leavening multiplication of the same issues. Prov. 18:13 NLT; Eccl. 8:11.

What is the Meaning of "Punishment" in the Scripture?
One hundred and seventy one times the Bible uses some form of the word, "punish." Of those one hundred and seventy one times, twenty seven times there is mentioned some form of the word, "punish," in the New Testament. Although the word has some emotive connotations, it is a word used by the Holy Spirit and as such, needs to be understood in its New Covenant application. Punishment is simply a painful consequence, exacted by another, on a person, who commits wrongdoing. In a temporal sense its purpose is meant to be redemptive and conciliatory. In an eternal sense it is an eternal separation. A few facts regarding the concept of "punishment" in the New Testament:

- The unrighteous who reject Christ's atoning work in their behalf, are sent at the end of time, into eternal punishment – Mt. 25:46; 2 Thes. 1:8, 9

- Teachers that are proud, self-promoting and take advantage of others for their own personal gain will be punished most severely Jesus said – Mark 12:38-40

- God's punishment and wrath against sin is partially exercised through earthly governmental authorities' punishment of violations of the civil law – Rom. 13:4, 5; 1 Pet. 2:14

- God's punishment comes on those who trample underfoot the Son of God – Heb. 10:29-31

- Great punishment comes upon the great prostitute, the Harlot, who is the opposite of the Bride of Christ – Rev. 17:1, 2

Judgment unto Redemption and Damnation
There is a Heaven and there is a Hell. Living in the light of these two realities, we persuade men. Some, in our day, want to dismiss the idea of Hell or the eternal judgment of the wicked because it does not fit their own idea of mercy or justice or their view of God. There is a day of reckoning or a day of judgment. Mt. 12:36. God is Who He is and all that He said He is. All of life is measured by what His Word has revealed about Him. He cannot deny Himself. He will not be conformed to any man's idea of whom or what He should be. He has made unmistakably clear Who He is. His judgments as the "Judge of all the Earth" are right and just. He is not fair as men define fairness from human reference points. Rom. 9:28; Rev. 9:14-21; Isa. 11:3. He expects us to fully embrace Him in all that He is and not choose one aspect to emphasise to the neglect of another dimension of His nature. He is both absolutely holy and absolutely loving. His holiness demands judgment while His love offers relationship.

Judgment unto damnation is refusing to accept God's mercy (mercy is not getting what you **do** deserve) and thus, by default, bringing on yourself the penalty for refusing

Leaders exercise judgment with great care, the Holy Spirit and biblical insight.

mercy. This is a judgment, by God, not in a particular moment, for a particular sin or a particular person but for sin and for all of mankind at the Cross. John 3:16 says, "…whoever believes on Him will not perish." To fail to believe to believe on Jesus is to receive the only other alternative—the judgment of eternal death.

God judged sin by placing all sin on Jesus and the judgment of all sin (which is death) on Jesus as well. This was judgment unto redemption—or a judging in order to redeem, not of Christ (who was/is sinless) but of mankind. When man ultimately forsakes God's judgment on sin, as rendered by the Cross, he comes into the consequence of that forsaking—eternal death.

God, who is rich in mercy, provided a "space to repent," in time, that man might accept God's judgment or designation of sin as sin and embrace the Saviour. God, who is rich in mercy, uses the negative consequences of sin to lead man to Himself. As a loving judge, He seeks to draw men in their brokenness to Himself, even while they are stubbornly resisting Him. Acts 9:4. The trouble and anguish that comes with sin is meant to be a redemptive sign that we are on the wrong path. Rom. 2:9. Just as pain in the human body causes us to investigate its cause, guilt, hardship and emotional pain cause us to seek the alleviation of it through the Saviour.

I met a man who was not a believer. He poured out a very significant catalogue of troubles, failures and deep disappointments. As I listened, I asked the Holy Spirit how to speak to him. I said, "It would appear that you have made a real mess of your life." He said, "I would have thought that as a pastor, you would have been more encouraging." I said, "What you need is not encouragement in the way you are going but a whole new way of living. All of us make a mess of our lives without Christ as the Bible says, 'The way of man is not in him.' It is also says that 'there is a way that seems right unto a man but end thereof is death.' Let me pray with you to receive the Saviour who is The Way." We knelt by the settee and he prayed to receive Christ. He was gloriously saved. His trouble served him, by being the pain that caused him to see that his own way, was not the way of Life and that he needed a saviour outside of himself.

The Great White Throne Judgment
The Bible speaks of the ultimate judgment by God upon all persons and things. Rev. 20:11-15 says, "Then I saw a great white throne and him who was seated on it. Earth and sky fled from his presence, and there was no place for them. And I saw the dead, great and small, standing before the throne, and books were opened. Another book was opened, which is the book of life. The **dead were judged** according to what they had done as recorded in the books. The sea gave up the dead that were in it, and death and Hades gave up the dead that were in them, and **each person was judged** according to what he had done. Then death and Hades were thrown into the lake of fire. The lake of fire is the second death. If anyone's name was not found written in the book of life, he was thrown into the lake of fire." Rom. 14:10; 2 Cor. 5:10. All that God has made comes to "give account" and judgment is to be rendered. Rom. 14:12. Seven

Leaders exercise judgment with great care, the Holy Spirit and biblical insight.

times the New Testament refers to "the Day of Judgment." Isa. 26:9-11 says, "…When your judgments come upon the earth, the people of the world learn righteousness. But when grace is shown to the wicked, they do not learn righteousness; even in a land of uprightness they go on doing evil and do not regard the majesty of the LORD. LORD, your hand is lifted high, but they do not see it. Let them see your zeal for your people and be put to shame; let the fire reserved for your enemies consume them." Five times the New Testament uses the phrase, "at the judgment." God, who is The Judge, will carry out the righteous judgment He has promised ultimately for all of creation. No person will escape that appointment. However, those clothed in the righteousness of the Son will be awarded what is theirs. Those not clothed in the righteousness of Christ will be judged unto eternal destruction along with death, Hell, Satan, the False Prophet, and the Beast. The Heavens and the Earth will be cleansed by fire.

Profile of a Judgmental Person and a Careless Person
For a host of reasons a person may be either a "judgmental" person or a "careless" person who has no regard for standards or the purpose of consequences for the violation of standards. Some believers have only been taught about sin and thus become more sin-focussed and sin-conscious rather than grace-focussed. Others have a misunderstanding of grace. Those that are sin-focussed tend to be condemning of both the **person** and the sin. Those that have a misunderstanding of grace tend to dilute or ignore the significance and impact of sin.

Leaders can ill afford to fall into either category but must wisely and carefully balance the necessity of having clear standards of right and wrong and the necessity of discipline, as a means of maintaining those standards, all the while loving the one who has sinned. Gal. 6:1 ESV. Whatever judgments they are required to make in concert with others, those decisions are filled with prayer, wisdom and collective guidance. They do not turn a blind eye to behaviour that leavens the Church as Eli did, nor do they have a legalistic condemnation of **people** who sin. They righteously decide that sin is sin and that people need help to recover themselves from it. Even if a person stubbornly refuses to repent, they still need the "tough love" that brings the love-based discipline that causes them to repent and find a new level of grace-enabled living!

Application

1. In small groups discuss why it is difficult to balance, in judging, both mercy and truth.

2. Discuss how elders or pastors might judge or bring loving discipline to a leader who is caught in an adulterous affair and refuses to repent based on Scripture.

Leaders exercise judgment with great care, the Holy Spirit and biblical insight.

Judgment Scriptures

Heb. 6:1-2 KJV
"Therefore leaving the principles of the doctrine of Christ, let us go on unto perfection; not laying again the foundation of repentance from dead works, and of faith toward God, of the doctrine of baptisms, and of laying on of hands, and of resurrection of the dead, and of **eternal judgment**."

Acts 15:37-41
"Barnabas wanted to take John, also called Mark, with them, but Paul did not think it wise to take him, because he had deserted them in Pamphylia and had not continued with them in the work. They had such a sharp disagreement that they parted company. Barnabas took Mark and sailed for Cyprus, but Paul chose Silas and left, commended by the brothers to the grace of the Lord. He went through Syria and Cilicia, strengthening the churches."

2 Tim. 4:11
"Only Luke is with me. Get Mark and bring him with you, because he is helpful to me in my ministry."

Rom 8:1
"Therefore, there is now **no condemnation for those who are in Christ Jesus**...."

1 John 3:19-21
"This then is how we know that we belong to the truth, and how we set our hearts at rest in his presence whenever our hearts condemn us. For God is greater than our hearts, and he knows everything." Dear friends, **if our hearts do not condemn us, we have confidence before God**."

1 Cor. 11:28-32 ESV
"Whoever, therefore, eats the bread or drinks the cup of the Lord in an unworthy manner will be guilty of profaning the body and blood of the Lord. Let a person examine himself, then, and so eat of the bread and drink of the cup. For anyone who eats and drinks without discerning the body eats and drinks **judgment on himself**. That is why many of you are weak and ill, and some have died. But **if we judged ourselves** truly, we **would not be judged**."

Gen. 31:36-53
"Jacob was angry and took Laban to task. 'What is my crime?' he asked Laban. 'What sin have I committed that you hunt me down? Now that you have searched through all my goods, what have you found that belongs to your household? Put it here in front of your relatives and mine, and **let them judge between the two of us.** 'I have been with you for twenty years now. Your sheep and goats have not miscarried, nor have I eaten rams from your flocks. I did not bring you animals torn by wild beasts; I bore the loss myself. And you demanded payment from me for whatever was stolen by day

Leaders exercise judgment with great care, the Holy Spirit and biblical insight.

or night. This was my situation: the heat consumed me in the daytime and the cold at night, and sleep fled from my eyes. It was like this for the twenty years I was in your household. I worked for you fourteen years for your two daughters and six years for your flocks, and you changed my wages ten times. If the God of my father, the God of Abraham and the Fear of Isaac, had not been with me, you would surely have sent me away empty-handed. But God has seen my hardship and the toil of my hands, and last night he rebuked you.' Laban answered Jacob, "The women are my daughters, the children are my children, and the flocks are my flocks. All you see is mine. Yet what can I do today about these daughters of mine, or about the children they have borne? Come now, let's make a covenant, you and I, and let it serve as a witness between us.' So Jacob took a stone and set it up as a pillar. He said to his relatives, 'Gather some stones.' So they took stones and piled them in a heap, and they ate there by the heap. Laban called it Jegar Sahadutha, and Jacob called it Galeed. Laban said, 'This heap is a witness between you and me today.' That is why it was called Galeed. It was also called Mizpah, because he said, 'May the Lord keep watch between you and me when we are away from each other. If you ill-treat my daughters or if you take any wives besides my daughters, even though no-one is with us, remember that God is a witness between you and me.' Laban also said to Jacob, 'Here is this heap, and here is this pillar I have set up between you and me. This heap is a witness, and this pillar is a witness, that I will not go past this heap to your side to harm you and that you will not go past this heap and pillar to my side to harm me. May the God of Abraham and the God of Nahor, the God of their father, **judge between us**. So Jacob took an oath in the name of the Fear of his father Isaac."

Ps. 119:66
"**Teach me** knowledge and **good judgment**, for I trust in your commands."

Prov. 24:3-4
"**By wisdom a house is built**, and through understanding it is established; through knowledge its rooms are filled with rare and beautiful treasures."

1 Kings 3:6 NKJV
"And Solomon said: "You have shown great **mercy** to Your servant David my father, because **he walked before You in truth**, in righteousness, and in uprightness of heart with You…."

Ps 25:10 NKJV
"All the paths of the Lord *are* **mercy and truth**, to such as keep His covenant and His testimonies."

Ps 85:10 NKJV
"**Mercy and truth have met together**; Righteousness and peace have kissed."

Leaders exercise judgment with great care, the Holy Spirit and biblical insight.

Prov. 16:6 NKJV
"In **mercy and truth atonement** is provided for iniquity; And by the fear of the Lord, *one* departs from evil."

1 Cor. 5:1-5 ESV
"It is actually reported that there is sexual immorality among you, and of a kind that is not tolerated even among pagans, for a man has his father's wife. And you are arrogant! Ought you not rather to mourn? Let him who has done this **be removed from among you**. For though absent in body, I am present in spirit; and as if present, **I have already pronounced judgment on the one who did such a thing**. When you are assembled in the name of the Lord Jesus and my spirit is present, with the power of our Lord Jesus, you are to **deliver this man to Satan for the destruction of the flesh, so that his spirit may be saved in the day of the Lord**."

1 Peter 4:17
"For it is time for **judgment to begin with God's household**; and if it begins with us, what will the outcome be for those who do not obey the gospel of God?"

1 Cor. 5:4-5
"So when you are assembled and I am with you in spirit, and the power of our Lord Jesus is present, hand this man over to Satan for the destruction of the flesh, so that **his spirit may be saved on the day of the Lord**."

2 Cor. 2:6-8
"The **punishment inflicted on him by the majority** is sufficient. Now instead, you ought to forgive and comfort him, so that he will not be overwhelmed by excessive sorrow. I urge you, therefore, to **reaffirm your love** for him."

Gen. 18:25
"Will not **the Judge of all the earth** do right?'

2 Peter 3:9-10
"The Lord is not slow in keeping his promise, as some understand slowness. Instead he is patient with you, not wanting anyone to perish, but everyone to come to repentance. But the day of the Lord will come like a thief. **The heavens will disappear with a roar; the elements will be destroyed by fire, and the earth and everything done in it will be laid bare**."

John 3:36
"Whoever believes in the Son has eternal life, but whoever rejects the Son will not see life, for **God's wrath remains on them.**"

Rom. 1:18
"The wrath of God is being revealed from heaven against all the godlessness and wickedness of people who suppress the truth by their wickedness…."

Leaders exercise judgment with great care, the Holy Spirit and biblical insight.

Rom. 2:4-8
"Or do you show contempt for the riches of his kindness, forbearance and patience, not realising that God's kindness is intended to lead you towards repentance? But because of your stubbornness and your unrepentant heart, you are storing up wrath against yourself for the day of God's wrath, **when His righteous judgment will be revealed**. God 'will repay to each person according to what they have done.' To those who by persistence in doing good seek glory, honour and immortality, he will give eternal life. But for **those who are self-seeking and who reject the truth and follow evil, there will be wrath and anger.**"

Heb. 10:29-31
"How much more severely do you think someone deserves to be punished who has trampled the Son of God underfoot, who has treated as an unholy thing the blood of the covenant that sanctified them, and who has insulted the Spirit of grace? For we know him who said, 'It is mine to avenge; I will repay,' and again, '**The Lord will judge his people.**' It is a dreadful thing to fall into the hands of the living God."

James 4:6 ESV
"But he gives more grace. Therefore it says, "God opposes the proud, but **gives grace to the humble.**"

Heb. 12:4-11
"In your struggle against sin, you have not yet resisted to the point of shedding your blood. And have you completely forgotten this word of encouragement that addresses you as a father addresses his son? It says, 'My son, do not make light of the Lord's discipline, and do not lose heart when he rebukes you, because the Lord disciplines the one he loves, and he chastens everyone he accepts as his son.' Endure hardship as discipline; God is treating you as his children. For what children are not disciplined by their father? If you are not disciplined—and everyone undergoes discipline—then you are not legitimate, not true sons and daughters at all. Moreover, we have all had human fathers who disciplined us and we respected them for it. How much more should we submit to the Father of spirits and live! They disciplined us for a little while as they thought best; but **God disciplines us for our good, in order that we may share in his holiness. No discipline seems pleasant at the time, but painful. Later on, however, it produces a harvest of righteousness and peace for those who have been trained by it.**"

Isa. 11:2-3
"The Spirit of the Lord will rest on him — the Spirit of wisdom and of understanding, the Spirit of counsel and of might, the Spirit of knowledge and fear of the Lord —and he will delight in the fear of the Lord. He will not judge by what he sees with his eyes, or decide by what he hears with his ears…."

Gen 31:53
"May **the God of Abraham** and the God of Nahor, the God of their father, **judge between us.**" So Jacob took an oath in the name of the Fear of his father Isaac."

Leaders exercise judgment with great care, the Holy Spirit and biblical insight.

Ex 6:6
"I am the Lord, and I will bring you out from under the yoke of the Egyptians. I will free you from being slaves to them, and I will redeem you with an outstretched arm and with **mighty acts of judgment**."

1 Cor.5:13
"**God will judge** those outside."

2 Tim. 4:1
"In the presence of **God** and of Christ Jesus, **who will judge the living and the dead**, and in view of his appearing and his kingdom, I give you this charge…."

Heb. 12:23
"You have come to **God, the judge** of all men…."

Heb. 13:4
"Marriage should be honoured by all, and the marriage bed kept pure, for **God will judge** the adulterer and all the sexually immoral."

Rom. 2:16
"This will take place on the day when **God will judge men's secrets** through Jesus Christ, as my gospel declares."

Rev. 11:18
"The nations were angry; and your wrath has come. **The time has come for judging the dead**, and for rewarding your servants the prophets and your saints and those who reverence your name, both small and great — and for destroying those who destroy the earth."

Rev. 20:7-15
"When the thousand years are over, Satan will be released from his prison and will go out to deceive the nations in the four corners of the earth — Gog and Magog — to gather them for battle. In number they are like the sand on the seashore. They marched across the breadth of the earth and surrounded the camp of God's people, the city he loves. But fire came down from heaven and devoured them. And the devil, who deceived them, was thrown into the lake of burning sulphur, where the beast and the false prophet had been thrown. They will be tormented day and night for ever and ever. Then I saw a great white throne and him who was seated on it. Earth and sky fled from his presence, and there was no place for them. And I saw the dead, great and small, standing before the throne, and books were opened. Another book was opened, which is the book of life. **The dead were judged according to what they had done** as recorded in the books. The sea gave up the dead that were in it, and death and Hades gave up the dead that were in them, and **each person was judged according to what he had done**. Then death and Hades were thrown into the lake of fire. The lake of fire is the second death. If anyone's name was not found written in the book of life, he was thrown into the lake of fire."

Leaders exercise judgment with great care, the Holy Spirit and biblical insight.

John 5:27-30
"And he has given him **authority to judge** because he is the Son of Man. "Do not be amazed at this, for a time is coming when all who are in their graves will hear his voice and come out — those who have done good will rise to live, and those who have done evil will rise to be condemned. By myself I can do nothing; I judge only as I hear, and my judgment is just, for I seek not to please myself but him who sent me."

Acts 17:31
"For he has set a day when **he will judge the world with justice** by the man he has appointed. He has given proof of this to all men by raising him from the dead."

Acts 10:42
"He commanded us to preach to the people and to testify that he is the one whom God appointed as **judge of the living and the dead**."

Isa. 11:3
"…he will delight in the fear of the Lord. He will not judge by what he sees with his eyes, or decide by what he hears with his ears…."

Heb. 12:11
"No discipline seems pleasant at the time, but painful. Later on, however, it produces a harvest of righteousness and peace for those who have been **trained by it**."

1 Sam. 3:13
"For I told him that I would **judge his family** for ever because of the sin he knew about; his sons made themselves contemptible, and **he failed to restrain them**."

Eph. 6:1
"Children, obey your parents in the Lord, for this is right."

Prov. 22:15 TLB
"A youngster's heart is filled with rebellion, but punishment will drive it out of him."

Prov. 20:11 NCV
"Even children are known by their behaviour; their actions show if they are innocent and good."

Col 3:20-21
"Children, obey your parents in everything, for this pleases the Lord. Fathers, do not embitter your children, or they will become discouraged."

1 Tim. 3:4, 12 NLT
"He must manage his own family well, **having children who respect and obey him**. For if a man cannot manage his own household, how can he take care of God's church?...A deacon must be faithful to his wife, and he must manage his children and household well."

Leaders exercise judgment with great care, the Holy Spirit and biblical insight.

1 Cor. 5:12, 13
"What business is it of mine to judge those outside the church? **Are you not to judge** those inside? **God will judge those outside**. "Expel the wicked man** from among you."

Eph. 4:15
"Instead, **speaking the truth in love, we will in all things grow up** into him who is the Head, that is, Christ."

1 Cor. 6:3-4
"Do you not know that we will **judge** angels? How much more the things of this life! Therefore, if you have disputes about such matters, **appoint as judges even men** of little account in the church!"

Gal. 6:1 ESV
"Brothers, if anyone is caught in any transgression, you who are spiritual should restore him in a spirit of gentleness. Keep watch on yourself, lest you too be tempted."

Rom. 3:24
"…and all are justified freely by his grace through the redemption that came by Christ Jesus."

1 John 2:1
"My dear children, I write this to you so that you will not sin. **But if anybody does sin**, we have one who speaks to the Father in our defence — Jesus Christ, the Righteous One."

1 John 1:9
"**If we confess our sins**, he is faithful and just and will forgive us our sins and purify us from all unrighteousness."

Matt. 6:12 NLT
"…and forgive us our sins, as we have forgiven those who sin against us."

James 4:6-7 ESV
"But he gives more grace. Therefore it says, "God opposes the proud, but gives grace to the humble."

2 Peter 3:9
"The Lord is not slow in keeping his promise, as some understand slowness. He is patient with you, not wanting anyone to perish, but everyone to come to repentance."

Rom. 2:8-9
"But for those who are self-seeking and who reject the truth and follow evil, there will be wrath and anger. **There will be trouble and distress for every human being who does evil**: first for the Jew, then for the Gentile…."

Leaders exercise judgment with great care, the Holy Spirit and biblical insight.

Ps. 66:18 NLT
"**If I had not confessed the sin** in my heart, the Lord would not have listened."

Rom. 2:4-6, 9
"Or do you show contempt for the riches of his kindness, tolerance and patience, not realising that God's kindness leads you towards repentance? But because of your stubbornness and your unrepentant heart, you are storing up wrath against yourself for the day of God's wrath, when his righteous judgment will be revealed. God "will give to each person according to what he has done". There **will be trouble and distress for every human being who does evil**: first for the Jew, then for the Gentile…."

1 Cor. 11:31-32
"**But if we judged ourselves, we would not come under judgment**. When we are judged by the Lord, we are being disciplined so that we will not be condemned with the world."

1 Sam. 16:7 ESV
"Man looks on the outward appearance but the Lord looks on the heart."

1 Cor. 13:7
"It always protects, **always trusts**, always hopes, always perseveres."

Prov. 21:2
"All a man's ways seem right to him, but **the Lord weighs the heart**."

1 Chron. 28:9
"…for **the Lord searches every heart and understands every motive behind the thoughts**."

1 Cor. 13:7
"It always protects, **always trusts**, always hopes, always perseveres."

Gal. 6:1 ESV
"Brothers, if anyone is caught in any transgression, you who are spiritual should restore him in a spirit of gentleness. Keep watch on yourself, lest you too be tempted."

Prov. 26:17 ESV
"**Whoever meddles in a quarrel not his own** is like one who takes a passing dog by the ears."

1 Tim. 5:19-20
"Do not entertain an accusation against an elder unless it is brought by two or three witnesses. Those who sin are to be rebuked publicly, so that the others may take warning."

Leaders exercise judgment with great care, the Holy Spirit and biblical insight.

1 Tim. 3:5
"If anyone does not know how to manage his own family, how can he take care of God's church?"

Isa. 11:3
"He will **not judge by what he sees with his eyes, or decide by what he hears** with his ears...."

Prov. 18:13 NLT
"Spouting off before listening to the facts is both shameful and foolish."

Eccl. 8:11
"When the **sentence for a crime is not quickly carried out**, the hearts of the people are filled with schemes to do wrong."

Matt. 25:46
"Then they will go away to eternal **punishment**, but the righteous to eternal life."

2 Thess. 1:8-9
"He will **punish** those who do not know God and do not obey the gospel of our Lord Jesus. **They will be punished** with everlasting destruction and shut out from the presence of the Lord and from the majesty of his power."

Mark 12:38-40
"As he taught, Jesus said, "Watch out for the teachers of the law. They like to walk around in flowing robes and be greeted in the market-places, and have the most important seats in the synagogues and the places of honour at banquets. They devour widows' houses and for a show make lengthy prayers. **Such men will be punished most severely**."

Rom. 13:4-5
"For he is God's servant to do you good. But if you do wrong, be afraid, for he does not bear the sword for nothing. He is God's servant, an agent of wrath **to bring punishment on the wrongdoer**. Therefore, it is necessary to submit to the authorities, not only because of **possible punishment** but also because of conscience."

1 Peter 2:14
"...or to governors, who are sent by him **to punish** those who do wrong and to commend those who do right."

Heb. 10:29-31
"How much more severely do you think a man deserves **to be punished** who has trampled the Son of God under foot, who has treated as an unholy thing the blood of the covenant that sanctified him, and who has insulted the Spirit of grace? For we know him who said, "It is mine to avenge; I will repay," and again, "The Lord will judge his people." It is a dreadful thing to fall into the hands of the living God."

Leaders exercise judgment with great care, the Holy Spirit and biblical insight.

Rev. 17:1-2
"One of the seven angels who had the seven bowls came and said to me, "Come, I will **show you the punishment of the great prostitute**, who sits on many waters. With her the kings of the earth committed adultery and the inhabitants of the earth were intoxicated with the wine of her adulteries."

Matt. 12:36
"But I tell you that men will have to give account on **the day of judgment** for every careless word they have spoken."

Rom. 9:28
"For **the Lord will carry out his sentence on earth** with speed and finality."

Rev. 9:14-21
"It said to the sixth angel who had the trumpet, "Release the four angels who are bound at the great river Euphrates." And the four angels who had been kept ready for this very hour and day and month and year were released to kill a third of mankind. The number of the mounted troops was two hundred million. I heard their number. The horses and riders I saw in my vision looked like this: Their breastplates were fiery red, dark blue, and yellow as sulphur. The heads of the horses resembled the heads of lions, and out of their mouths came fire, smoke and sulphur. A third of mankind was killed by the three plagues of fire, smoke and sulphur that came out of their mouths. The power of the horses was in their mouths and in their tails; for their tails were like snakes, having heads with which they inflict injury. The rest of mankind that were not killed by these plagues still did not repent of the work of their hands; they did not stop worshipping demons, and idols of gold, silver, bronze, stone and wood — idols that cannot see or hear or walk. Nor did they repent of their murders, their magic arts, their sexual immorality or their thefts."

Isa. 11:3
"…and he will delight in the fear of the Lord. He will not judge by what he sees with his eyes, or decide by what he hears with his ears…."

Acts 9:4
"He fell to the ground and heard a voice say to him, "Saul, Saul, why do you persecute me?"

Rom. 2:9
"There will be trouble and distress for every human being who does evil: first for the Jew, then for the Gentile…."

Rev. 20:11-15
"Then I saw a great white throne and him who was seated on it. Earth and sky fled from his presence, and there was no place for them. And I saw the dead, great and small, standing before the throne, and books were opened. Another book was opened, which is the book of life. The **dead were judged** according to what they had done as

Leaders exercise judgment with great care, the Holy Spirit and biblical insight.

recorded in the books. The sea gave up the dead that were in it, and death and Hades gave up the dead that were in them, and **each person was judged** according to what he had done. Then death and Hades were thrown into the lake of fire. The lake of fire is the second death. If anyone's name was not found written in the book of life, he was thrown into the lake of fire."

Rom. 14:10
"You, then, why do you judge your brother? Or why do you look down on your brother? **For we will all stand before God's judgment seat**."

2 Cor. 5:10
"For **we must all appear before the judgment seat of Christ**, that each one may receive what is due to him for the things done while in the body, whether good or bad."

Rom. 14:12
"So then, each of us will give an account of himself to God."

Gal. 6:1 ESV
"Brothers, if anyone is caught in any transgression, you who are spiritual should restore him in a spirit of gentleness. Keep watch on yourself, lest you too be tempted."

Leaders exercise judgment with great care, the Holy Spirit and biblical insight.

The Leader and.....

Legalism

Ever since sin entered the human race, in the Garden of Eden, man has been preoccupied with the search for acceptability. He is born with the instinct to seek approval and acceptance from others and from within himself. God made clear that man's efforts to be approved by God could only come by responding to God's work on man's behalf—not by man's efforts to be approved or accepted by God. He rejected man's attempt to be acceptable in the Garden when He chose to cover Adam and Eve in the blood-shedding sacrifice of an animal skin, instead of their own self-made fig-leaf covering. Man, apart from God's redemptive work of unmerited favour, still seeks to be whole, clean and approved by his own strenuous efforts.

One of the characteristics of all the world's major religions is the emphasis on "good works." Religion is a belief, that if you show you are good enough, by doing enough good works, you will be accepted by God and make it to Heaven or have some other good end after this life is over. Yet for all of his efforts, mankind is still filled with doubt about his "goodness." His lingering guilt or condemnation lead him to think, despite all he may have done in the "good column," it never is enough. Thus religion or legalism is a superhuman effort to attain acceptability from God by doing good works and making every human effort to refrain from evil. Unwittingly, legalism is an idol of human effort—the subconscious worship of what "I can do" to be accepted or justifiably make it to Heaven when I die.

The Old Covenant law, a lower standard than the New Covenant standard, was impossible to keep by human effort. **Only by faith in the Lawkeeper**, living inside the believer, will the believer keep the higher New Covenant standard.

Prov. 28:1 says, "The wicked man flees though no-one pursues, but the righteous are as bold as a lion." This tells us that a person with guilt (based on wrong acts committed or simply being born a "sinner") or condemnation (believing he is guilty still, wrong, or sinful) is "fleeing" in life. Inside themselves, the wicked or sinners, are running away from 'themselves' in effect. The "bad" is the person they are, in their minds, and they instinctively are trying to "get away" from the bad. Their lives are secretly consumed with a constant war with themselves. For some, they eventually stop even trying to refrain from sin (which they have found impossible). They simply try to compensate for it by working hard at doing more "good works." This ultimately becomes their self-sanctifying religion.

Leaders help others move out of the chains of legalism into grace.

The only solution to guilt is confession and repentance, accompanied by receiving God's impartation of forgiveness and favour. The only solution to condemnation (passing a sentence on myself that God does not pass) is to fully *receive* by faith God's forgiveness and favour (grace). Favour is, in one sense, God's current assessment of me. He loves me and He likes me because of what He has done to make me His own.

Heb. 9:14 says, "How much more, then, will the blood of Christ, who through the eternal Spirit offered himself unblemished to God, *cleanse* our consciences from acts that lead to death, so that we may serve the living God!" Our conscience is the inner faculty of man that "accuses or excuses" our behaviour according to the law of God written within man. Rom. 2:15. Our conscience is the inner "judge" that announces to us that we have done something wrong. It functions, however, not only instinctively, but according to information by which it is informed concerning what is right, wrong and acceptable. It can make, occasionally, wrong judgments about our behaviour based on a wrong standard or law it attempts to apply. It functions on the basis of a law inside us, informed or ignorant, that we believe is God's view of our hearts and behaviour. 1 John 3:21.

Many times, believers who recognise they have been saved by grace (God's work, not theirs—Eph. 2:8-9), strangely live their on-going, day-to-day life in a works-based self-effort to *keep* from sinning. They fear that falling into a single sin cancels their salvation and their ticket to Heaven. They may have come from a tradition that is constantly reminding them of sin and thus they are more conscious of sin, and who they used to be, than grace, and who they are now in Christ. This kind of lifestyle leads to all kinds of problems in judging self, judging others and in failing to walk consistently in the reality of whom they have become in Christ. Their self-effort without faith, cancels the freely-given power of grace to live in righteousness. Unwittingly, their faith is more invested in what they are doing more than in what He has done.

Leaders recognise any form of legalism in themselves and rid themselves of it through the application of grace. They do this to live in the blessing and the freedom of grace as well as to correctly help others to walk in grace. There is so much striving and attempted superhuman effort amongst believers that God wrote a whole book of the Bible (Galatians) to help us discern it and replace it. Apparently in Paul's day, some leaders were requiring the new converts, to conform to many of the Old Covenant laws, in order to be approved of by God. Paul makes clear that it is not the external that is in view in God's mind, but the internal. Rom. 13:8-10. Outward circumcision of the flesh (Old Testament command) does not make you holy. It is the inward circumcision of the heart (putting to death the old nature by the Spirit-Rom. 8:13 NLT) that enables us to live holy and the imputation of Christ's righteousness that makes a person holy. Heb. 8:10; Phillip. 2:13. We have received what we could not earn and we are enabled by His inner working.

Leaders help others move out of the chains of legalism into grace.

Legalism Defined

Legal-ism has to do with law. Law is a required or demanded *standard* of behaviour. Laws are meant to be obeyed. God gave The Law as a revelation of His holiness and to show what He expected of man at the time of its giving. This revelation of God was to endure up to the time of the coming of a *higher* Law—that of Christ Jesus. Every believer is now measured not by the Ten Commandments, but by Jesus. Our lives are measured by how we match up to the One who is the Holiness of God personified, who lives within us. Thus we learn to walk in a **relationship of love** rather than a will-enforced, duty-demanded, fearful conformity to a set of regulations. John 14:23 says, "Jesus replied, "If anyone loves me, he will obey my teaching. My Father will love him, and we will come to him and make our home with him."

We move from sin-consciousness to relationship-consciousness. People who are said to be greatly romantically "in love" with each other give little thought to the sacrifice and effort necessary to express that loving—almost without thinking, they give, plot and plan how they can please the one they love. Believers, sometimes, may not give much thought to being "in love" with Jesus because they are working so hard to try to keep inside the boundaries. These are two greatly divergent lifestyles.

Legalism is the publication and expectation of a standard of behaviour demanded of adherents **without the power** to actually perform to that standard. There are standards for living both in the Old Testament and in the New Testament. The standards of the Old Testament are *superseded* by the standards of the New Testament. These New Covenant standards are higher standards than the standards of the Old Testament. The Old Testament says, "You shall not commit adultery." Ex. 20:14 KJV. The New Testament has a higher standard that God *requires* of believers expressed in the statement "not to look at a woman to lust after her." The Old Testament focusses on the behaviour and the New Testament focuses on the mind activity that leads to the sinful behaviour. There is a greater standard required in dealing with the inner thought life than refraining from external behaviour. Most people would not murder another person, however, the New Testament says that the inward heart of anger (one of the primary motivations of murder) is grounds for judgment. Mt. 5:21-22 TMV.

Some, in an attempt to avoid being criticised for being legalistic, cast aside any discussion or consideration of a standard. They repeat the oft-heard mantra, "Don't be legalistic." However, God is holy and thus measures man and His ways whether a believer or a sinner. It is not as though God throws away holiness or the requirement to be holy once you give your life to Christ. 1 Pet. 1:15-17 was written to believers. On the contrary, God holds New Covenant believers to a higher standard than the Old Testament standard. It is, like the Old Testament, an impossible standard to comply with by mere human effort. The Lawgiver must become, *on the inside*, the Law Keeper, for every believer. Gal. 3:2-3 NLT.

The Law of the Old Covenant was the "teacher" that brings us to Christ because, we, like Paul, recognise we had to have Divine help to keep the standard God requires.

Leaders help others move out of the chains of legalism into grace.

Rom. 7:6-7. Paul saw that although he was able to keep the outward standards of the Ten Commandments, one of them he stumbled over. It was the inner, heart-based commandment—"you shall not covet." Since one is guilty of failing the whole Law by failing in one part, (James 2:10), Paul knew he had to have help to live the standard that God requires. He, like everyone else, needed a change in nature. He had to have the very nature of God, the Lawgiver, to be the Lawkeeper within him. 2 Pet. 1:3-4 ESV. This higher law, the person of Jesus, had to be "written in his heart."

What Grace Is Not:

> The absence of *any* standard of conduct or holy living – the standard "under grace" is Jesus. He is the standard and He is the One inside us living His holy life through us.

Characteristics of Legalism:

1. Lifelong striving in human effort to maintain righteousness – Heb. 2:15; Heb. 9:9

2. Residual sense of false guilt or condemnation that never really goes away – Heb. 10:22 NASU; 10:1-2

3. Harsh judgment of others and sometimes self for sins committed – Col. 2:23

4. Attempts to create an impassable wall of boundaries to prevent failure -- Col. 2:23 says, "…such regulations…lack any value in restraining sensual indulgence."

5. Fear of going to Hell for any sins left unconfessed

6. Needing to get saved all over again after committing a sin of any kind

7. Preoccupation with self because of an abiding sense of failure and condemnation

8. Negative focus on self, life and others because of a greater consciousness of sin rather than a greater consciousness of Jesus

9. Lack of abiding joy because of failure or the fear of failure – Rom. 14:17

10. Falling into the same sins that others are harshly judged for – Gal. 6:1 ESV; James 5:9

11. Pride in spiritual position of "greater holiness" than others due to comparison – 1 Cor. 1:12; Gal. 6:4

12. Often a broken, morbid, mournfulness of spirit that is viewed as humility but really masks an abiding sense of failure and lack of confidence in God's abiding grace and one's new identity in Christ -- Neh. 8:9-10

Leaders help others move out of the chains of legalism into grace.

13. A preoccupation with deliverance amongst believers when it seems no addiction to sin can be broken – the deep and wide exploration of generational curses, soul-ties, demonic connections and demonic possession that becomes a path believed to relieve the incidence of failure and secure a spiritual freedom. This has led to so many self-created "ministers" (both male and female) of deliverance who often "deliver" over and over and over the same people from the same alleged demonic bondages.

14. Apparent lack of recognition given to any "crucifying of the flesh" by the power of the Holy Spirit in doctrine and teaching – Rom. 8:12, 13 NLT

15. Living in "sin-consciousness" not "grace-consciousness"

The message of grace is that the believer has a *new* nature! The great message of grace is that the believer *does* have the law of God written within! The great message of grace is that the believer has the very *life of God* within him! The One who keeps God's holy standard is co-mingled in spirit with the believer to live His holy life! 1 Cor. 6:17.

Two Great Confusions
There are two great confusions connected with legalism: (1) the actual law or standard by which our lives are measured and (2) the activity of judging. What is the confusion connected with the actual law by which our lives are measured by God? Let us break down the Law of the Old Testament into its three component parts and then look at how each part is to be treated in the New Testament according to Scripture. John 1:17.

1. Ceremonial law. In general terms, the ceremonial law was what God required of Israel in the Old Testament that had to do with the festivals and sacrifices that God gave Moses.

2. Moral law. The moral law had to do with specific commands of righteous living that God had commanded. It is fundamentally the Ten Commandments.

3. Civil law. The civil law governed the administration of justice in civil and criminal matters.

All of the law of the Old Testament comes to a major reference point at the Cross. John 1:17; Matt. 11:13 says, "For all the Prophets and the Law prophesied until John." The Law spoke (prophesied) along with the Prophets until the coming of Christ (John, the Introducer). At that point all of the Old Testament that comes to the Cross where Christ, the fulfilment of all the Law, was crucified, undergoes a change. The ceremonial law was all fulfilled in Christ's sacrifice so the sacrifices of sheep and goats ends. The civil law today is not practised today by any nation although it provided the moral compass for all of modern Western legal thought. The moral law or the Ten Commandments are all repeated in the New Testament **except** the law of the Sabbath *day*.*

Leaders help others move out of the chains of legalism into grace.

The Ten Commandments, although repeated in the New Testament, except one, were to be kept by New Covenant believers but not in the same way as in the Old Testament. The New Covenant believer can keep all the Ten Commandments and the much higher standard of New Testament commands by the indwelling Christ—not by screwing up the will in self-forced, self-made attempts. Gal. 3:5 AMP says, "Then does He Who supplies you with His marvelous [Holy] Spirit and works powerfully *and* miraculously among you do so on [the grounds of your doing] what the Law demands, or because of your believing in *and* adhering to *and* trusting in *and* relying on the message that you heard?" It is faith in the Lawkeeper within that enables the New Covenant believer.

> *The principle of Sabbath or rest is expressed in the life of faith that is the believer's life but it is not expressed in a duty to worship on a specific day. The necessity of a particular day is no longer stipulated in the New Testament. Col. 2:16, 17. Soon after the Resurrection the church began to worship on the *first* day of the week and Paul noted this in his Epistles. 1 Cor. 16:1, 2; Acts 20:7. As most churches follow this pattern, the believer does not take it on himself to establish some rule for worshipping for himself but goes along with all other worshippers to gather with them in worship. It isn't the *day* that matters in the New Covenant but the practise of corporate worship that matters. Rom. 14:5, 6 NLT.

Two key phrases: "you are not under the law but under grace" (Rom. 6:14 NKJV) and "the handwriting of ordinances that was against us, which was contrary to us, and took it out of the way, nailing it to his cross…." (Col. 2:14 KJV). Clearly understanding these two phrases is vital to grasping the essence of legalism. What does it mean "not under the law but under grace?" Law is a standard of righteous behaviour that God requires. The Old Testament law was a standard of righteous behaviour that God required. It would be foolish to suggest that there is no standard of righteous behaviour that God requires a New Covenant believer. It is, however, a reference to the particular law given under the older, lesser covenant. It was a law given *without the ability to keep it*. In contrast to the "law" of the Old Testament, the New Covenant (a higher standard of righteous behaviour), comes **with** "the power to live it" as the Lawgiver is the Lawkeeper within. The standard of righteous behaviour under the era of grace is a standard or a law that carries the power to live it, as the Holy One, the Holy Spirit, inhabits the believer. It is not simply a standard in the believer's mind but it is the indwelling Holy One, living out His holy life. Phil. 2:13 says, "…it is God who works in you *to will and to act* according to his good purpose." 2 Thess. 3:3 NKJV.

The law of the Old Covenant is connected to what Scripture refers to in Romans as the "law of sin and death." The law of the New Covenant (also a law or standard of righteous behaviour) is connected to the "law of the Spirit of life." The new nature of the believer, has inherent in that new nature, the desire,

Leaders help others move out of the chains of legalism into grace.

will and ability to keep the higher standard or law of the New Covenant. It is an identity, nature, and behaviour that is released by faith in God. It is the "righteousness that comes by faith" (Rom. 4:13) as we walk daily with the Holy One. It is a relationally-released righteousness, not an externally forced, sense of religious obligation. John 14:15 says, "If you love me, you will do what I command." A love relationship with God releases His power to live pleasing Him. This is part of the "package of grace" or Divine enablement that comes to the believer in new creation relationship.

The second phrase, "handwriting of ordinances that was against us" must also be understood. How could the law given by God to His people be something that was "against them?" It was "against" their success because it condemned their behaviour as they had no power to live up to the law or prevent its consequences. It was designed to reveal to them their utter and total dependence upon God for success in a righteous relationship to Him. The Lawgiver led them to Himself by revealing their total inability to live without Him.

This "unkeepable" standard was actually a gracious provision of God in two ways: it was the means by which man could, by faith-based sacrifices, approach God and receive mercy. It also provided the growing realisation, that keeping the holy standard that God required, was not humanly possible. It subsequently prepared man to receive the New Covenant message of grace. Gal. 3:24 NASU. In the dimension of grace offered under the New Covenant, the sacrifices had all been done by Christ's work on the Cross. Man's approach to God was no longer based on his own animal sacrifices. Mercy is granted not on the basis of what man has done but what Christ has done in man's behalf. Eph. 2:8-9; Titus 3:5-7. This New Covenant grace also moved the standard from being kept by man's sheer will power and the threat of death, to a change in nature. The new nature has inherent within it the power to keep the higher holy standard of the New Covenant. 2 Pet. 1:2-4; Rom. 8:4-5, 9 NLT.

4. New Covenant Standards. Often mankind has sought to write down some standard of behaviour that it is believed is acceptable to God. God, Himself, provided a base line or foundational standard in the giving of the Law, but proceeded to raise that standard under the New Covenant to a much higher level. It is a law written *within,* instead of a law on paper. It is the Spirit of Holiness which is the Spirit of Jesus. A voice within us tells us to say, "No" to ungodliness instead of simply trying to stay by human effort alone inside the Ten Commandments. The One who is full of grace is that voice. Titus 2:11-12; Isa. 30:21.

Often movements have endeavoured to write out a code of practice that exceeds the Ten Commandments so as to preserve the purity of what God is doing among them. However, that is doomed to fail, as God has designed the basis of right living is in a *relationship* with Jesus. You cannot live continuously in

Leaders help others move out of the chains of legalism into grace.

union and intimacy and love with The Holy One and walk in sin. It is this faith-based union and relationship that **enables** righteous living. Live a distant, cold, intellect-centred life and you will walk in sin. This relationship with Jesus is not without objective clarity, however. There are numerous passages of Scripture in the New Testament that name specific sins, so we have no doubt whatsoever about those sins. However, all sin starts inwardly and then manifests outwardly. Thus the remedy of replacement of focus is absolutely necessary—no more sin-conscious living but Christ-conscious living.

The second confusion regarding legalism has to do with judgment or the activity of judging. Some would assert that any attempt to judge another's behaviour in *any* regard is to step into legalism. However, the Scripture makes clear over and over that there is a dimension in which we are **not allowed** to judge and a dimension in which we are **commanded** to judge. Leaders must understand these two dimensions lest they take wrong steps in dealing with others. This issue will be discussed in another lesson.

Application

1. Read aloud to yourself the entire book of Galatians in The Message Version. Give some thought to how legalism or the attempt to be approved by God by your own efforts has been a part of your life. Make a list of the ways. Make a list of grace statements to put next to the list of your own efforts to counteract those tendencies.

2. Read the book, "The Grace Awakening" by Chuck Swindoll.

3. In small groups discuss how legalism may have affected your life and how you have begun to deal with it.

4. Read the book, "What Do You Mean? I Am Not Under Law, I Am Under Grace," by Kevin J. Conner.

Leaders help others move out of the chains of legalism into grace.

Legalism Scriptures

Rom. 2:15
"...since they show that the requirements of **the law are written on their hearts**, their consciences also bearing witness, and their thoughts now accusing, now even defending them."

1 John 3:21
"Dear friends, if our hearts do not condemn us, we have confidence before God...."

Eph. 2:8-9
"For it is by grace you have been saved, through faith — and this not from yourselves, it is the gift of God — not by works, so that no-one can boast."

Rom. 13:8-10
"Let no debt remain outstanding, except the continuing debt to love one another, for he who loves his fellow-man has fulfilled the law. The commandments, "Do not commit adultery," "Do not murder," "Do not steal," "Do not covet," and whatever other commandment there may be, are summed up in this one rule: "Love your neighbour as yourself." Love does no harm to its neighbour. Therefore love is the fulfilment of the law."

Rom. 8:12, 13 NLT
"Therefore, dear brothers and sisters, you **have no obligation to do what your sinful nature urges you to do**. For if you live by its dictates, you will die. But if **through the power of the Spirit you put to death the deeds of your sinful nature**, you will live."

Heb. 8:10
"This is the covenant I will make with the house of Israel after that time, declares the Lord. I will put my laws in their minds and write them on their hearts. I will be their God, and they will be my people."

Phil. 2:13
"...for **it is God who works in you to will and to act** according to his good purpose."

Matt. 5:21-22 TMV
"You're familiar with the command to the ancients, 'Do not murder.' I'm telling you that anyone who is so much as angry with a brother or sister is guilty of murder."

1 Peter 1:15-17
"But just as he who called you is holy, so be holy in all you do; for it is written: "Be holy, because I am holy." Since you call on a Father who judges each man's work impartially, live your lives as strangers here in reverent fear."

Leaders help others move out of the chains of legalism into grace.

Gal. 3:2-3 NLT
"Let me ask you this one question: Did you receive the Holy Spirit by obeying the law of Moses? Of course not! You received the Spirit because you believed the message you heard about Christ. How foolish can you be? After starting your Christian lives in the Spirit, why are you now **trying to become perfect by your own human effort**?"

Rom. 7:6-7
"But now, by dying to what once bound us, we have been released from the law so that we serve in **the new way** of the Spirit, and **not in the old way** of the written code. What shall we say, then? Is the law sinful? Certainly not! Nevertheless, I would not have known what sin was had it not been for the law. For I would not have known what coveting really was if the law had not said, 'Do not covet.'

James 2:10
"…or whoever keeps the whole law and yet stumbles at just one point is guilty of breaking all of it."

2 Peter 1:3-4 ESV
"His divine power has granted to us **all things that pertain to life and godliness**, through the knowledge of him who called us to his own glory and excellence, by which he has granted to us his precious and very great promises, so that through them you may become **partakers of the divine nature**, having escaped from the corruption that is in the world because of sinful desire."

Heb. 2:15
"…and free those who all their lives were held in slavery by their fear of death."

Heb. 9:9
"This is an illustration for the present time, indicating that the gifts and sacrifices being offered were not able to clear the conscience of the worshipper."

Heb. 10:22 NASU
"…let us draw near with a sincere heart in full assurance of faith, having our hearts sprinkled *clean* from an evil conscience and our bodies washed with pure water."

Heb. 10:1-2
"The law is only a shadow of the good things that are coming — not the realities themselves. For this reason it can never, by the same sacrifices repeated endlessly year after year, make perfect those who draw near to worship." Otherwise, would they not have stopped being offered? For the worshippers would have been cleansed once for all, and would no longer have felt guilty for their sins."

Col. 2:23
"Such **regulations** indeed have an appearance of wisdom, with their self-imposed worship, their false humility and their harsh treatment of the body, but **they lack any value in restraining sensual indulgence**."

Leaders help others move out of the chains of legalism into grace.

Rom. 14:17
"For the kingdom of God is not a matter of eating and drinking, but of righteousness, peace and joy in the Holy Spirit...."

Gal. 6:1 ESV
"Brothers, if anyone is caught in any transgression, you who are spiritual should restore him in a spirit of gentleness. Keep watch on yourself, lest you too be tempted."

James 5:9
"Don't grumble against one another, brothers and sisters, or you will be judged. The Judge is standing at the door!"

1 Cor. 1:12
"What I mean is this: one of you says, 'I follow Paul'; another, 'I follow Apollos'; another, 'I follow Cephas'; still another, 'I follow Christ.'

Gal. 6:4
"Each one should test their own actions. Then they can take pride in themselves alone, without comparing themselves to someone else...."

Neh. 8:9-10
"Then Nehemiah the governor, Ezra the priest and teacher of the Law, and the Levites who were instructing the people said to them all, 'This day is holy to the Lord your God. Do not mourn or weep.' For all the people had been weeping as they listened to the words of the Law.' Nehemiah said, 'Go and enjoy choice food and sweet drinks, and send some to those who have nothing prepared. This day is holy to our Lord. Do not grieve, for the joy of the Lord is your strength.'

Rom. 8:12, 13 NLT
"Therefore, dear brothers and sisters, you have **no obligation to do what your sinful nature urges you to do**. For if you live by its dictates, you will die. But if **through the power of the Spirit you put to death the deeds of your sinful nature**, you will live."

1 Cor. 6:17
"But whoever is united with the Lord is one with him in spirit.

John 1:17
"For the law was given through Moses; **grace and truth** came through Jesus Christ."

Col. 2:16-17
"Therefore **do not let anyone judge you** by what you eat or drink, or with regard to a religious festival, a New Moon celebration or **a Sabbath day**. These are a shadow of the things that were to come; the reality, however, is found in Christ."

Leaders help others move out of the chains of legalism into grace.

1 Cor. 16:1-2
"Now about the collection for the Lord's people: do what I told the Galatian churches to do. **On the first day of every week**, each one of you should set aside a sum of money in keeping with your income, saving it up, so that when I come no collections will have to be made."

Acts 20:7
"On **the first day of the week we came together to break bread**. Paul spoke to the people and, because he intended to leave the next day, kept on talking until midnight."

Rom. 14:5-7 NLT
"In the same way, some think one day is more holy than another day, while others think every day is alike. You should each be fully convinced that whichever day you choose is acceptable. Those who worship the Lord on a special day do it to honor him. Those who eat any kind of food do so to honor the Lord, since they give thanks to God before eating. And those who refuse to eat certain foods also want to please the Lord and give thanks to God."

Rom. 6:14 NKJV
"For sin shall not have dominion over you, for you are not under law but under grace."

Col. 2:14 KJV
"Blotting out the handwriting of ordinances that was against us, which was contrary to us, and took it out of the way, nailing it to his cross...."

2 Thess. 3:3
"But the Lord is faithful, and he will strengthen you and protect you from the evil one."

Rom. 4:13
"...through the righteousness that comes by faith...."

Gal. 3:24 NASU
"Therefore the Law has become our tutor *to lead us* to Christ, so that we may be justified by faith."

Eph. 2:8-9
"For it is by grace you have been saved, through faith — and this is not from yourselves, it is the gift of God — not by works, so that no-one can boast."

Titus 3:5-7
"...he saved us, not because of righteous things we had done, **but because of his mercy**. He saved us through the washing of rebirth and renewal by the Holy Spirit, whom he poured out on us generously through Jesus Christ our Saviour, so that, having been justified by his grace, we might become heirs having the hope of eternal life."

Leaders help others move out of the chains of legalism into grace.

2 Peter 1:2-4

"Grace and peace be yours in abundance through the knowledge of God and of Jesus our Lord. His divine power has given us everything we need for a godly life through our knowledge of him who called us by his own glory and goodness. Through these he has given us his very great and precious promises, so that through them you may **participate in the divine nature and having escaped the corruption in the world caused by evil desires.**"

Rom. 8:4-5, 9 NLT

"He did this so that the just requirement of the law would be fully satisfied for us, who no longer follow our sinful nature but instead follow the Spirit. Those who are dominated by the sinful nature think about sinful things, but those who are controlled by the Holy Spirit think about things that please the Spirit…But you are not controlled by your sinful nature. You are controlled by the Spirit if you have the Spirit of God living in you."

Titus 2:11-12

"For the grace of God that brings salvation has appeared to all people. **It teaches us to say 'No' to ungodliness and worldly passions**, and to live self-controlled, upright and godly lives in this present age…."

Isa. 30:21

"Whether you turn to the right or to the left, your ears will hear a voice behind you, saying, 'This is the way; walk in it.'

Leaders help others move out of the chains of legalism into grace.

The Leader and.....

The Fear of The Lord

Introduction
We live in a world that has little or no respect for God as the Creator of all that exists. There is no fear in the hearts of unregenerate man that there is a God who holds the power of life and death. They do not see a God who will preserve men, or punish those who refuse to recognise Him for Whom He is. Ps. 36:1-4. They do not see a god who is all-powerful and holy. The fragility and futility of their lives is no clear message that informs their relationship to their Creator. Only when great disasters occur, does it seem that mankind stops to reflect on the possibility of an awesome and mighty God. Even believers can be subtly lulled into a careless mode of living and move away from a life-shaping respect and reverence for God and His power. Heb. 12:28, 29 NKJV (written to believers) says, "Therefore, since we are receiving a kingdom which cannot be shaken, let us have grace, by which we may serve God acceptably with reverence and **godly fear**. For our God *is* a consuming fire."

Record church attendance was recorded in America, for a season, right after the 9-11 attacks on the World Trade Center. Men and women were profoundly reminded that the only refuge on this planet is a close and intimate relationship with the Creator of the planet. One part of this close relationship to God that we are to have is what the Bible calls, "the fear of the Lord."

God uses fear. Once not long after the 9-11 attacks on the World Trade Center, I visited Pakistan to minister to the lost. Great efforts were made for our security. The other American pastor and I were told that all Westerners had fled and that there was a bounty of two million dollars on each of our heads. We were never alone. A Special Forces type of guard was next to us with a machine gun and grenades and challenged everyone who came near. Soldiers of various kinds were all around us. However, just before we were to preach the gospel in some crusade services, we were told the following story. The police superintendent called all of his policeman together and assigned them to guard us saying, "If one hair of these men is damaged, America will bomb this city off the map!" Needless to say, they were diligent because of fear. God used their fear to protect us. Josh. 2:8, 9.

On another occasion a couple came for counsel. The wife was a believer and the husband was not. He was quite wealthy and owned a large company listed on the stock market. The wife complained that her husband was quite cruel, selfish and uncaring. I asked him if this was true. He said, "Yes." I tried to show him the way of salvation and how God would help him to live in marriage and life, with His

Leaders live, like Christ, in the fear of the Lord. Isa. 11:2-3.

life. He rejected the notion. He seemed proud and arrogant. Just as I was about to dismiss them with prayer I felt the Lord prompt me to give him a gentle warning. I told him that his wife was God's daughter and that God did not take lightly someone mistreating His daughter, so he should revise his approach to her, for God would act in her behalf. He left with her. A year later I saw them after a morning service. They lived several hundred miles away so it was unusual for me to see them. The husband rushed over to see me and with a great smile warmly shook my hands and engaged me in conversation like we were old friends.

When he finished, he pressed some piece of paper into my hand and walked away. When I took the time to look at it, it was a cheque for two hundred and fifty dollars. It seemed strange until I saw his wife and she told me the story. When they had returned home, he went back to his same old ways of neglect, selfishness, and abuse. However, as soon as he did, the stock in his company inexplicably plummeted. It looked like he could go under financially. The message got home to him. He rushed home and told his wife to get herself ready that they were going out to dinner. He began to buy her things and do everything he could to make her happy. After a few days, the stock in his company inexplicably rose again and he was back doing well financially. He continued to bless and care for his wife and according to her, wanted to make sure everything was okay with God, thus the cheque to me as His "agent."

God used the fear of financial failure, allowed by God, as a consequence of mistreating one of His kids, to turn a man's mind and behaviour. Although not a believer at that time, he had an encounter with the fear of the Lord that was the beginning of wisdom for him.

The Bible speaks of the "fear of the Lord." It is not understood as something that is negative but something that is positive and vital to wholesome Christian living. One dimension of the Spirit upon Jesus was the "fear of the Lord." Isa. 11:2. Jesus delighted in the fear of the Lord (Jehovah). Isa. 11:3. Leaders subscribe to the fear of the Lord that they might sustain their spiritual longevity.

Arrows fly to subvert the heart in the most subtle of ways. Temptations come of varying kinds, in the varying seasons of our lives. Living out of our true identity enables us to see with spiritual discernment, decide with holy fervour, and deal with every one of those arrows. The fear of the Lord is one dimension of our internal disposition that insures that spiritual discernment, caution and carefulness is present in all the seasons. The Bible refers to the "fear of the Lord" as a particular phrase, twenty-two times and "the fear of God," nine times. It speaks of fearing God 387 times. The fear of the Lord is portrayed as something beautiful, preserving, blessing, enabling, protecting, providing and delivering. It is something every leader should covet and embrace.

Sometimes believers may unwittingly and wrongly attempt to "humanise" God. There are biblical terms that define and describe human relationships that also define

Leaders live, like Christ, in the fear of the Lord. Isa. 11:2-3.

and describe our relationship to God as believers. Yet it must be understood that our relationship to God is unlike, in its totality, any other relationship we have as believers with other believers. God is our closest friend, our lover, and our Father. However, there is no one on earth that is our Maker, our Redeemer, The Creator, and The Saviour. All of the aforementioned characteristics wonderfully and *uniquely* make up our relationship to God. Although it is not central to the work of this text to fully explore this subject, as wonderful as it is, there is a fundamental difference (generally, there are some exceptions) between **how** God has related to man under the Old Covenant and **how** God has related to man under the New Covenant. God is still the same (Mal. 3:6) but the way He conducts His relationship to His offspring is different under the New Covenant. Ez. 36:26, 27.

Under the Old Covenant, God was **externally** perceived. His voice, His acts, and His appearance were experienced **externally**. He shook the earth and men, when He appeared. Often God's people were so terrified that they wanted to be away from such an awesome God. They were so filled with fear that they told Moses to approach God on their behalf. They did not have "God" within them and thus His greatness, power, and holiness staggered their minds. Under the New Covenant, God is **internally** perceived and experienced. We have come to know Him on the **inside**. Now we know Him so personally and so intimately and He is so wonderfully close to us. We are, as the Scripture says, *in Him*, and He is *in us*. John 14:20.

However, God is still God, no matter that He is within us. It is *all* that the Scripture has to say about Him that informs and defines our relationship to Him. We live balancing or holding in "tension," both the greatness of God and the nearness of God. We value and enjoy the intimacy we have with Him but we also live in a profound respect and awe that has no earthly relationship parallel. To live without one or the other, is to live in destitution or danger. We live in great spiritual and relational poverty, if we do not experience and relate to God as our deepest intimate friend. We live in danger of pride and spiritual carelessness, if we do not experience and relate to God as the Almighty Creator of Heaven and earth and the Judge of all things.

There are two theological terms that describe the primary dimensions of our relationship to God or how we relate to God. Those two terms are: transcendence and imminence. They refer to the greatness of God and the nearness of God. Balancing the two…loving Him and fearing Him. Close to Him but in awe of Him. Intimate with Him, but staggered by the weight of Who He is.

What Is the Fear of the Lord?
There are three Hebrew words translated "fear" in the Old Testament. They are: Yare, Mowra, and Yirah. They are used in a combined total of 387 times. They have a various range of meanings including: To be afraid, stand in awe, or fear. These terms are expressed as a belief or response, to God Himself, other persons, situations, Divine places or qualities, to God's mighty acts of destruction, a result of sinful guilt, or a general state of mind.

Leaders live, like Christ, in the fear of the Lord. Isa. 11:2-3.

The Fear of Man
Prov. 29:25 says, "Fear of man will prove to be a snare…." This type of fear is a strong **belief that a negative consequence will come** to a person's life as a result of the negative opinion of others. Even as faith is a powerful life-shaping force in the life of a believer, so also this "negative faith" is a life-shaping power for robbing the believer of life and blessing. Often it is this fear that causes men to calculate a perceived outcome as the basis for doing something or not doing something. The issue is not decided on the basis of right and wrong but on the basis of fear of the perceived outcome. Mt. 21:26; John 19:38.

This powerful belief in possible negative consequences is a spiritual cowardice, a sin, and a paralysing belief. Rom. 14:23b; Rev. 21:8. The other half of Prov. 29:25 quoted above, is the antidote to this condition of mind and life-robbing fear. It says, "…but whoever trusts in the Lord is kept safe." Prov. 29:25. Trusting in the Lord is a belief. It is a powerful belief that is our safety from life-destroying consequences and the fear of them. In the Old Testament, this trust is also described as a fear—the proper "fear of the Lord" that destroys all other fears. Ps. 112 reveals all the amazing benefits of this fear/trust. A wise leader will make a thorough study of this chapter and meditate it into his inner man.

In the New Testament there are several words used for fear:

1. Phobos – this is the word from which we get the English word, "phobia." It has a wide range of definitions also covering both positive and negative applications. It is used 47 times.

    - It is used of something scary or a fear of the unknown as in the case of the disciples when they saw Jesus walking on the water but thought it was a ghost. Matt. 14:26.

    - It is used to describe the guards' responses when the Angel of the Lord appeared and rolled the stone away from Christ's grave. Matt. 28:2-4.

    - It also describes the two Marys' responses as they went to share the awesome news of the resurrection—they went with fear and great joy. Mt. 28:8.

    - Great manifestations of God's power were often met by fear. Acts 2:43.

    - It is also used of mankind's response, in the last days, to the prospect of what is coming on the earth that causes men to die from sheer terror. Luke 21:26.

    - It is used to describe a fear of what others will think. John 19:38.

Leaders live, like Christ, in the fear of the Lord. Isa. 11:2-3.

- It is also used to describe reaction to the judgment exercised upon Ananias and Sapphira in the Early Church. Acts 5:5, 11.

- It also described a lifestyle of living in the fear of the Lord in the Early Church. Acts 9:31; 19:17; Phil. 2:12.

- It also describes the nature of wicked men who have no fear of God before their eyes. Rom. 3:18.

- It is translated, "respect" in the NIV in reference to people in authority. Rom. 13:7

- It is part of the inner culture from which Paul preached. 2 Cor. 5:11.

- It is part of what helps us to perfect holiness…translated "reverence." 2 Cor. 7:1.

2. Deilia – a fearfulness that is not from God that is expressed in timidity and cowardice. 2 Tim. 1:7 KJV; John 14:27.

3. Eulabeia – used twice in Heb. 5:7 and Heb. 12:28. Used to express reverence and godly fear.

In our world today it is clear to see that men (in general) have no fear or life-altering respect for the holiness, greatness or power of God. Rom. 3:12-18. They live with a self-focussed, self-projecting, self-worshipping promotion of themselves and their desires. Only disasters cause them to pause and reflect that there are events and circumstances that are outside of their control. In those moments, they are reminded of their own fragility and smallness. If they do not turn to God in an attempt to preserve their own lives by crying out to their Maker, they carry on in their deception, in effect, "thumbing their nose" or "stiff-arming" God out of their lives. They have no abiding sense of what is expressed in the New Testament that says, "worship God acceptably with reverence and awe, for our 'God is a consuming fire.' Heb. 12:28-29; Isa. 30:30.

There are other manifestations of fear mentioned in the Bible. One such manifestation is the condition or state mind that accompanies guilt. Gen. 3:10; Lev. 26:16-17. Because Adam was living in guilt, he was afraid. It was this fear-belief that prompted him to hide from the most loving and powerful person in his life—God. He ran and hid. Prov. 28:1 NKJV says, "The wicked flee when no one pursues but the righteous are bold as a lion." The presence of a guilty conscience causes men to be in "perpetual flight or hiding." All men are born into this world, because of sin, with varying levels of fear. Satan comes with the "spirit of fear" to enhance this "belief system" and use it to destroy a person's life.

Leaders live, like Christ, in the fear of the Lord. Isa. 11:2-3.

What the Fear of the Lord is Not

The fear of the Lord is not:

- A perspective of a God who is sitting with a disposition or attitude of severe judgment, waiting to bring the impending circumstances of that judgment, and to crush the one who sins (His sons and His daughters).

- The caricature of God that believes God's acceptance of us is based on our absolute perfect performance in spirit, attitude and behaviour. Because we don't walk in perfect sinlessness every day, His frown must be constantly upon us—disapproving, condemning, disappointed and angry.

- The view that any unconfessed sin committed by a believer immediately erases his salvation and he is at that moment on his way to Hell. Yes, sin should always be acknowledged and confessed and forgiveness received. No loving earthly father disowns his son or daughter because of their sins or mistakes—neither does our great, loving, Heavenly Father.

The Fear of the Lord Defined

- The attitude or disposition that has deep respect or reverence for the holiness, power and ability to judge that Almighty God has – Luke 12:4-5; 1 Pet. 1:17 says, "Since you call on **a Father who judges each person's work** impartially, live out your time here in *reverent fear*." 2 Cor. 7:1; Rev. 11:18.

- To hate evil is the fear of the Lord – Prov. 8:13. Wherever evil is found, the believer chooses to hate *it*, not the doer of *it*.

- A restraint to do evil – Gen. 20:11. If men believe that God is a holy judge who can punish their evil deeds, they pause and reflect on their considered behaviour. Col. 3:22 NASU; Prov. 14:27; Prov. 16:6; Ecc. 12:13-14 says, "...fear God and keep his commandments, for this is the duty of all mankind. For God will bring every deed into judgment, including every hidden thing, whether it is good or evil."

- An attitude and an approach in worship and prayer that is full of deep respect for whom God is – Heb. 12:28; Heb. 5:7. Sometimes believers can relate to the Presence of God in public meetings casually, lightly, carelessly or flippantly. Leaders have a deep respect for the Presence, which is God Himself, and they reflect that in how they lead. They are careful, not careless. They are deeply respectful, not casual, in their lifestyle of worshipping God and in corporate worship services.

- Wisdom and knowledge – Job 28:28; Ps. 111:10; Prov. 1:7. It is God's intelligence given to man (wisdom) to fear the Lord, even as Christ lived as a man, in the spirit of the fear of the Lord. Isa. 11:2-3.

Leaders live, like Christ, in the fear of the Lord. Isa. 11:2-3.

Love and the Fear of the Lord.
The believer is meant to live in loving intimacy with God but have a very deep respect for Who He is. In human relationships, men and women may have a close relationship with others but they don't have the same profound respect for them that they have for the Lord. This is simply because our relationship with God, although it has many of the same dimensions as we have in our relationships with others, is signally different in this aspect: He is God Almighty, our Creator, our Redeemer, our greatest Lover, and our ultimate Judge. No earthly relationship even comes close to being equal to these descriptions. We recognise the negative impact that fear has on relationships with other believers but we should also recognise the great value that respect has on them as well.

God judges in mercy and love, yet He still judges. No one can, with impunity, afford to ignore the power of God to righteously punish or exercise judgments that are crushing and painful. To respect His omniscience (all-knowing), His infinite wisdom, His righteousness and His mighty power, is to live in a vital component of relationship to our Redeemer. All of God's ways are right and just. He is always fair as He defines fairness by Himself. When He judges, it is always right and appropriate. It is always in conjunction with another dimension of His nature: love.

In theological terms, we are aware of two dimensions in which we experience and interact with God: His transcendence (the infinite, measureless dimension of Him who created all and fills all and is yet beyond all that is) and His imminence (the ability to be immediately present with us and be ours and others' most intimate friend). These two dimensions of our relationship to God make it a relationship like no other. We are close to Him who so deeply loves us and who is absolutely all-powerful, total purity and the very definition of holiness. He knows all, sees all and is in total control of all that He chooses.

In the Old Testament we see the Father God ruling in the affairs of men with great power, in such ways, that man was often terrified when He appeared. In the New Testament we see Jesus who lived, talked, ate and slept among His disciples sharing the deepest secrets of His heart. They are one and the same God. It is vital that both dimensions of God be held in equal tension—not so familiar with Him that we forget that He is the Creator of all things and not so distant that we fail to have intimacy with Him. On one occasion Jesus' said speaking to His disciples, "Do not be afraid of those who kill the body but cannot kill the soul. Rather, be afraid of the One who can destroy both soul and body in hell." Matt 10:28. The original Greek word used in this passage is from the word, *phobeo,* from which we get the word, phobia, in English. It actually means fear. Fear is a belief. Just as faith is believing, in a positive sense, so also is fear a believing—most of the time in a negative sense, but in relation to God, a positive sense. It is the fear or belief that drives away all other fears. Ps. 112:1, 7-8.

I once was present when a volcano erupted nearby. I saw the sheer terror that gripped men and women as they sought to run from the massive shift of earth, water, and trees

Leaders live, like Christ, in the fear of the Lord. Isa. 11:2-3.

rushing toward them like a massive torrent. Yet the One who made it all was not for a moment ill at ease. He had allowed this event. All the men and women, including myself, seemed pretty small in those moments. Only the One who is in charge of all things could preserve us from the potential imminent devastation.

Many men and women unwittingly live without a deep sense of who they are in relation to Him. Yes, every believer is great in beauty and power but the Lord our God is so hugely greater and more powerful. Yes, we reign with Him but He is still the King of Kings. Our humility is vested in this recognition. We are so amazingly privileged to reign with Him while knowing deep down inside of us that there is only one awesome God! Someone has said, "Two foundational facts of human enlightenment: 1) There is a God and 2) You are not Him." God must always be magnified by us in order that we would never allow the insidious pride that prompts careless living to grow inside us. Dan. 11:36; Luke 1:46 NKJV; Acts 10:46 NKJV.

The Purpose of the Fear of the Lord
God desires always for us to see Him as He is. When we see Him as He truly is, we live in accordance with that perspective. If it is a narrow or incomplete perspective that we hold, we have a relationship affected by that lack. Those that see God only as a severe judge, live in self-paralysing fear. Those that only see God as loving (as they define loving), live in unwitting carelessness. God is a loving judge. He is our very best friend but He is also the absolute and final judge. What then is the purpose of walking in the fear of the Lord?

- It causes us to live with a carefulness and a diligence that we need. 2 Cor. 7:1 NASU says, "Therefore, having these promises, beloved, let us cleanse ourselves from all defilement of flesh and spirit, *perfecting holiness in the fear of God.*"

- It causes us to have endurance in our leadership, when success comes, because we walk in humility. "When he takes the throne of his kingdom, he is to write for himself on a scroll a copy of this law, taken from that of the Levitical priests. It is to be with him, and he is to read it all the days of his life so that he may learn **to revere the LORD his God** and follow carefully all the words of this law and these decrees and **not consider himself better than his fellow Israelites and turn** from the law to the right or to the left. Then he and his descendants **will reign a long time** over his kingdom in Israel." Deut. 17:18-20.

Two Tendencies
Often, depending on a believer's upbringing and particular spiritual journey, he or she can have a tendency to lean one way or another in their relation to God. Some naturally seem to interact with God as a loving Father more than as a judge. Others seem to naturally interact with God as the righteous judge more than as a loving Father. Both need balance. Great men and women have backslidden and suffered terrible consequences because they did not walk in the fear of the Lord.

Leaders live, like Christ, in the fear of the Lord. Isa. 11:2-3.

I have watched "small men" become "great men." When they became great (great in influence, gifts and fruitfulness), they lost the carefulness they had "on the way up" and became careless. In their carelessness, they lost accurate perspective of who they were in relation to God. They did this unwittingly, but nevertheless they did it. It wasn't as if they, all of a sudden, had a loss of conscience or did not know right from wrong. They had stopped living in the "fear of the Lord." In the end, they finished in shame and reproach which they never envisioned when they were "small." The sorts of judgments they experienced were very hard to swallow. Does God forgive them when they repent? Of course, He does. Are they still His sons and daughters that He loves and is ready to restore? Yes, of course, they are. Ps. 103:11-13.

Many, on the other hand, have lived their entire lives like the older brother in Luke 15, deficit of the Father's love, blessing and provision simply because they did not feel they *deserved* it. They often "feel" condemned by God and never find the place of deep acceptance, love and intimacy that God so desires for them. Their view of God distances Him so far from them they never have "felt" His hug or loving embrace. Their Christian life is often joyless, smile-less, morbid, and a lot of disappointing hard work. They soldier on, hoping to "make it to Heaven" and somehow attain His approval. They live without a perception of the smile of God abiding on them.

The Early Church married both of these two great truths of the fear of the Lord and the love of God. Acts 9:31 KJV says, "Then had the churches rest throughout all Judaea and Galilee and Samaria, and were edified; and walking in the **fear of the Lord**, and **in the comfort of the Holy Ghost**, were multiplied."

Application
Discuss in small groups how your own journey has impacted your view of God in relation to His great loving and His power to judge. Share any experiences that reveal how God spoke to you of His love and perhaps, how He lovingly disciplined you.

Read through Psalm 112 and discuss how a right fear has so many benefits and blessings—a vital foundation for the life of the believer.

Read three good books on the fear of the Lord.

Leaders live, like Christ, in the fear of the Lord. Isa. 11:2-3.

The Fear of the Lord Scriptures

Ps. 36:1-4
"I have a message from God in my heart concerning the sinfulness of the wicked: **There is no fear of God before their eyes**. In their own eyes they flatter themselves too much to detect or hate his sin. The words of their mouths are wicked and deceitful; they fail to act wisely and to do good. Even on theirs bed they plot evil; they commit themselves to a sinful course and do not reject what is wrong."

Josh. 2:8-9
"Before the spies lay down for the night, she went up on the roof and said to them, 'I know that the Lord has given this land to you and that **a great fear of you has fallen on us,** so that all who live in this country are **melting in fear** because of you."

Isa. 11:2
"The Spirit of the Lord will rest on him — the Spirit of wisdom and of understanding, the Spirit of counsel and of might, the Spirit of the knowledge and **fear of the Lord**...."

Isa. 11:3
"...and **he will delight in the fear of the Lord**. He will not judge by what he sees with his eyes, or decide by what he hears with his ears...."

Mal. 3:6
'I the Lord **do not change**.'

Ezek. 36:26-27
"I will give you a new heart and put a new spirit in you; I will remove from you your heart of stone and give you a heart of flesh. And I will **put my Spirit in you** and move you to follow my decrees and be careful to keep my laws."

John 14:20
"On that day you will realise that I am in my Father, and **you are in me, and I am in you**."

Matt. 21:26
"But if we say, "Of human origin" — **we are afraid of the people**, for they all hold that John was a prophet.'

John 19:38
"Later, Joseph of Arimathea asked Pilate for the body of Jesus. Now Joseph was a disciple of Jesus, but **secretly because he feared the Jewish leaders**."

Rom. 14:23
"...and everything that does not come from faith is sin."

Leaders live, like Christ, in the fear of the Lord. Isa. 11:2-3.

Rev. 21:8
"But the **cowardly**, the unbelieving, the vile, the murderers, the sexually immoral, those who practise magic arts, the idolaters and all liars — they will be consigned to the fiery lake of burning sulphur. This is the second death.'

Matt. 14:26
"When the disciples saw him walking on the lake, they were terrified. 'It's a ghost,' they said, and **cried out in fear**."

Matt. 28:2-4
"There was a violent earthquake, for an angel of the Lord came down from heaven and, going to the tomb, rolled back the stone and sat on it. His appearance was like lightning, and his clothes were white as snow. **The guards were so afraid of him that they shook** and became like dead men."

Matt. 28:8
"So the women hurried away from the tomb, **afraid yet filled with joy**, and ran to tell his disciples."

Acts 2:43
"**Everyone was filled with awe** at the many wonders and signs performed by the apostles."

Luke 21:26
"**People will faint from terror**, apprehensive of what is coming on the world, for the heavenly bodies will be shaken."

John 19:38
"Later, Joseph of Arimathea asked Pilate for the body of Jesus. Now Joseph was a disciple of Jesus, but **secretly because he feared the Jewish leaders**. With Pilate's permission, he came and took the body away."

Acts 5:5, 11
"When Ananias heard this, he fell down and died. And **great fear seized all who heard what had happened**." ...Great fear seized the whole church and all who heard about these events."

Acts 9:31
"Then the church throughout Judea, Galilee and Samaria enjoyed a time of peace and was strengthened. **Living in the fear of the Lord** and encouraged by the Holy Spirit, it increased in numbers."

Acts 19:17
"When this became known to the Jews and Greeks living in Ephesus, **they were all seized with fear, and the name of the Lord Jesus was held in high honour**."

Leaders live, like Christ, in the fear of the Lord. Isa. 11:2-3.

Phil. 2:12
"Therefore, my dear friends, as you have always obeyed — not only in my presence, but now much more in my absence — continue to **work out your salvation with fear and trembling**...."

Rom. 3:18
'There is **no fear of God before their eyes.**'

Rom. 13:7
"Give to everyone what you owe them: if you owe taxes, pay taxes; if revenue, then revenue; **if respect, then respect**; if honour, then honour."

2 Cor. 5:11
"Since, then, **we know what it is to fear the Lord, we try to persuade others**. What we are is plain to God, and I hope it is also plain to your conscience."

2 Cor. 7:1
"Therefore, since we have these promises, dear friends, let us purify ourselves from everything that contaminates body and spirit, **perfecting holiness out of reverence for God.**"

2 Tim. 1:7 KJV
"For God hath not given us **the spirit of fear**; but of power, and of love, and of a sound mind."

John 14:27
"Peace I leave with you; my peace I give you. I do not give to you as the world gives. Do not let your hearts be troubled and **do not be afraid.**"

Heb. 5:7
"During the days of Jesus' life on earth, he offered up prayers and petitions with fervent cries and tears to the one who could save him from death, and he was heard because of his **reverent submission.**"

Heb. 12:28
"Therefore, since we are receiving a kingdom that cannot be shaken, let us be thankful, and so **worship God acceptably with reverence and awe**...."

Rom. 3:12-18
"All have turned away, they have together become worthless; there is no-one who does good, not even one.' 'Their throats are open graves; their tongues practise deceit.' 'The poison of vipers is on their lips.' 'Their mouths are full of cursing and bitterness.' 'Their feet are swift to shed blood; ruin and misery mark their ways, and the way of peace they do not know.' '**There is no fear of God before their eyes.**'

Leaders live, like Christ, in the fear of the Lord. Isa. 11:2-3.

Heb. 12:28-29
"Therefore, since we are receiving a kingdom that cannot be shaken, let us be thankful, and so worship God acceptably **with reverence and awe, for our 'God is a consuming fire.'**

Isa. 30:30
"The Lord will cause people to **hear his majestic voice and will make them see his arm coming down with raging anger and consuming fire**, with cloudburst, thunderstorm and hail."

Gen. 3:10
"He answered, 'I heard you in the garden, and **I was afraid** because I was naked; so I hid.'

Lev. 26:16-17
"…then I will do this to you: I will bring on you **sudden terror**, wasting diseases and fever that will destroy your sight and sap your strength. You will plant seed in vain, because your enemies will eat it. I will set my face against you so that you will be defeated by your enemies; those who hate you will rule over you, and **you will flee even when no-one is pursuing you.**"

Prov. 28:1
"The wicked flee **though no-one pursues**, but the righteous are as bold as a lion."

Luke 12:4-5
'I tell you, my friends, do not be afraid of those who kill the body and after that can do no more. But **I will show you whom you should fear: fear him who, after your body has been killed, has authority to throw you into hell. Yes, I tell you, fear him.**"

2 Cor. 7:1
"Therefore, since we have these promises, dear friends, let us purify ourselves from everything that contaminates body and spirit, **perfecting holiness out of reverence for God.**"

Rev. 11:18
"The nations were angry, and your wrath has come. The time has come for judging the dead, and for rewarding your servants the prophets and your people **who revere your name, both small and great** — and for destroying those who destroy the earth.'

Prov. 8:13
"**To fear the Lord is to hate evil**; I hate pride and arrogance, evil behaviour and perverse speech."

Gen. 20:11
"Abraham replied, 'I said to myself,' "There is surely **no fear of God in this place**, and they will kill me because of my wife."'

Leaders live, like Christ, in the fear of the Lord. Isa. 11:2-3.

Col. 3:22 NASU
"Slaves, in all things obey those who are your masters on earth, **not with external service**, as those who *merely* please men, but with sincerity of heart, **fearing the Lord**."

Prov. 14:27
"The fear of the Lord is a fountain of life, turning a person from the snares of death."

Prov. 16:6
"Through love and faithfulness sin is atoned for; **through the fear of the Lord evil is avoided**."

Heb. 12:28
"Therefore, since we are receiving a kingdom that cannot be shaken, let us be thankful, and so worship God acceptably **with reverence and awe**…."

Heb. 5:7
"During the days of Jesus' life on earth, he offered up prayers and petitions with fervent cries and tears to the one who could save him from death, and he was heard because of his **reverent submission**."

Job 28:28
"And he said to the human race, '**The fear of the Lord — that is wisdom**, and to shun evil is understanding.'"

Ps. 111:10
"The fear of the Lord is the beginning of wisdom; all who follow his precepts have good understanding. To him belongs eternal praise."

Prov. 1:7
"The fear of the Lord is the beginning of knowledge, but fools despise wisdom and instruction."

Isa. 11:2-3
"The Spirit of the Lord will rest on him — the Spirit of wisdom and of understanding, the Spirit of counsel and of might, the Spirit of the knowledge and **fear of the Lord** — and **he will delight in the fear of the Lord**. He will not judge by what he sees with his eyes, or decide by what he hears with his ears…."

Ps. 112:1, 7, 8
"Praise the Lord. **Blessed are those who fear the Lord**, who find great delight in his commands." "They will have **no fear of bad news**; their hearts are steadfast, trusting in the Lord. Their hearts are secure, **they will have no fear**; in the end they will look in triumph on their foes."

Leaders live, like Christ, in the fear of the Lord. Isa. 11:2-3.

Ps 103:11-13

"For as high as the heavens are above the earth, so great is his love for those who fear him; as far as the east is from the west, **so far has he removed our transgressions from us.** As a father has compassion on his children, **so the Lord has compassion on those who fear him**...."

Leaders live, like Christ, in the fear of the Lord. Isa. 11:2-3.

The Leader and.....

Favour and Grace

Introduction

One of the most liberating truths of Scripture and Christian living is the truth of God's grace or favour. Without having a deep knowledge and experience of grace, the leader will suffer lack and make poor judgments or decisions regarding others. To be a gracious leader you must understand grace. To help others live under the favour of God, you must understand and live under that favour yourself. Grace or favour has to do with both *being* and *doing* as a Christian, as result of Christ's great redemptive work. Much of Christian experience is self-effort-centred, in an attempt to please God, by *doing*. Every believer should want to please God, but pleasing God, should arise out of loving Him. Rom 5:2 says, "...we have gained **access by faith into this grace** in which we now stand." The believer is *in* grace or *in* the favour of God. He stands *in* grace. God looks upon him with favour. Every day that he gets out of bed, he lives in God's gracious favour. It is this favour that says, "this (the believer) is my beloved son," just as God the Father said it about Christ.

The new creation that the believer has **become,** by believing in the finished work of Christ, is where grace begins to unfold magnificently in his or her life. The church is a community of grace—a family of believers in intimate relationship to God and with each other. This family lives together by His unmerited favour, expressed and experienced in the work of redemption. The leader learns to see himself and all others through the "glasses" of redemptive grace.

Grace and Favour Defined

Grace is such a large word theologically that it takes numerous other words to define it. It involves the following:

- Grace has to do with the means by which you were saved—it was **by grace.** Eph. 2:8-9. God took the initiative to save you from the destruction and death of sin, not by anything you merited or did but simply because He wanted to and chose to do so. There was nothing about you that warranted God's redeeming love—He simply chose to love on you despite your totally unlovely state. Titus 3:5-7. He took the initiative and made the invitation that gave you a revelation of Him and His love for you.

- Grace has to do with your standing, position or place before God. Rom. 5:1-2. How do you stand before God? What is your relationship to the One who is all holiness, all power and all knowledge? It is the unmerited, unwarranted,

Leaders live in the abundance of God's amazing grace!

unearned favour of God's grace that has taken you, from being a sinner into being a son, from being an orphan to being an heir, and from being the unlovely, to being a greatly loved one. Your state before God is said to be a "justified state." You didn't just receive a pardon, but the *record* of who you were and what you did, was expunged or destroyed for eternity. You could only arrive at such a position because of His marvellous, amazing grace! God cherishes you. As a leader you must fully (as much as one can) embrace this great truth in order to reflect this value to others about themselves in the ways that you relate to them. 1 Pet. 4:10 NCV says, "Each of you has received a gift to use to serve others. *Be good servants of God's various gifts of grace.*" As a leader, you are a grace-filled believer, ministering God's favour to others. You are a gracious person and a "grace-giver" to others.

- Grace has to do with the power or ability you now have to live a life pleasing to God. Acts 13:43; Phil. 2:13. Just as you were saved by grace, you live in the power of that grace, as your faith, in that grace, releases the power of righteousness within you. Your ability to choose right and your actual right choices come from the reservoir of grace within you, released by your believing. **All of grace is released by faith**. Rom. 5:2; Rom. 1:17; Rom. 4:13; 9:30. The righteousness we have received is not only a static state of our standing before God, but a righteousness released, moment by moment, in our love walk with Him, as we live connected by faith. If your faith is in your own ability to choose rightly, you unwittingly live by law—the mere intellectual recognition of right and wrong and the attempt to logically choose right. This results in failure. Only by faith in Him and His provided grace (ability) can you live making right choices continually. Gal. 3:2-5 NLT.

- Grace has to do with special privileges, opportunities, and blessings God bestows upon you. Moses, whose life was threatened as an infant was "graced" to become leader of Israel. Gideon, an ordinary Israelite, was "graced" to become a great leader of Israel. Esther the orphan, was "graced" to become Queen on a throne. David, the shepherd boy, was "graced" to become the King of Israel. Christ, was "graced" to move from a manger to the Throne. Saul, was "graced" to move from being a murderer to become a great apostle. 1 Cor. 15:9-10.

- Grace has to do with God's disposition toward you as his son or daughter. Gen. 6:8. It could be said that God has an attitude of grace or a gracious attitude toward you. As a loving Father, He looks to release the favour He has provided for all, on all.

- Grace has to do with gifts or abilities to function in a specific way in the family of God or the Body of Christ. Eph. 4:7-13; 1 Cor. 12:4-6 says, "There are different kinds of *gifts*, but the same Spirit distributes them. There are different kinds of *service*, but the same Lord. There are different kinds of *working*, but in all of them and in everyone it is the same God at work." The original Greek word

Leaders live in the abundance of God's amazing grace!

translated for "gifts" in this passage is the word, "charisma," which means "grace gifts or gifts of grace." These Divinely-given abilities and instincts are designed to enable every believer to serve the Body of Christ and the Lost according to the specific ability they possess. They are *received* gifts, not earned gifts, as there is no such thing as an "earned gift." 1 Cor. 4:7.

- Grace has to do with supernatural abilities God grants you as an expression of His love and power to demonstrate the miraculous. Acts 4:33; Acts 14:3.

- Grace has to do with the actual presence of power and ability when the believer seems to feel his weakest and most vulnerable. 2 Cor. 12:9-10. Often a leader "feels" the weakness of his humanity but that is not his reality. His Bible-based reality is that he is actually in the presence of great power in that moment. He acts in faith in that revelation. Subsequently, circumstances and conditions are radically altered because he is acting out of the truth of who he is and the amazing grace that is **now present**. He is, in that "grace-bestowed-moment," not acting out of the message of his weak humanity. Matt. 19:26; Matt. 17:20. With man, many things are impossible but the leader is not merely a man and thus nothing is impossible for him. This is the position and power of grace. It is the life and lifestyle of the leader.

- Grace has to do with power to finish a great mission, given by God, released at times by simply shouting, "Grace, Grace!" to it. Zech. 4:7 NKJV. Grace mentioned twice here. Once at the beginning and once at the end. Grace to begin and grace to finish--that is the life of a leader.

Access into This Amazing Grace

Although grace is unwarranted, unmerited, and unearned, it must be accessed. In redemption, there are two dimensions: provision and application. God has, in His gracious favour, provided all of the amazing benefits we saw mentioned above. It remains for man to apply those benefits that have been provided by the means that God has designed. He said, "It is finished." Now it remains for all of mankind to receive what has been provided. If he chooses not to receive what has been provided, in the only ways it can be received, he lives outside the benefits that the grace of God provides. God loves the sinner. However, if the sinner rejects that loving, he ultimately denies the grace provided and ends up in Hell. The Scripture explains, that grace in all of its many forms, is received and applied to our lives through two means:

1. Humility. James 4:6 ESV. The opposite of humility is pride, independence, self-will, self-effort and self-dependence. When we yield to Whom God is and what He says, we exhibit humility and become a candidate for His grace and favour. You cannot resist God in self-will or self-dependence and receive grace. God resists the proud. He does not reward them or "grace" them. He did grant you grace in the deception of your sinful state prior to becoming a believer. That grace was a favour of *revelation* to invite you into relationship with Him.

Leaders live in the abundance of God's amazing grace!

However, He will not continue to pour gracious favour upon you if you walk in prideful independence as a believer. 1 Pet. 5:5-6 NKJV; Matt. 23:12; Phil. 2:8-9. Pride is automatically a resistance of God and His grace. In the barren place of pride, we discover our inner bankruptcy and return to the outpouring of His gracious help. He always is there, ready to help but sometimes may have to wait until we "re-discover" humility, and call upon Him. Parents can often see their children struggling but not wanting any help from their parents. While still loving them, they wait until the child looks up from the struggle and calls for help. Grace or help, in this sense, is always available but temporarily unused because of self-dependence. Grace is accessed by humility.

An important distinction must be made here. God gives great and powerful gifts to men and women. Those gifts operate through men and women who walk humbly or proudly. They produce simply because they are expressions of God's power that He will not recall. They are powerful measures of grace that flow *from* ministries who may be walking in pride. They are, even though expressed through self-important, prideful ministries, expressions of God's love to those who are the recipients. However, the ministry who walks in prideful independence will eventually implode, painfully illustrating the truth of God's resistance of pride. Dan. 4:37. It was pride that caused a great ministry in Heaven to fall—Lucifer became the Devil. Ez. 28:13-17. Grace or the ability to express God in power and blessing to others, can flow **from** a leader as he/she expresses their "grace-gifts" or grace-enabled abilities. However, grace flows **into** our hearts as we walk in humility with the Lord. Many a "great ministry" has fallen eventually, while doing amazing things, because of their inner heart attitude. They had "stuff" going on even while they were ministering powerfully. The leader who walks in pride, uses his gifts, but his inner poverty of grace, will eventually bring him to disgrace. He implodes. 2 Sam. 1:19. Sustaining humility, we sustain the flow of His grace to us on the *inside* and our lives, families and ministries are sustained.

2. Faith. Rom. 5:1-2. One of the great truths of Christian living is the abiding constant of *availability*. The grace to be, do, and to accomplish is always available. It is simply there—inside the believer. The believer doesn't have to search for it, call for it, stress for it, or work for it—it is simply abiding all the time. Like the human heart inside each person, you never wonder if you have one. You never go out to find one. You can't work to get one. It simply is there, inside you, receiving blood and pumping blood out to every part of your body. You believe this happens. The same is true with grace. You have a grace-filled spirit that is transforming you, enabling you, and enlarging you every day as you simply believe. You have access to that abiding grace as Rom. 5:1 declares, "Therefore, since we have been justified through faith, we have peace with God through our Lord Jesus Christ, through whom **we have gained access by faith into this grace** in which we now stand." Every dimension of grace is accessed and enabled by the exercise of faith. It is not accessed and enabled by knowledge,

Leaders live in the abundance of God's amazing grace!

but by the exercise of faith. Are you believing every day and every moment that His grace is *on* you, *in* you, and flowing *from* you? Are you "standing" in His grace? Grace can be said to be activated by the exercise of our faith or by our believing. I wear the "glasses of faith" and live each day looking for and expecting the manifestation of His favour.

Leaders Living in Grace, Expressing Grace-Gifts and Being Gracious
Leaders are meant to live in the grace that Christ died to bring them. They are not to have merely occasional experiences of the vast resource of grace provided for them. Their entire lives are to be an expression of the grace of God.

1. They **live** in grace. Rom. 5:1-2; 2 Cor. 6:1-2. A leader's sufficiency is not in themselves but in Him, in His grace. They don't live in inadequacy, excuses, weakness or fear. Rom. 5:17. Living from the inside out, they avail themselves of grace every day through their humility, dependence and faith. 1 Cor. 15:10.

2. They **minister to others** out of the great reservoir of grace. Standing in grace, they minister out of grace. 1 Pet. 4:10 NCV. You give away what you have received. Matt. 10:8 NASU. A leader has power and spiritual authority to change our world—those resident gifts, are grace-gifts, to minister to others for the glory of God. Rom. 12:6; 15:15-16.

3. They are **gracious in their speech**. Eph. 4:29, 30 NKJV. Leaders are those that use their amazing "word-power" to build the lives of others. They enquire, they bless, they mediate, they dial down tension, fear, anger and confusion, they affirm, they encourage, they pray, and build the lives of others with their words. Leaders release the disposition and power of God's favour into the lives of others through their words.

4. They **model** grace. 2 Cor. 1:12; 2 Cor. 12:9. Living as examples, they understand and lean on the grace of God to do so. Even in their weak areas, they discover the presence and availability to succeed, silencing the voice of weakness, inadequacy, and fear.

5. They **excel** in the grace of giving financially. 2 Cor. 8:7; 9:8. Leaders make certain their material existence is anchored in a Heavenly value system by living a generous lifestyle where money is concerned.

6. They **recognise** and **affirm** the unique and special giftings of grace that others possess so that God's great plan is accomplished. Gal. 2:9. There is no spirit of competition, comparison or insecurity among them.

Leaders live in the abundance of God's amazing grace!

Application
In small groups discuss how the grace of God has impacted you as a person in the following areas:

- Your view of yourself

- Your view of your own abilities

- Your ministry to others

- Your view of others, especially those so, so different from you and those you think are so much more greatly gifted than you are (wrongful comparison)

- Your response to challenging or overwhelming situations or opportunities

Read the book, "What's So Amazing About Grace?" by Phillip Yancey.

Leaders live in the abundance of God's amazing grace!

Favour and Grace Scriptures

Eph. 2:8-9
"For it is **by grace you have been saved**, through faith — and this is not from yourselves, it is the gift of God — not by works, so that no-one can boast."

Titus 3:5-7
"…he saved us, **not because of righteous things we had done**, but because of his mercy. He saved us through the washing of rebirth and renewal by the Holy Spirit, whom he poured out on us generously through Jesus Christ our Saviour, so that, having been **justified by his grace**, we might become heirs having the hope of eternal life."

Rom. 5:1-2
"Therefore, since we have been justified through faith, we have peace with God through our Lord Jesus Christ, through whom we have gained **access by faith into this grace** in which we now stand. And we boast in the hope of the glory of God."

Acts 13:43
"When the congregation was dismissed, many of the Jews and devout converts to Judaism followed Paul and Barnabas, who talked with them and **urged them to continue in the grace of God**."

Phil. 2:13
"…for it is **God who works in you to will and to act** in order to fulfil his good purpose."

Rom. 5:2
"…through whom **we have gained access by faith into this grace** in which we now stand. And we boast in the hope of the glory of God."

Rom. 1:17
"For in the gospel the righteousness of God is revealed--**a righteousness that is by faith from first to last,** just as it is written: 'The righteous will live by faith.'

Rom. 3:22 AMP
"…the **righteousness of God which comes by believing**…."

Rom. 9:30
"What then shall we say? That the Gentiles, who did not pursue righteousness, have obtained it, a **righteousness that is by faith**…."

Gal. 3:2, 3, 5 NLT
"Let me ask you this one question: Did you receive the Holy Spirit by obeying the law of Moses? Of course not! You received the Spirit **because you believed** the message

Leaders live in the abundance of God's amazing grace!

you heard about Christ. How foolish can you be? After starting your Christian lives in the Spirit, why are you now trying to become perfect by your own human effort?...I ask you again, does God give you the Holy Spirit and work miracles among you because you obey the law? Of course not! It is because you **believe the message you heard about Christ.**"

1 Cor. 15:9-10
"For I am the least of the apostles and do not even deserve to be called an apostle, because I persecuted the church of God. But **by the grace of God I am what I am, and his grace to me was not without effect.** No, I worked harder than all of them yet not I, but the grace of God that was with me."

Gen. 6:8
"But Noah found **favour in the eyes of the Lord.**"

Eph. 4:7-13
"But **to each one of us grace has been given** as Christ apportioned it. This is why it says: 'When he ascended on high, he took many captives and **gave gifts to people.**' (What does 'he ascended' mean except that he also descended to the lower, earthly regions? He who descended is the very one who ascended higher than all the heavens, in order to fill the whole universe.) So Christ, himself gave the apostles, the prophets, the evangelists, and the pastors and teachers, to equip God's people for works of service, so that the body of Christ may be built up until we all reach unity in the faith and in the knowledge of the Son of God and become mature, attaining to the whole measure of the fullness of Christ."

1 Cor. 4:7
"For who makes you different from anyone else? What do you have that you did not receive? And if you did receive it, why do you boast as though you did not?"

Acts 4:33
"With great power the apostles continued to testify to the resurrection of the Lord Jesus, and **God's grace was so powerfully at work in them all.**"

Acts 14:3
"So Paul and Barnabas spent considerable time there, speaking boldly for the Lord, **who confirmed the message of his grace by enabling them to do perform signs and wonders.**"

2 Cor. 12:9-10
"But he said to me, 'My **grace is sufficient for you, for my power is made perfect in weakness.**' Therefore I will boast all the more gladly about my weaknesses, so that Christ's power may rest on me. That is why, for Christ's sake, I delight in weaknesses, in insults, in hardships, in persecutions, in difficulties. For when I am weak, then I am strong."

Leaders live in the abundance of God's amazing grace!

Matt. 19:26
"Jesus looked at them and said, '**With man this is impossible**, but with God all things are possible.'

Matt. 17:20
"He replied, 'Because you have so little faith. Truly I tell you, if you have faith as small as a mustard seed, you can say to this mountain, "Move from here to there" and it will move. **Nothing will be impossible for you.**'

Zech. 4:7 NKJV
"'Who *are* you, O great mountain? Before Zerubbabel *you shall become* a plain! And he shall bring forth the capstone, with shouts of **"Grace, grace to it!"**

James 4:6 ESV
"But he gives more grace. Therefore it says, "**God opposes the proud, but gives grace to the humble.**"

1 Peter 5:5 NKJV
"God resists the proud but gives **grace to the humble.**"

Matt. 23:12
"For those who **exalt themselves will be humbled, and those who humble themselves will be exalted.**"

Phil. 2:8-9
"And being found in appearance as a man, **he humbled himself** by becoming obedient to death — even death on a cross! **Therefore God exalted him** to the highest place and gave him the name that is above every name…."

Dan. 4:37
"Now I, Nebuchadnezzar, praise and exalt and glorify the King of heaven, because everything he does is right and all his ways are just. And **those who walk in pride he is able to humble.**"

Ezek. 28:13-17
"You were in Eden, the garden of God; every precious stone adorned you: carnelian, chrysolite and emerald, topaz, onyx and jasper, lapis lazuli, turquoise and beryl. Your settings and mountings were made of gold; on the day you were created they were prepared. You were anointed as a guardian cherub, for so I ordained you. You were on the holy mount of God; you walked among the fiery stones. You were blameless in your ways from the day you were created till wickedness was found in you. Through your widespread trade you were filled with violence, and you sinned. So I drove you in disgrace from the mount of God, and I expelled you, O guardian cherub, from among the fiery stones. **Your heart became proud** on account of your beauty, and you corrupted your wisdom because of your splendour. So I threw you to the earth; I made a spectacle of you before kings."

Leaders live in the abundance of God's amazing grace!

2 Sam. 1:19
"How the mighty have fallen!"

Rom. 5:1-2
"Therefore, since we have been justified through faith, we have peace with God through our Lord Jesus Christ, through whom **we have gained access by faith into this grace in which we now stand.** And we boast in the hope of the glory of God."

2 Cor. 6:1-2
"As God's fellow-workers we urge you **not to receive God's grace in vain**. For he says, 'In the time of my favour I heard you, and in the day of salvation I helped you.' I tell you, **now is the time of God's favour**, now is the day of salvation."

Rom. 5:17
"For if, by the trespass of the one man, death reigned through that one man, how much more will those who receive **God's abundant provision of grace and of the gift of righteousness reign in life** through the one man, Jesus Christ!"

1 Cor. 15:10
"But by the grace of God I am what I am, and his grace to me was not without effect. No, I worked harder than all of them yet not I, but the grace of God that was with me."

1 Peter 4:10 NCV
"Each of you has received a gift to use to serve others. Be good servants of God's various **gifts of grace.**"

Matt. 10:8 NASU
"Heal *the* sick, raise *the* dead, cleanse *the* lepers, cast out demons. **Freely you received, freely give."**

Rom. 12:6
"We have different gifts, according to the grace given to each of us. If your gift is prophesying, then prophesy in accordance with your faith."

Rom. 15:15-16
"Yet I have written to you quite boldly on some points, as if to remind you of them again, because **of the grace God gave me to be a minister** of Christ Jesus to the Gentiles. He gave me the priestly duty of proclaiming the gospel of God, so that the Gentiles might become an offering acceptable to God, sanctified by the Holy Spirit."

Eph. 4:29-30 NKJV
"Let no corrupt word proceed out of your mouth, but what is good for necessary edification, that **it may impart grace to the hearers.**"

Leaders live in the abundance of God's amazing grace!

2 Cor. 1:12
"Now this is our boast: Our conscience testifies that **we have conducted ourselves in the world, and especially in our relations with you, with integrity and godly sincerity**. We have done so not according to worldly wisdom but **according to God's grace**."

2 Cor. 12:9
"But he said to me, '**My grace is sufficient** for you, for my power is made perfect in weakness.' Therefore I will boast all the more gladly about my weaknesses, **so that Christ's power may rest on me**."

2 Cor. 8:7
"But since you excel in everything — in faith, in speech, in knowledge, in complete earnestness and in the love we have kindled in you — see that you also **excel in this grace of giving**."

2 Cor. 9:8 ESV
"And God is able to make **all grace abound to you**, so that having all sufficiency in all things at all times, **you may abound in every good work**."

Gal. 2:9
"James, Peter and John, those reputed to be pillars, gave me and Barnabas the right hand of fellowship when **they recognised the grace given to me. They agreed that we should go to the Gentiles, and they to the Jews.**

Leaders live in the abundance of God's amazing grace!

The Leader and.....

Fathers

Introduction
One of the most significant parts of a leader's life is his or her relationship to a spiritual father, even as they relate to their Heavenly Father. Observing and working with so many leaders over the last forty years, I have seen the multitude of father-less leaders we have today. We live in a world that is increasingly characterised by rejection, betrayal, rebellion and hurt. Matt. 10:21 says (of the last days), 'Brother will betray brother to death, and **a father his child; children will rebel against their parents** and have them put to death.'

However, Jesus said in John 14:18, "I will not leave you as orphans...." Paul referred numerous times to his spiritual son, Timothy, and how eventually Timothy became a "fellow-worker." Rom. 16:21. The prayer that Jesus taught His disciples to pray begins with, "Our **Father**...."

As the family is the "manufacturing plant of society," and there are so many dysfunctional and fragmented families, so many believers enter into leadership life with major deficits in themselves. It is not their fault that they grew up without a good father figure in their lives. However, they often are even unaware of what is missing from their lives as a result of their father-less upbringing. Fatherless leaders fail to be fathers and the cycle of "fatherlessness" continues. The Bible makes clear the need we all have for spiritual fathers. Mal. 4:6 NKJV. One of the primary ways God has of expressing His relationship to us as His children is to describe Himself as Father. Jesus taught us to pray, "Our Father...." It is in this relationship to God as our Father, that we find so many great insights of the need and practice of fathering or spiritual parenting. Ex. 3:15. 2 Cor. 6:18. There is a necessary and unique grace transferred to a life from a spiritual father that is absolutely essential to life and ministry.

1 Cor. 4:14-17 NCV says, "I am writing this to give you a *warning* **as my own dear children**. For though you may have ten thousand teachers in Christ, **you do not have many fathers**. Through the Good News **I became your father in Christ** Jesus, so I beg you, please follow my example. That is why I am sending to you **Timothy, my son in the Lord**. I love Timothy, and he is faithful. He will help you remember my way of life in Christ Jesus, just as I teach it in all the churches everywhere."

Great preachers and teachers are not necessarily "spiritual fathers." Sincere, passionate, would-be leaders are not necessarily good spiritual sons and daughters. All too often believers do not know how to be sons or daughters. Leaders often do not know how to

Leaders embrace spiritual fathers, their wisdom and the mantle they carry.

be spiritual parents. They model to others what has been modelled to them out of their earthly parents and the leaders they have worked under. The leader should suspect that if they did not have a good earthly father, they may well have some "father" deficiencies in their lives. These deficiencies will need to be addressed in order for them to succeed in life and be able to encourage the maturity of others. Ps. 68:5 tells us that God is a "Father to the fatherless" and thus leaders learn to become "fathers" and "mothers" to those who had no father or did not have a good father or mother in growing up naturally and spiritually.

Characteristics of Fatherless Leaders and Fatherless Sons and Daughters
The Bible speaks of fathers over 1,612 times. It must be important. Across the globe there are hundreds of thousands of men and women in places of leadership in ministry. Many of them grew up "fatherless" in one dimension or another. No matter how proficient and effective they are, when they are functioning in the grace residing in their giftings, they struggle to produce, in their most promising followers, anything other than greatly-skilled leaders. Because they themselves have inherent weaknesses, due to fatherlessness, they reproduce "after their kind." Many painful experiences come needlessly to them and those that work or attempt to work alongside them. The ones that revere them the most for their great gifts, come to places of hurt and offence. Often this is because they cannot negotiate a stable, trusting, secure, enduring relationship with their great leader. This is an unnecessary tragedy. The following are some of the results of fatherlessness in ministry life:

- Rebellion, in a spiritual son or daughter, is sometimes based in their perception of being rejected by the spiritual father. The attempts that are made to correct or adjust them are met with resistance and rebellion—an instinctive response to an earlier rejection. "To protect myself from hurt, I reject all hurtful things without conscious reference to the nature of what is hurting and why I feel the pain." They do not distinguish their need for correction and adjustment and subsequently take the correction as a message that they are being rejected as a person.

  They fail to realise that the "flesh" or carnal nature will always feel the painful penetration of the sword of the Spirit which is the Word. Heb. 12:11. The pain of "sword-word" penetration is ok and necessary. It is fundamentally *different* from personal rejection. No one *is* a flaw but everyone has flaws. Denying the validity of any correction that is given or attempted to be given, the "fatherless" son or daughter moves inward and/or geographically to a place where there is no such pain to be encountered—they hope. However, wise, secure leaders realise the necessity of living in the old adage, "accountable, available, flexible and adjustable," so they will become fully who God has made them to be. They receive correction not as rejection but as loving improvement. Prov. 12:1; Ps. 141:5.

Leaders embrace spiritual fathers, their wisdom and the mantle they carry.

- Relational poverty is the result, as the insecure, uncorrectible person holds others outside of real and transparent relationships. Fatherless believers or leaders are unwittingly, self-protecting (based in fear) instead of self-giving (based in love). They learn to *manage* relationships at a level that enables them, so they believe, to succeed. Inwardly and secretly they long for the fulfilment and safety of deep relationships, however. They struggle to trust anyone deeply.

- Comparison—leading to jealousy or self-denigration. Unwittingly striving for the position they think validates or affirms who they are as a person, they are constantly looking at the opportunities others receive. The result of this activity is either to be jealous and angry or discouraged with their own apparent lack. Even their own successes do not leave them with a sense of value, worth, or confidence in whom they are in Christ. What they do just isn't good enough, powerful enough, great enough or skilful enough to get them, what others seem to have so easily.

- Works-based attempts at approval. Fatherless believers and leaders have a great struggle to believe they have value, worth and are capable of making significant contribution. The lie, that they are of little or no value, is deeply embedded in their thinking. Because this deception is so painful, they are always working to gain some relief from it and secure the place of esteem, appreciation and praise that others are receiving. They work hard to gain this and get angry when they don't succeed or others receive the praise or credit for what they, in their minds, are due. They desperately want what every person that is born wants: a father's approval that says, "Well done!" Unfortunately, all of the praise and commendation that does come their way seems to go into a "black hole of nothingness" that brings no relief and peace to their unwitting quest for value and significance. They ride a "roller-coaster" of disappointment. Unwittingly, their inner motivation to gain, robs them of the blessing that can only come from pure, selfless giving. *The best way to gain approval is to selflessly give it to others.*

- Sometimes leaders who have been "fatherless" for various reasons live in a "drifting mode." They seem to lack any *firmness of purpose* or drive to complete a mission. They may be kind, helpful and even loving, but are often not faithful in tasks or in communication with those over them. They desire to be fruitful but there is no "inner push" to overcome difficulties, pursue a calling and take great responsibility. They sometimes resist adjustment, taking all correction as a personal attack on themselves. They live in a "cocoon" of self-protection, yet all the while wanting to be greatly productive. They can wander from church to church seeking the "magic bullet" for their malaise or frustration with themselves.

The aforementioned problems that arise out of fatherlessness often cause men and women to leave churches and look for another place to "settle." They carry hurts

Leaders embrace spiritual fathers, their wisdom and the mantle they carry.

and wounds from their previous experience. Those wounds affect their perspective on the new place they attend. Somewhere and sometime, in the great expanse of Christendom, they will have to **sit** down and **trust** someone enough to place their lives in their hands so they can be healed and progress in fruitfulness. A good spiritual father and good spiritual mother are best able to help them as they humbly trust their lives to them.

Portrait or Profile of A Spiritual Father
The truth of "father" must be a huge truth to absorb, as God Himself, describes Himself to us all as, The Father. The truth of "sonship" must be huge, as the second person of the Trinity is The Son, who lives in constant relationship to The Father. God also designed earthly families with this structure and relationship design. Job 29:1-25; Jer. 31:9. The following are some characteristics of a spiritual father:

- Compassionate – Ps. 103:13
- Gift-giving – Mt. 7:11
- Loving – 1 John 3:1; Mk. 1:11
- Lovingly correcting – Heb. 12:9
- Providing revelations and insights – Mt. 11:25
- Encouraging – 1 Thes. 2:11, 12
- Comforting – 1 Thes. 2:11, 12
- Urging on to success – 1 Thes. 2:11, 12
- Providing a father's prophetic blessing – Gen. 49:28; Heb. 11:20, 21
- Defending and responding to the cause of the fatherless – Deut. 10:18
- Passing a spiritual heritage to their sons and daughters – Josh. 4:21-24 ESV
- Showing kindness – 2 Sam. 10:2
- Providing an example in ministry and worship – 1 Chron. 25:3, 6
- Meeting needs – Job 29:16
- Instructing – Prov. 1:8
- Delighting in sons and daughters – Prov. 3:12
- A heart "turned toward" sons and daughters – Mal. 4:6 NKJV

Leaders embrace spiritual fathers, their wisdom and the mantle they carry.

- Merciful – Luke 6:36

- Giving their inheritance to their sons – Luke 15:31

- Are affectionate – Luke 15:20

- Are celebrators – Luke 15:23, 24

- Are forgivers – Luke 23:34

- Are a safe place for the lives of sons and daughters – Luke 23:46

- A trainers – Eph. 6:4

- Proud to serve alongside their sons – Phil. 2:22

- Knowing the Lord and allowing their sons to know them – 1 John 2:13; 1 Thes. 2:8; Col. 4:7

- Affirming their sons/daughters – Luke 3:22

Portrait of a Spiritual Son or Daughter

- Honouring their fathers – Mal. 1:6; Matt. 19:19

- Loving unconditionally – Mt. 5:44, 45

- Having prophetic capacity – Acts 2:17

- Are led by the Spirit – Rom. 8:14 NKJV

- Have a spirit of "sonship" (adoption as sons) – Rom. 8:15 NASU; Gal. 4:6

- Live separated from evil – 2 Cor. 6:16-18; 1 Thes. 5:5

- Possessing an amazing inheritance – Gal. 4:5 ESV

- Receiving hardship as training – Heb. 12:7 ESV

- Possessing a permanent place in the family – John 8:35

- Serving with their fathers – Phil. 2:22

Fathers With Sons and Daughters and Daughters and Sons With Fathers
Philippians 2:22. All relationships are comprised of three major components: time, words and actions. To develop a father-son relationship there must be time spent together, significant words exchanged and actions that grow and cement the bonds of such a potentially powerful and loving relationship. It is a loving friendship that is **built**

Leaders embrace spiritual fathers, their wisdom and the mantle they carry.

by the effort and contribution from both sides. It is not based in demand, expectation, or striving but in a mutual respect and valuing on both sides. The father invests, the sons and daughters receive—both end up beautifully blessed. The father leaves a greater legacy and the sons and daughters receive the wisdom and encouragement that enables their lives to be so much more enhanced, than they would have been. Often church structures unwittingly work against this kind of development by the unintended restriction of availability of spiritual parents. They simply do not make the task of "spiritual parenting," a priority.

How To Connect With a Spiritual Father or Mother
Simply meet up with a potential spiritual father or mother and ask them if they would consent to being a spiritual father or mother to you. Think about what you want or would expect from them, taking into account that they have others they "father," "mother," or mentor as well. Tell them what you are thinking in tentative terms. Let them say what they can do and if they are willing (most of the time they are), get on with scheduling your first meeting. Be appreciative of their time and input, love and care. Respond in generosity and acts of kindness that let them know that you are not simply selfishly expecting them to do something that they are not obligated to do. Communication of your major decisions, challenges, dreams, struggles, and blessings provides an opportunity for them to release grace into your life. Give them opportunity to affirm you, love on you, celebrate you and advise you.

How To Replace Your Own "Fatherlessness" With a Fathering Grace
Fathers are unselfish lovers *not looking* for something to reward their love. They know that love is always right and because it is meant to produce growth and maturity in others, it will--despite the amount of time necessary to bring it about. They see beyond today and the current distress, to a day of great blessing, peace, fulfilment and fruitfulness. Let a father's unique grace flow into your life by mutual arrangement. You will begin to see that what they do blesses and adds to you and you will eventually reach into that reservoir and bless others with the same. Imitate their loving and caring in your relationships with others, while you are receiving the wisdom of your spiritual parents.

Being A Spiritual Father or Mother As A Leader
Paul wrote that often believers had many instructors but not many fathers. He described a great need that is even in sharper focus in our day as so many believers come from homes that had no father or a dysfunctional one. Leaders will learn to live and act as spiritual parents before anyone actually refers to them as "Dad" or "Mom" in a spiritual sense. The purpose of spiritual fathers and mothers is to raise sons and daughters **to also be spiritual parents**. Leaders grow up, in a relationship to their spiritual parents, to *become* spiritual parents.

Spiritual sons and daughters are capable of discerning the spirit of love, protection, and care that comes from spiritual parents. They instinctively want to be close to them, especially, if they were lacking such closeness with their own parents. How

Leaders embrace spiritual fathers, their wisdom and the mantle they carry.

does a leader act like a "father" or "mother?" The following are some guidelines for the "parenting" role that leaders are to have in the lives of others.

1. Don't act parental in the same way or sense as biological parents would approach their children. Adults don't usually require all the simple instructions that natural parents give over and over. If your tone of voice is "parental" instead of loving advice, you will not be the fresh, objective voice of a loving spiritual parent but perhaps, the voice of someone, that hurt, neglected, or abused them.

2. Encourage and advise. Don't tell them what to do.

3. Don't give advice about everything. Let them ask for advice or counsel.

4. Celebrate their successes.

5. Remind them of all their many assets and capabilities and the grace that is on their lives.

6. Don't assume anything. If you think something, ask about it. However, don't assume they want to open up about everything all at once or ever. Let them, in God's timing and prompting, share their hearts with you. Don't be overly intrusive.

7. Love on them…verbally, with holy hugs, and kindnesses.

8. Pray for them. Allow the Holy Spirit to give you insights and words to give them at the right time.

9. Be extremely careful about adjusting a spiritual son or daughter. If they have had a reactive response to authority earlier in their lives, they can hear another's voice in your voice and run away like they did last time.

10. Remember that deep trust takes time to build. Your level of compassion, desire to help and encourage, may not be the same as their level to receive in the early stages.

11. Be safe. Meet in public places or if in a home, only when others are in the building. It is always good to err on the side of caution in maintaining the most transparent activity. Keeping relationships with spiritual sons or daughters of the opposite sex spiritually and emotionally healthy is wise. Making sure that your spouse is both aware, in agreement and is most often present is best. These simple steps protect both parties.

Some years ago I received a phone call. I answered to hear the voice of a stranger who identified himself as a believer who had gotten my telephone from a friend of a friend in Australia. He was, at that moment, standing by the side of the road carrying

Leaders embrace spiritual fathers, their wisdom and the mantle they carry.

a briefcase and a small duffel bag. He needed a place to stay. He had been sleeping on the settee of a friend's acquaintance but now was required to move on. He asked would I come and get him. I said, "Yes." In short, he was a Christian young man who had had a broken relationship with his father and had left Australia to get away from him. He stayed a short period in our home. He went on to say of the hurts he had with his father. I asked him what he wanted to do for the Lord. He said he wanted to be the administrator of a Christian school but there were no such jobs available. I lovingly explained that he was a "prodigal son" who needed to return to Australia and reconcile with his father. He did. Three months later he wrote. He had gone to his father and reconciled. His father received him and made radical changes in the way he related to his son. He immediately asked him to go fishing with him—something the boy had always wanted to do but had never been invited. He went. Their relationship began to be very close. He got a job as an administrator of a Christian school. It all started with re-connecting with his father.

Application

In small groups discuss the impact your father has had on your life and ministry. Pray for each other as you identify weaknesses and strengths.

In small groups discuss how you can take a "fatherly" or "motherly" role in another's life without coming across like their parents perhaps did when they were a teenager.

Decide on pursuing a "spiritual father" if you have not had one. If you do have one, pursue him in an enlightened way for greater impact in your life and ministry.

Read "The Father You Have Been Waiting For," by Mark Stibbe.

Leaders embrace spiritual fathers, their wisdom and the mantle they carry.

Father Scriptures

Rom. 16:21
"Timothy, **my co-worker**, sends his greetings to you, as do Lucius, Jason and Sosipater, my fellow Jews."

Mal. 4:6 NKJV
"And he will turn the **hearts of the fathers** to the children, and the **hearts of the children** to their fathers, Lest I come and strike the earth with a curse."

Ex. 3:15
"God also said to Moses, 'Say to the Israelites, "The Lord, **the God of your fathers** — the God of Abraham, the God of Isaac and the God of Jacob — has sent me to you."' 'This is my name for ever, the name you shall call me from generation to generation."

2 Cor. 6:18
"And, '**I will be a Father to you**, and you will be my sons and daughters, says the Lord Almighty.'

Heb. 12:11
"No discipline seems pleasant at the time, but painful. Later on, however, it produces a harvest of righteousness and peace for those who have been trained by it."

Job 29:1-25
"Job continued his discourse: 'How I long for the months gone by, for the days when God watched over me, when his lamp shone on my head and by his light I walked through darkness! Oh, for the days when I was in my prime, when God's intimate friendship blessed my house, when the Almighty was still with me and my children were around me, when my path was drenched with cream and the rock poured out for me streams of olive oil. 'When I went to the gate of the city and took my seat in the public square, the young men saw me and stepped aside and the old men rose to their feet; the chief men refrained from speaking and covered their mouths with their hands; the voices of the nobles were hushed, and their tongues stuck to the roof of their mouths. Whoever heard me spoke well of me, and those who saw me commended me, because I rescued the poor who cried for help, and the **fatherless** who had none to assist them. The one who was dying blessed me; I made the widow's heart sing. I put on righteousness as my clothing; justice was my robe and my turban. I was eyes to the blind and feet to the lame. I was a father to the needy; I took up the case of the stranger. I broke the fangs of the wicked and snatched the victims from their teeth. 'I thought, "I shall die in my own house, my days as numerous as the grains of sand. My roots will reach to the water, and the dew will lie all night on my branches. My glory will not fade, the bow will be ever new in my hand." 'People listened to me expectantly, waiting in silence for my counsel. After I had spoken, they spoke no more; my words fell gently on their ears. They waited for me as for showers and drank in my words as the spring rain. When I smiled at them, they scarcely believed it; the light of

Leaders embrace spiritual fathers, their wisdom and the mantle they carry.

my face was precious to them. I chose the way for them and sat as their chief; I dwelt as a king among his troops; I was like one who comforts mourners."

Jer. 31:9
"They will come with weeping; they will pray as I bring them back. I will lead them beside streams of water on a level path where they will not stumble, **because I am Israel's father, and Ephraim is my firstborn son.**"

Ps. 103:13
"As a **father has compassion** on his children, so the Lord has compassion on those who fear him…."

Matt. 7:11
"If you, then, though you are evil, know how to give good gifts to your children, how much more will **your Father in heaven** give good gifts to those who ask him!"

1 John 3:1 KJV
"Behold, what manner of **love the Father** hath bestowed upon us, that we should be called the sons of God: therefore the world knoweth us not, because it knew him not."

Mark 1:11
"And a voice came from heaven: **'You are my Son, whom I love; with you I am well pleased.'**"

Heb. 12:9
"Moreover, we have all had human **fathers who disciplined us** and we respected them for it. How much more should we submit to the Father of spirits and live!"

Matt. 11:25
"At that time Jesus said, 'I praise you, Father, Lord of heaven and earth, because you have hidden these things from the wise and learned, and **revealed them to little children.**'"

1 Thess. 2:11-12
"For you know that we dealt with each of you as a **father** deals with his own children, **encouraging, comforting and urging you to live lives worthy** of God, who calls you into his kingdom and glory."

Gen. 49:28
"All these are the twelve tribes of Israel, and this is what their **father** said to them when **he blessed them, giving each the blessing appropriate** to him."

Heb. 11:20-21
"By faith **Isaac blessed Jacob and Esau in regard to their future.** By faith Jacob, when he was dying, **blessed each of Joseph's sons**, and worshipped as he leaned on the top of his staff."

Leaders embrace spiritual fathers, their wisdom and the mantle they carry.

Deut. 10:18
"**He defends the cause of the fatherless** and the widow, and loves the foreigner residing among you, giving them food and clothing."

Josh. 4:21-24 ESV
"And he said to the people of Israel, "When your children **ask their fathers** in times to come, 'What do these stones mean?' then you shall let your children know, 'Israel passed over this Jordan on dry ground.' For the LORD your God dried up the waters of the Jordan for you until you passed over, as the LORD your God did to the Red Sea, which he dried up for us until we passed over, so that all the peoples of the earth may know that the hand of the LORD is mighty, that you may fear the LORD your God forever."

2 Sam. 10:2
"David thought, 'I will show kindness to Hanun son of Nahash, just as his **father showed kindness to me**.'

1 Chron. 25:3, 6
"As for Jeduthun, from his sons: Gedaliah, Zeri, Jeshaiah, Shimei, Hashabiah and Mattithiah, six in all, **under the supervision of their father Jeduthun, who prophesied**, using the harp in thanking and praising the Lord." All these men were **under the supervision of their father for the music of the temple** of the Lord, with cymbals, lyres and harps, for the ministry at the house of God. Asaph, Jeduthun and Heman were under the supervision of the king."

Job 29:16
"I was a **father to the needy**; I took up the case of the stranger."

Prov. 1:8
"Listen, my son, to **your father's instruction** and do not forsake your mother's teaching."

Prov. 3:12
"…because the Lord disciplines those he loves, **as a father the son he delights in**."

Mal. 4:6 NKJV
"And he will **turn the hearts of the fathers to the children**, and the hearts of the children to their fathers, Lest I come and strike the earth with a curse."

Luke 6:36
"Be merciful, just as your **Father is merciful**."

Luke 15:31
"'My son," the father said, "you are always with me, and **everything I have is yours**."

Leaders embrace spiritual fathers, their wisdom and the mantle they carry.

Luke 15:20
"So he got up and went to his father. 'But while he was still a long way off, his father saw him and was filled with compassion for him; **he ran to his son, threw his arms round him and kissed him.**"

Luke 15:23-24
"Bring the fattened calf and kill it. Let's have a feast and celebrate. For this son of mine was dead and is alive again; he was lost and is found." **So they began to celebrate.**"

Luke 23:34
"Jesus said, '**Father, forgive them**, for they do not know what they are doing.'

Luke 23:46
"Jesus called out with a loud voice, '**Father, into your hands I commit my spirit.**'

Eph. 6:4
"**Fathers**, do not exasperate your children; instead, **bring them up in the training and instruction of the Lord.**"

Phil. 2:22
"But you know that Timothy has proved himself, because **as a son with his father he has served with me in the work** of the gospel."

1 John 2:13
"I am writing to you, **fathers, because you know him** who is from the beginning. I am writing to you, young men, because you have overcome the evil one. I write to you, **dear children, because you know the Father.**"

1 Thess. 2:8
"…because we loved you so much, we were delighted **to share with you** not only the gospel of God but **our lives as well**, because you had become so dear to us."

Col. 4:7
"Tychicus will **tell you all the news about me**. He is a dear brother, a faithful minister and fellow servant in the Lord."

Luke 3:22
"And a voice came from heaven: 'You are my Son, whom I love; **with you I am well pleased.**'

Mal. 1:6
"**A son honours his father**, and a slave his master. If I am a father, where is the honour due to me?"

Matt. 19:19
"…**honour your father** and mother.…"

Leaders embrace spiritual fathers, their wisdom and the mantle they carry.

Matt. 5:44-45 NKJV
"But I say to you, **love your enemies**, bless those who curse you, do good to those who hate you, and pray for those who spitefully use you and persecute you, that you may be **sons of your Father** in heaven…."

Acts 2:17
"'In the last days, God says, I will pour out my Spirit on all people. Your **sons and daughters will prophesy**, your young men will see visions, your old men will dream dreams."

Rom. 8:14 NKJV
"…for as many as are **led by the Spirit** of God these **are sons** of God."

Rom. 8:15 NASU
"For you have not received a spirit of slavery leading to fear again, but you have received **a spirit of adoption as sons** by which we cry out, "Abba! Father!"

Gal. 4:6
"Because **you are his sons**, God sent **the Spirit of his Son into our hearts**, the Spirit who calls out, 'Abba, Father.'

2 Cor. 6:16-18
"What agreement is there between the temple of God and idols? For we are the temple of the living God. As God has said: 'I will live with them and walk among them, and I will be their God, and they will be my people. Therefore, 'come out from them and be separate, says the Lord. **Touch no unclean thing**, and I will receive you.' And, '**I will be a Father to you, and you will be my sons and daughters**, says the Lord Almighty.'

1 Thess. 5:5 NASU
"…for you are all **sons of light and sons of day**. We are not of night nor of darkness."

Gal. 4:5 ESV
"…to redeem those who were under the law, that we might receive **adoption as sons**."

Heb. 12:7 ESV
"It is for **discipline that you have to endure**; God is treating you **as sons**. For what son is there that his father does not discipline?"

John 8:35
"Now a slave has no permanent place in the family, but **a son belongs to it for ever.**"

Phil. 2:22
"But you know that Timothy has proved himself, because as **a son with his father he has served with me in the work** of the gospel."

Leaders embrace spiritual fathers, their wisdom and the mantle they carry.

The Leader and.....

The Authority You Possess and Use

Introduction
This lesson is concerned with spiritual authority—not ecclesiastical, hierarchical, or political authority. As there are two spiritual kingdoms pitted against each other, the subject of authority is crucial. If you never discover and utilise your spiritual authority as a believer and as a leader, you will always be a victim to things that God never meant you to suffer from. John 10:10 says, "(Satan), the thief comes to steal, kill and to destroy." If you are not greater in everyday living and in ministry to others than that Thief, you will be his prey all of your days.

Many believers have some notion that the Greater One lives inside of them but do not live as though He does. This lesson is intended to be a part of the "hearing process" that enables your faith to be energised to live authoritatively in this life. If you have authority and you truly believe you possess it, you operate from that place of authority and do not live in doubt and fear no matter what seems to be taking place. Prayer and faith are not some "roulette wheel" that you hope will result in your "lucky number win." Because you believe, you are confident, and your practice, based in the eternal Word of God, produces supernatural change.

- You learn to live as Christ, "destroying the works of the evil one." 1 John 3:8.

- Progressively, the "yes, buts" go away—as He had none. Your doctrinal foundation is not meant to be a mix of "hit and miss" theology but is to be based on the Word, not your **past** experience or **ignorance** of truth.

Many Christians see life, more through the lens of where they have been, than the Word of God. Unwittingly, they, in effect, live in the past. They do not bring to the present, the amazing and powerful arsenal of world-shaping, life-transforming weapons that Christ used and gave to us. Unwittingly, even as they "try their hardest," they live inwardly in "que sera, sera." Strong confidence, powerful faith being exercised, and uncommon victory still elude them. There are some issues, they have in discouragement, surrendered to, in defeat. When they fail, they don't suspect there is some knowledge that will give them the success that has eluded them, so they live in perpetual discouragement. 2 Pet. 3:18 tells us to grow (increase) in *grace* and *knowledge*. What is it that you do not know that has hindered the 'greater grace' from flowing to you and from you?

Leaders exercise authority and power in the spirit realm to change the world.

Some observe those who operate in the authority they have been given by Christ and criticise them verbally or inwardly as arrogant—yet they secretly (and rightly) covet the same results. It is *uncommon* in our world to connect to a person who fears nothing (but the Lord in a right sense), and boldly commands conditions to conform to the standard of living that is in Heaven. Matt. 6:10.

The Possession of Authority
The complete understanding of any truth in the Bible is all that the Bible has to say about that truth. When you study a Bible truth, study it from Genesis to Revelation, even if you only use a portion of what you study in public discourse.

- 76 times the NIV mentions the word, "authority," in the New Testament and twelve times in the Old Testament.

- Dictionary definition of authority -- the power to determine, adjudicate, or otherwise settle issues or disputes; jurisdiction; the right to control, command, or determine.

- Jesus operated in authority – He had an authority in teaching. (Authority in teaching is a Spirit-released, compelling ring of authenticity that invites the hearers to faith—it is not "mind-to-mind" intellect transfer embellished by human charisma). Mt. 7:29; 1 Cor. 2:13 NLT. He also had an authority in doing miracles. Mt. 21:24, 27. One of the distinguishing features of Christ's ministry was that He operated in a realm of authority that was different from the Scribes and Pharisees. They recognised that He operated a 'kind' and a 'source' of authority that they did not possess thus they asked Him about the source of His authority. They understood authority had to be *given*. They had an ecclesiastical authority. Where was His authority coming from?

- Authority, in human terms, is the ability to command in a realm or sphere of operation. In spiritual terms, authority is the right and the ability to command *in a spiritual realm* with the confidence that the command will be obeyed—circumstances and conditions will conform to the command given – Mt. 21:19; Mt. 9:6-8 ESV; Mt. 8:3; Mk. 1:25-27, – (evil spirits have to obey the authority over them – a house divided cannot stand). *It requires authority to operate in an invisible, spiritual realm.* Mark 11:33 says, "Jesus said, 'Neither will I tell you *by* what authority I am doing these things.'" The King of the Kingdom lives inside of us and exercises His authority through commands *we give* that change conditions supernaturally.

- To exercise authority you must **believe** you have (actually possess) that authority, right and power. Mark 11:24. Peter said, "…what I do **have**, I give you." Acts 3:6. Authority is given in the new creation construct—you are born into the Kingdom as a new creation with the authority to command. Your commanding ability is a possession. You have to immerse yourself in the consciousness

Leaders exercise authority and power in the spirit realm to change the world.

of that conviction—you have "command-ability." You must see yourself in a superior position to evil spirits and their works. You have resident within you the authority over them and their works. 1 John 3:8 ("...to destroy the works of the evil one."). You have "command-ability, heal-ability, deliverance-ability and change-ability." Christ did what He did by virtue of the authority He possessed. We are to do these things also by that same authority, as it is The authority, the only authority that we possess. It is, in effect, the Lord operating through us to bring glory to His Name! Joined to Him as one (1 Cor. 6:17) He uses our words (Jesus-words) spoken from our mouths, with the authority that we have (us and Him) to accomplish the supernatural. 1 John 2:6 ESV says, "Whoever says he abides *in Him* ought to *walk* in the same way *as* He walked." Matt. 9:8 ESV says God gave "authority to men." Say aloud, "I have authority!"

- Authority in a spiritual realm operates *with* power to produce supernatural effect – Luke 4:36; Luke 10:19. It is not an "empty" order but an order that carries within itself the conforming power to accomplish. Acts 16:18 says, "...he turned round and **said to the spirit**, 'In the name of Jesus Christ I command you to come out of her!' At that moment the spirit left her."

- Authority is initially expressed in words--*orders or commands* given – Luke 4:36. This is distinct from permission or request. Permission and request are not a protocol of operation of authority in spiritual realms. In relationships they are vital values of cooperation, respect, and goodwill. "I say what *I have* because I have *what I say.*" Acts 3:6; Mark 11:23, 24.

- God has given believers the same kind of authority that Jesus had to teach and to do in a supernatural way– Matt. 9:6-8 ESV (authority to men); Mark 3:14, 15; Mark 6:7; Luke 9:1,2. Read the Gospels with the concept of our 'union' in mind. John 14:20. All that He did, we are to do. 1 John 2:6 ESV.

- Authority operates within a structure or hierarchy – "a man *under* authority." Thus authority operates in conjunction *with* the One over it and within the stated boundaries of permission. Matt. 8:9; John 3:35; Luke 4:6 reveals that even Satan was given authority, (by man, "the king," submitting to his seduction and rejecting the King of Kings) but thus a limited authority—the one who has the authority to give authority, is greater than the authority given and the one to whom it is given.

- Authority is given without lessening the authority of the one who gave it. Num. 27:20. Believers sometimes give a 'greater authority' to Satan by believing his lies and thus unwittingly come under his authority—rather than exercising their God-given 'greater authority' subjugating the Devil. Luke 10:19; Rom. 6:16.

- The spirit realm operates on the basis of authority – Satan's subjects operate according to his limited authority. That authority is superseded by the believer's

Leaders exercise authority and power in the spirit realm to change the world.

authority (a higher authority) by virtue of its Word-stated certification (Luke 10:19). Demons respond to their authority head (Satan himself) and afflict, torment, oppress, possess, harass, etc. Believers, exercising a greater authority, dispatch those demons just as Christ did—with "finger effort." They live positionally, "far above all principalities and powers." Eph. 1:20, 21; Eph. 2:6.

- Jesus was given "all authority" – we are given *some* authority as those *under* His authority. Matt. 28:18-20. Believers have the authority to do what Christ did and whatever He tells them to do. On some occasions He will tell them to do things greater than He did. John 14:12. We heal the sick, raise the dead, cast out demons, cleanse lepers, move mountains of opposition, release provision and resources, calm storms, transform substances from one form into another, nullify poison, paralyse danger, walk on water, translate to other locations, escape capture, send miracles remotely, heal the paralysed, rebuke fevers, feed multitudes, grant requests for miracles, restore severed parts of the body, etc. Jesus intended that his followers move from impossibility thinking into a supernatural norm of regular operation. Matt. 17:20.

- We are *commanded* to **command**. Matt. 28:19, 20; Matt. 10:8. Because the nature of ministry is in a spirit realm primarily, it requires a shift that only can be accomplished by the exercise of authority. The invisible realm undergoes radical change as commanding "words of authority and power" are spoken and the visible realm registers the effect. You cannot operate in the invisible realm as a "commander" with success, without having the authority and power to do so.

    - Creation came **by words**.
    - Salvation came **by words**.
    - Jesus is/was **the Word 'spoken'** by the Father to the world.
    - Jesus delivered from demons **by words**.
    - Jesus raised the dead **by words**.
    - Jesus calmed the storm **by words**.
    - Jesus rebuked a fever **by words**.
    - Jesus cursed a fig tree **by words**.
    - Jesus healed **by words**.
    - Jesus cleansed lepers **by words**.
    - Jesus opened blind eyes **by words**.

All of these words were 'commanding words' or commands given. What do you think He expects us to use to exercise the authority we have been given? Words. 2 Cor. 4:13; Isa. 44:26; Isa. 51:16; Isa. 59:21; Deut. 18:18; Jer. 1:9; Jer. 5:14.

All the miracles of the Gospels were commands. How are we to do miracles and the 'greater' things? By words full of authority and power!

Leaders exercise authority and power in the spirit realm to change the world.

- Authority is exercised and power is demonstrated in spiritual gifts through the flow of the Spirit. 1 Cor. 12:8, 9. "…by means of the same Spirit." Jesus did what He did by obeying the Spirit's voice. His Father's words and works flowed from Heaven to earth by the voice or the prompting of the Holy Spirit.

Spiritual Authority and Confidence and Boldness

In our world today it is uncommon for believers to operate in confidence and boldness. However, when we truly grasp our position in Christ, the powerful weapons we possess, and the world-changing keys of the Kingdom, we operate in this life with confidence and boldness. We speak certain that our words are filled with power to make happen what we say. We are not boasting in our ability but simply doing what He told us to do, with the inner disposition He has defined. Acts 3:12, 16; Acts 4:29, 31; Acts 9:28; Acts 14:3; Heb. 11:1 NCV.

Summary:

1. There is authority manifested in teaching and doing.

2. The authority I have is *given* and thus it must have been *received*.

3. The authority I have is made to operate in the spiritual, invisible realm. The nature of the authority that I have been given, is such that it gives me access to the invisible realm and the power to effect change—as all that is in the visible world is controlled by the invisible world.

4. I *possess* command-ability.

5. The authority I have *is* the confidence that what is commanded **will be,** because inherent *in the command* is the power to make it happen—whether it is healing, change, transformation, creation, supply or deliverance.

6. The hierarchy of authority means I am *positioned* **above** with the right to command what is **beneath**—Satan, circumstances, conditions, earthly matters. I can/must destroy the works of Satan. I can move mountains, heal bodies, deliver the oppressed, and release provision because *I possess the authority and power* to do so.

7. My **words** release the exercise of authority and the dispatch of power into circumstances and conditions making the world a better place to the glory of God.

8. I am *commanded to command*—that is, I am under **orders to order** the supernatural to take place. Matt. 10:8 is a command.

9. It is a primary function of the Spirit who indwells my spirit **to speak through me the words** that make miracles.

Leaders exercise authority and power in the spirit realm to change the world.

10. I believe, speak and act (the primary components of faith) as though **I am who I am** and **I have what I have**, in Christ.

BSA – Believe, speak, and act as though you have authority and power, exercising authority in the spirit realm—sanctioned by One who commissioned you to do so.

Application

- Begin to take this vital truth of your authority into your own world of operation.

- Begin to hear and speak **to** issues and conditions with boldness and authority.

- Begin today by speaking to someone in your group's situation.

- Use the smallest amount of words—Jesus only used three words in commanding the storm in Mark 4:39. You don't need to "talk something into happening"—you are commanding it!

- Read "Releasing the Supernatural," by David Oyedepo. Highlight the book as you read to maximize your meditative intake of the material.

Leaders exercise authority and power in the spirit realm to change the world.

Scriptures for the Authority You Have and Use

1 John 3:8
"...The reason the Son of God appeared was **to destroy the devil's work.**"

2 Pet. 3:18
"But **grow in the grace and knowledge** of our Lord and Saviour Jesus Christ."

Matt. 6:10
"...your kingdom come, **your will be done, on earth as it is in heaven.**"

Matt. 7:29
"...he **taught as one who had authority, and not as their teachers** of the law."

1 Cor. 2:13 NLT
"When we tell you these things, we do not use words that come from human wisdom. Instead, we speak **words given to us by the Spirit, using the Spirit's words to explain** spiritual truths."

Matt. 21:24, 27
"Jesus replied, 'I will also ask you one question. If you answer me, I will tell you **by what authority I am doing** these things...they answered Jesus, 'We don't know.' Then he said, 'Neither will I tell you **by what authority I am doing these things.**"

Matt. 21:19
"Seeing a fig-tree by the road, he went up to it but found nothing on it except leaves. Then **he said to it,** 'May you never bear fruit again!' **Immediately the tree withered.**"

Mark 9:6-8 ESV
"But that you may know that the Son of Man has authority on earth to forgive sins"—he then said **to the paralytic**—"Rise, pick up your bed and go home." And **he rose and went home.** When the crowds saw it, they were afraid, and they glorified **God, who had given such authority to men.**"

Mt. 8:3
"Jesus reached out his hand and touched the man. 'I am willing,' he said. **'Be clean!'** Immediately he was cleansed of his leprosy."

Mark 1:25-27
'Be quiet!' said Jesus sternly. 'Come out of him!' The impure spirit shook the man violently and came out of him with a shriek. The people were all so amazed that they asked each other, 'What is this? **A new teaching—and with authority!** He even gives **orders to impure spirits and they obey him.**'

Leaders exercise authority and power in the spirit realm to change the world.

Mark 11:24
"Therefore I tell you, whatever you ask for in prayer, **believe that you have received it**, and it will be yours."

1 Cor. 6:17
"But whoever is united with the Lord is one with him in spirit."

1 John 2:6 ESV
"…whoever says he abides in him ought to walk in **the same way in which he walked**."

Luke 4:36
"All the people were amazed and said to each other, 'What words these are! With authority and power he gives orders to impure spirits and **they come out!**'

Luke 10:19
"I have given you authority to trample on snakes and scorpions and **to overcome all the power of the enemy; nothing will harm you**."

Luke 4:36
"All the people were amazed and said to each other, 'What words these are! With authority and power **he gives orders** to impure spirits and **they come out!**'

Acts 3:6
Then Peter said, 'Silver or gold I do not have, but **what I do have** I give you. In the name of Jesus Christ of Nazareth, walk.'

Mark 11:23-24
'Truly I tell you, if anyone says to this mountain, "Go, throw yourself into the sea," and does not doubt in their heart but **believes that what they say will happen, it will be done for them**. Therefore I tell you, whatever you ask for in prayer, believe that you have received it, and it will be yours."

Mark 9:6-8 ESV
"But that you may know that the Son of Man has authority on earth to forgive sins"—he then said **to the paralytic**—"Rise, pick up your bed and go home." And **he rose and went home**. When the crowds saw it, they were afraid, and they glorified **God, who had given such authority to men**."

Mark 3:14, 15
"He appointed twelve that they might be with him and that he might send them out to preach and **to have authority to drive out demons**."

Mark 6:7
"Calling the Twelve to him, he began to send them out two by two and **gave them authority over** impure spirits."

Leaders exercise authority and power in the spirit realm to change the world.

Luke 9:1-2
"When Jesus had called the Twelve together, **he gave them power and authority to drive out all demons and to cure diseases**, and he sent them out to proclaim the kingdom of God and **to heal those who were ill**."

John 14:20
"On that day you will realise that I am in my Father, and **you are in me**, and **I am in you**."

1 John 2:6 ESV
"…whoever says he abides in him ought to walk in **the same way in which he walked**."

Matt. 8:9
"For I myself am **a man under authority**, with soldiers under me. I tell this one, "Go," and he goes; and that one, "Come," and he comes. I say to my servant, "Do this," and he does it.'

John 3:35
"The Father loves the Son and has placed **everything in his hands**."

Luke 4:6
"And he said to him, 'I will give you all their authority and splendour; **it has been given to me**, and I can give it to anyone I want to."

Num. 27:20
"**Give him some of your authority** so that the whole Israelite community will obey him."

Luke 10:19
"**I have given you authority** to trample on snakes and scorpions and **to overcome all the power of the enemy**; nothing will harm you."

Rom. 6:16
"Don't you know that when you **offer yourselves to someone as obedient slaves**, you are slaves of the one you obey—whether you are slaves to sin, which leads to death, or to obedience, which leads to righteousness?"

Eph. 1:20, 21; Eph. 2:6
"…he exerted when he raised Christ from the dead and **seated him at his right hand in the heavenly realms, far above all rule and authority, power and dominion**, and every name that is invoked, not only in the present age but also in the one to come… And **God raised us up with Christ and seated us with him** in the heavenly realms in Christ Jesus…."

Leaders exercise authority and power in the spirit realm to change the world.

Luke 10:19
"**I have given you authority** to trample on snakes and scorpions and **to overcome all the power of the enemy**; nothing will harm you."

Matt. 28:18-20
"Then Jesus came to them and said, '**All authority in heaven and on earth has been given to me**. Therefore go and make disciples of all nations, baptising them in the name of the Father and of the Son and of the Holy Spirit, and teaching them to obey everything I have commanded you. And surely I am with you always, to the very end of the age.'

John 14:12
"Very truly I tell you, whoever believes in me will do the works I have been doing, and **they will do even greater things than these**, because I am going to the Father."

Matt. 17:20
"He replied, 'Because you have so little faith. Truly I tell you, if you have faith as small as a mustard seed, you can say to this mountain, "Move from here to there," and it will move. **Nothing will be impossible for you.**'

Matt. 28:19, 20
"Therefore go and make disciples of all nations, baptising them in the name of the Father and of the Son and of the Holy Spirit, and teaching them **to obey everything I have commanded you**. And surely I am with you always, to the very end of the age.'

Matt. 10:8
"**Heal** those who are ill, **raise the dead, cleanse those who have leprosy, drive out demons**. Freely you have received; freely give."

2 Cor. 4:13
"It is written: 'I believed; therefore I have spoken.' **Since we have that same spirit of faith, we also believe and therefore speak**...."

Isa. 44:26
"...**who carries out the words of his servants and fulfils the predictions of his messengers**...."

Isa. 51:16
"I have put **my words in your mouth**...."

Isa. 59:21
'As for me, this is my covenant with them,' says the LORD. 'My Spirit, who is on you, will not depart from you, and **my words that I have put in your mouth will always be on your lips, on the lips of your children and on the lips of their descendants**—from this time on and forever,' says the LORD."

Leaders exercise authority and power in the spirit realm to change the world.

Deut. 18:18
"I will raise up for them a prophet like you from among their fellow Israelites, and **I will put my words in his mouth. He will tell them everything I command him.**"

Jer. 1:9
"Then the LORD reached out his hand and touched my mouth and said to me, **'I have put my words in your mouth.**'"

Jer. 5:14
"Therefore this is what the LORD God Almighty says: 'Because the people have spoken these words, **I will make my words in your mouth a fire** and these people the wood it consumes.'"

Acts 3:12, 16
"When Peter saw this, he said to them: 'Fellow Israelites, why does this surprise you? **Why do you stare at us as if by our own power or godliness** we had made this man walk?'… By faith in the name of Jesus, this man whom you see and know was made strong. It is Jesus' name and the faith that comes through him that has completely healed him, as you can all see."

Acts 4:29, 31
"Now, Lord, consider their threats and enable your servants **to speak your word with great boldness**… After they prayed, the place where they were meeting was shaken. And they were all filled with the Holy Spirit and **spoke the word of God boldly**."

Acts 9:28
"So Saul stayed with them and moved about freely in Jerusalem, **speaking boldly** in the name of the Lord."

Acts 14:3
"Paul and Barnabas spent considerable time there, **speaking boldly** for the Lord, who **confirmed the message of his grace by enabling them to perform signs and wonders.**"

Heb. 11:1 NCV
"**Faith means being sure** of the things we hope for and knowing that something is real even if we do not see it."

Matt. 10:8
"**Heal those who are ill, raise the dead, cleanse those who have leprosy, drive out demons.** Freely you have received; freely give."

Mark 4:39
"He got up, rebuked the wind and said to the waves, **'Quiet! Be still!'** Then the wind died down and it was completely calm."

Leaders exercise authority and power in the spirit realm to change the world.

Summary

Now that you have finished this course of training, sit down and read the entire book again from beginning to end **five** times taking a highlighter pen to emphasise everything that the Holy Spirit emphasises to you. This will help you develop and sustain what you have learned. Matt. 12:35 says, "The good man brings good things out of the good **stored up in him**...." Well done! May His grace continue to take you higher and deeper in Him as He leads you to lead others. On to the next level!